SUMMER THEOLOGY

SUMMER THEOLOGY

SUMMER THEOLOGY

Rediscovering
Judaism

Rediscovering Judaism

REFLECTIONS ON
A NEW THEOLOGY

EDITED WITH AN INTRODUCTION BY

ARNOLD JACOB WOLF

CHICAGO
QUADRANGLE BOOKS
1965

Contents

Introduction 7

1 LOU H. SILBERMAN: The Task of Jewish Theology *15*

2 JAKOB J. PETUCHOWSKI: The Dialectics of Reason and Revelation *29*

3 EMIL L. FACKENIIEIM: The Revealed Morality of Judaism and Modern Thought *51*

4 MONFORD HARRIS: Israel: The Uniqueness of Jewish History *77*

5 EUGENE B. BOROWITZ: The Individual and the Community in Jewish Prayer *109*

6 ARNOLD JACOB WOLF: Psychoanalysis and the Temperaments of Man *133*

7 ZALMAN M. SCHACHTER: Patterns of Good and Evil *163*

8 MAURICE FRIEDMAN: Christianity and the Contemporary Jew *211*

9 STEVEN S. SCHWARZSCHILD: A Jewish Perspective on International Relations *245*

Notes *271*

A Note on the Contributors *287*

Introduction

AN UNFRIENDLY CRITIC might say that this book is neither new nor Jewish nor theology. He would not be entirely wrong. Our hypothetical critic correctly notes that there is not one absolutely new idea in this whole volume; if there were, he suspects its author would try to prove that it was really only a restatement of Biblical or rabbinic doctrine. Indeed, one of the most characteristic features of these essays is their attempt to root themselves without qualification in authoritative tradition. Our critic would say, too, that either we are not Jewish or that Jews have never written theological texts (our *Summa* is a law code; our Church Fathers were story-telling Haggadists), and that to the extent we have achieved theology we have left Judaism behind. Or (perhaps inconsistently, *and*), to the extent that we have remained Jewish thinkers, we have, he might claim, failed theology. He will discover the *midrashic* commentary in our essays, the homiletic *aperçu*, legalistic instruction, philosophical logic-chopping. All this may be interesting, our critic might say, but it is still by no means theology.

We cannot quite concede his argument. We insist paradoxically (and paradox, too, is one of the characteristics of these essays) that because we are old, we are new. Nothing is more radical, in the strict sense of the word, than naked tradition. Novelty inheres in our recovery of Biblical categories, the refurbishing of Talmudic direction, straight pre-

7

sentation of philosophic insights from the Middle Ages. None
of our basic ideas is really ours. At most, we have fought
our way back to an ancient conviction, and in that consists
our novelty.

For we are not old-fashioned Jews. We have grown up on
the American continent (where most of us were born),
studied in secular universities (where most of us now teach),
assimilated the pragmatism, optimism, and scientism of our
century. If we assert traditional doctrine, it is not because
we know no alternative. For us, Judaism is not so much a
heritage as an achievement. Or, perhaps more accurately, to
make it our heritage has become our decisive task.

Nor are we simply new men with old ideas. For each of
us, tradition is a problem as well as a gift. We take the Bible
and tradition seriously, but not literally. We confront the
sacred texts in reverence, but we do not believe that they
came from God unmediated by man. We honor the old, but
we do not feel compelled to repeat it.

I am fairly certain, too, that we are honestly Jewish. A few
of us are called Orthodox, most Conservative or Reform.
Such labels mean little in the world of ideas. One of the most
radical essays in this collection is the work of a traditional
rabbi whose life style is gracefully but strictly orthoprax.
One of the most "Jewish" is by a layman whose Jewish education before college was entirely in a Reform Sunday school in
Oklahoma. Nearly all of us are rabbis, but I am the only
one who spends most of his time serving a congregation, and
I suppose that I, too, could be had. On the other hand, the
total number of years spent as congregational rabbis by several contributors would surely reach a hundred.

One of the reasons we think we are Jews, despite our pen-
chant for theology and other Western European imports, is
that we recognize each other as Jews. Within our separate
sectarian movements we find suspiciously humanist or suspiciously irrational types who may be Jews but whose ideas
seem to us either recalcitrant or banal, and frequently both.

When we talk to one another, however, we disagree, but always within and upon a basic consensus. We validate each other's truth.

Our Judaism is for us an attempt to permit the Living God to address us severally and as a sacred community. We put to God directly and through the mediation of our precedents all the agonized questions of modern life; we let Him answer us His way, and then we try to speak without distortion what we hear. This may sound more "mystical" than it is. What, in fact, we look like we are doing is studying, reflecting, praying, speaking, listening, saying. Phenomenologically, that signifies for us revelation. How much of what we say is spoken through us by Him, we cannot know. It is, we hope, far more than we suspect. But even if not revealed truth, our search for the God of Abraham, Isaac, and Jacob must be conceded to be Judaism. That much we certify to one another and to our readers. You may find us wrong, sometimes perhaps profoundly wrong, but do not presume to call us disloyal.

I am least sure that we are theologians, and least care. While theologians came rather late to Judaism, no scholar would deny the title to Franz Rosenzweig and Martin Buber in our century, and many would ascribe it to Maimonides and Judah Halevi 800 years ago. To the extent that theology is *logos*, the science of God, it may be a Greek betrayal of Biblical insight. The greatest modern Christian thinkers are themselves suspicious of theology; we have no desire to embrace theology at the very time it may be jettisoned by the Church. But, to the extent that theology is simply thinking about God in some ordered way, the Jews were the first and greatest theologians and we only wish we could be their proper successors.

What we teach is not called Theology by our schools. They call it Philosophy or Jewish Thought or the History of Ideas. Their reticence may reflect a proper feeling that Judaism does not fit neatly into Aristotelian (or Kantian or

Hegelian or Kierkegaardian) categories; it may be a tribute to
the truth that Judaism is no system but a life, not catechism
but direction. But refusing to call us theologians may also be
an evasion. Some say that Judaism is more than a religion but
only mean that it is less. To label as Christianizing all Jewish
thinking about God and His *Torah* is ignorant where it is not
also vicious. We may no longer quite know what the word
signifies, but we are not ashamed to attempt theology.

All of us practice theology in roughly the same way,
though we start with different premises and come to different
conclusions. None of us here attempts to prove the existence
of God or the superiority of Judaism. We do not believe that
God spoke to our people only at Sinai, or only in Frankfort,
Vilna, or New York. We do not flee the witness of the past
nor the problem which constitutes the present. We try not
to summarize, systematize, or explain away. We do not pretend we are rare spirits hovering over the real world of men
like wraiths; we know our flesh and our failings, and we
speak out of both. We do not seek paradox for its own sake,
but we are not surprised when we fail to understand nearly
everything the Almighty does. We are humble before God
when we succeed, and before men who do not unfairly tax us
with being too prolix or too poetic to be right. We all share
a cause, a mood, a crisis; but we respond separately and alone.

We have had the same teachers: the Baal Shem Tov, Maimonides, Schelling, Exodus, Akiba, the *Midrash;* but they
teach us variously and with varying results. We have all been
moved and instructed by the rebirth of Jewish thinking during
this century under Rosenzweig and Buber. In a sense, we are
only their American continuators. But the area they marked
out is too large for two men or for one generation to
explore. It will be the work of a thousand years to respond
adequately to their discoveries. We do not feel like epigones,
but only like disciples.

We are also under the tutelage of American philosophy,
liberal religion, and existentialism. If the latter word did not

connote Sartrian nihilism as well as the profoundest religion of modern times, and if the greatest existentialists did not (like Buber) eschew the title, we might arrogate it to ourselves. So far as existentialism signifies openness, personalism, a philosophy for life and not for textbooks, we should like to believe we are existentialists. But we are not thereby committed to Sartre's slogan "existence prior to essence," nor to Kierkegaard's *midrash* on the Binding of Isaac. Nor are we confined by the attempts to systematize philosophy's greatest anti-system. We assert the primacy of meeting God in *Torah* and of authentic response. We plead for a tragic view of life instead of a merely pathetic one, for a messianic optimism rather than the pretense of progress. We consider our Judaism ineluctable, and yet we insist on our right to choose to be Jews. We are human, failed, inconsistent. We are also theological, Jewish, and new (or neoclassical). If this be existentialism, let our critics make the most of it!

The reader will find in this book contemporary answers to the classical problems of Jewish theology. The answers are different in different essays, but not wholly so. Some essays are largely historical in method, some purely constructive. Some are centered on one great religious text; others are almost exclusively personal response. But a lack of footnotes in one essay should not deceive the reader into missing its scholarship, nor elaborate documentation in another into escaping its deeply personal conviction. Since we are all teachers, we are accustomed to the paraphernalia of scholarship. Since we are all men, we speak in a context of love and struggle, death and hope.

We welcome our reader to consider what we have written, but much more what we have heard and have tried to become.

Arnold Jacob Wolf

Rediscovering Judaism

LOU H. SILBERMAN

The Task of Jewish Theology [1]

An Introductory Admission

IN HIS CHALLENGING open letter to Martin Buber, *Die Bauleute*, Franz Rosenzweig acclaimed his friend for his disclosure to that generation of the true nature of Torah, "the Teaching." "You have," he wrote, "saved the Teaching from the splendiferous poverty of basic principles to which the nineteenth century—not in the first but in the most specific and far-reaching attempt—sought to reduce it." No distinctions *a priori* were to be countenanced; the whole of the Tradition, not any predetermined segment, became the object of study (*Lernstoff*) and became also potentially Torah, to be actualized by choosing so that it became truth.

This understanding of Torah has been, almost from the moment I read Rosenzweig's esssay, the basic method of my own studies. It has formed my interests and informed my concerns. It has, sadly enough, uprooted loyalties and unwillingly brought about alienation. But it has opened for me vistas previously shut off and granted me insights previously denied.

I. *A Critical Appraisal*

More than ten years ago, as part of a symposium on "The State of the Reform Movement," I read a paper before the Central Conference of American Rabbis dealing with "The

Recent History of Reform Philosophy." It was critical in its approach, negative in its conclusions, and avoided complete pessimism only by following the tradition of ending on a note of eschatological hopefulness. The intervening decade has, sadly enough, not softened the criticism nor erased the negativism. It has, however, deepened the pessimism and confirmed my most desperate imaginings concerning the intellectual desert in which liberal Judaism has set up its tents. Continued probing into the past and examination of its records have shattered illusion after illusion and revealed the precarious state of our foundations. The liberation Rosenzweig claimed as Buber's gift has not become our possession. The substance of our thinking has, for the most part, been borrowed in a totally indiscriminating fashion from prevailing non-Jewish positions. These, far from being mastered and disciplined by an indigenous methodology, have been thrown together helter-skelter, enveloped in vagueness, and swathed in homiletic veils. Although Gershom Scholem [2] may have gone to or beyond the boundaries of sound judgment, there is no doubt that much of what I have described is due to the fact that *Die Wissenschaft des Judentums*, the nineteenth century liberal scholarship in which Reform Judaism has its roots, often was not the instrument of intellectual liberation but the tool of bourgeois social and political programs, and frequently was not even that but only a sterile and ineffectual academic pastime. The *a priori* self-limitations rooted in nineteenth century bias and prejudice of which Rosenzweig wrote have dangerously narrowed our vision and distorted our perspective. Yet when, within the last generation, a total repudiation of the bourgeois definition of the nature of the people of Israel espoused by the Reform movement was forced upon us by the tragic history of our times, we replaced it with a melange of western European romantic nationalism and eastern European messianism which we call Zionism, and we have submitted uncritically to the emotional appeal of mere sentiment. Time after time, like all tired liberals, we cling tenaciously to positions regarding issues that have moved through and beyond their crucial stages. The old positions may or may not have been sound; now they are irrelevant. Nor is what I have said limited in any way to liberal Judaism. Irrelevance is not our possession alone; we share it graciously with all our brethren.

Nothing that anyone can say will change that which lies behind; and, though to face today and to move into tomorrow one needs to understand yesterday, to make of that task more than a prolegomenon is to retire to academic desuetude.

II. *The Problematic Nature of the Undertaking*

The task I have set for myself in this paper is the examination of a program of study and work that can lead to a meaningful statement of Judaism, intellectually sound and spiritually relevant in and for the generation to which it is addressed. There is, unfortunately, a frustration built into this enterprise, for there is no static body of given propositions which can be merely rearranged or restated. One is caught up in a dynamic process which constantly shows forth new meanings, so that, in a very real sense, whatever one manages to say is rendered obsolete in its saying. Rosenzweig, in the letter quoted above, wrote: ". . . Torah [this is what he means by "die Lehre"] itself is not known once and for all but is always something in the future. Thus the question of him who asks for it today is perhaps already a part of the answer that will be given to another man tomorrow and at some time in the future will surely become the keyword of the answer given to him who today is the questioner." One must reckon at the outset with the dissolution of a theological statement at its moment of utterance, and must do so bravely and indeed thankfully.

The point of departure for this journey is, as I have already suggested, the open confrontation of the Tradition in its vastness, unfettered as far as humanly possible by prejudg-

ments as to what is essential and what is peripheral. It is clear
at once that the fulfilment of such a task is beyond the
competence of any living man today, but this inability does
not invalidate the basic supposition, that one dare not make
unsupported prejudgments. One must be prepared to say yes
as widely as possible, embracing contradiction and paradox,
not for their own sake but because they are the very stuff
of the Tradition that one must face, so that it may become
his truth. This is what *Die Wissenschaft des Judentums*,
Jewish scholarship, must mean. It is not to be the drawing
up of accounts and the closing of books, as some nineteenth
century scholars imagined, bringing to an end and dismissing
to dusty shelves large areas of the Tradition. It is the opening
up of ever new realms that have been hidden under the dust
of centuries, so that we may know again the magnitude of
our past and thus be challenged to an equally broad tomorrow.

One must be ready to face the multiplicity and complexity
of the Tradition and, as scholar, seek to penetrate, to understand, and to make one's own that which is encountered. At
this point, it seems to me, one must acquire that method
so forthrightly exhibited by Leo Baeck, the technique of
Nacherleben derived from his teacher Wilhelm Dilthey's
Verstehende Psychologie, in which one seeks to understand a
totality, a *Gestalt*. Recognizing the polarity of the Jewish
religious experience, one affirms the tension and makes it one's
own. This requires that one throw into question the choices
and conclusions of yesterday, not arrogantly, but with the
humbling knowledge that nothing is ours until we make
it ours.

III. *History and Dogma*

As a theologian, then, one begins with history, for there
it is that one beholds the affirmations and the refusals of
the people of Israel confronted by God and His Word. These
affirmations and refusals as action in political, economic, and

social life; affirmations and refusals made in the field of legal
structure, in worship, in prophetic utterance and popular
response, in historical narrative and poetic art, in mystic con-
templation and philosopher's dialectic, in legend and in song;
these affirmations and refusals are the "stuff," the material
with which the theologian labors. He needs to know them.
Through the risk of his own affirmation and his own refusal
they become in his life, and perhaps through him in the life
of others, Torah. To affirm or refuse, not in isolation, not
cut off from the community, but in its midst, with it, requires
that we know what the Jewish people has affirmed and what
it has refused in its existence.

These affirmations and refusals are the dogmas of Judaism.
By dogmas I mean *emūnōt* which, as Alexander Altmann has
pointed out, is Ibn Tibbon's translation of Saadya's Arabic
amānat and denotes doctrines "accepted by an act of religious
faith." The whole question of dogma has been so clouded by
"apologetic thinking" that only the most determined effort
can free us from our liberal prejudices. We have been so
thoroughly bemused by formal considerations, so naively
entrapped by nineteenth century bias, that we have failed
to recognize that from the very beginning our literature is
shot through with theological affirmations. Where these occur
and what they are thus become a crucial part of the theologian's task.

IV. *Liturgy and Dogma*

One of the most important contributions of contemporary
biblical scholarship has been the recognition of the role of
the *Credo*, the liturgical confession, in the Bible. I find the
term *Credo* not entirely satisfactory, but a mistake in labeling
does not change the nature of what is labeled. What else is
at the beginning of *Ki Tavo*, that most familiar passage in
Deuteronomy (26:1-11)? One is commanded to come before
the Lord and to say, "I am making a declaration unto the

Lord [your] my God today because I have come into the
land which He swore unto our fathers to give to us." What
does he declare? He narrates a story, the story of his people
that is at the same time his own story. In the course of it
he makes three theological affirmations: "He heard our cry;—
He brought us forth from Egypt;—He brought us unto this
place."

Here we see the *Sitz im Leben*, the living situation in which
the theological affirmations of the Israelite community were
made, the liturgical or cultic act. Here too, we learn the
structure or the form in which these affirmations are clothed,
the historical narrative. This form, although it does not conform to our expectation that dogmatic credal statements will
be framed as abstract propositions, is explicitly a creed, a
normative affirmation by the Israelite community. Thus this
passage and others like it provide one with the clue to the
discovery of the dogmas of Judaism and the recognition that
the superbly articulated narrative that begins with the opening
verses of Genesis and culminates in the stirring covenant-
making scene in Joshua 24, is one great theological affirmation
proclaiming the Creator God who is the Lord of history and
the *Melekh* of Israel.

It is against the background of these affirmations that the
prophetic movement in Israel gains its meaning. Only in a
community where the dogma of a Creator God who rules
history and is Sovereign of the people has been accepted and
affirmed does the pattern of prophetic warnings and promise
make sense. Both the warnings of punishment and the promises of restoration are but workings-out of the meaning of
divine lordship over history and divine sovereignty over
Israel. At the same time, the narrative of the going forth
from Egypt is the paradigm of fulfilment, for He is a God
who saves.

These affirmations grew up and continued to find their
expression within the liturgical structure of Israel in literary
forms that reflected that structure. Israel's worship of God

expressed what Israel affirmed about God. In contemporary
New Testament scholarship it is generally accepted that the
earliest theological formulation of nascent Christianity is the
kerygma, the *Haggadah*, the proclamation of the acts of God.
Apostolic preaching was quite clearly a brief narrative of
what the Church understood to be the crucial act of God in
history. C. H. Dodd has pointed out that it is in the great
liturgies of the Church that this *kerygma*, this proclamation,
is retained in its purity. In this direction one must seek for
the basic formulation of Jewish dogmas. Dogmas already
explicit in the whole of the Bible now provided a clear and
unmistakable structure.

Pharisaic Judaism brought together and made explicit its
comprehension of Israel's theological affirmation just as the
Scripture had done time and time again through liturgical
formulation. But, as we have said, the form of expression
in no way mitigates its dogmatic content. Indeed, the form
underscores its dogmatic and binding nature. Professor
Finkelstein has shown that the various prayers of the *Tefillah*
also serve the function of dogmatic definition. In discussing
the role of the second benediction, *Geburot*, he wrote, "The
emphasis on the Resurrection in this benediction is too clear
to be missed, and it can only be taken as a confession of
faith in Pharisaism as opposed to Sadduceeanism."

Elbogen put the whole matter succinctly when he wrote
that the service of worship "expressed that which the community held in common, the confession of faith. The formulation of belief that united all the members of the community
provided the primary element of the public liturgy around
which the other elements, as around a natural center, ranged
themselves." Thus, there can be no doubt that the order of
worship was indeed the basic statement of belief of Pharisaic-
rabbinic Judaism, not derived from philosophic propositions
but proclaiming as existential truth the various ways in which
Israel had been confronted by God.

These were not only Judaism's dogmas; this was, contrary

to Rosenzweig (who said, "*Judentum hat . . . nämlich zwar Dogmen, aber keine Dogmatik*"), Judaism's dogmatic, a systematic and integrated statement of the fundamental affirmations of Pharisaic-rabbinic Judaism, resting ultimately on the authority of Scripture. While the exact date of the emergence of this formulation is uncertain, there is every reason to believe that it took place before the rise of Christianity. Because of the dogmatic liturgy, the direction and task of its tradition within Judaism became normative. In a very real sense what one may call Jewish theology is a vast commentary upon the affirmations here set down. Anyone who is at all concerned with an intellectually sound and spiritually relevant statement of Judaism must, therefore, begin with a recognition and acceptance of the dogmatic structure of Judaism. Each theologian does not, of course, necessarily deal with all of these affirmations; he may limit himself to a discussion of one or several; but whatever he deals with must be thought of in the presence of all the others.

V. *The Dogmatic Undertaking*

The task of the theologian now is the discovery of the explicit and implicit meaning of these affirmations within the Tradition, in all their detail. He must investigate and chart the route or routes by which this statement of the faith of Israel emerged out of the encounter and dialogue between God and the people of Israel. Beginning with what scholarship can demonstrate to be the earliest full articulation of the liturgical-creedal structure here outlined, he is obligated to disclose by a meticulous *explication de texte* the possibilities and probabilities that lie within it, recognizing all along the presence of ambiguities and lost nuances. Thus Scripture and its interpretation, *Midrash*, must be carefully scrutinized in order to recognize how the Pharisaic-rabbinic community understood the language which was embodied in its theological formulation.

The theologian must allow himself to be confronted by the Tradition in all of its variety. At the end, having before him at least in theory the dominant direction this affirmation has taken, together with a map of the side-roads, cul-de-sacs, and detours, he is able to make a statement about the authentic position of the synagogue that will not be a homiletic conceit, a partial truth (hence partially untrue), or even a well-informed guess. He will have disclosed with all the rigor of scientific method the structure and the dynamic of a fundamental affirmation of the synagogal tradition as it has emerged.

The methodology sketched here points the way toward the construction of a systematic statement of the Tradition. Following the liturgical dogmatic, this statement begins with the doctrine of Creator and Creation, of God and man; moves to the doctrine of the Lord of history and His covenant with the people of Israel, which will include the doctrine of commandment (*mitzvah*) and response, i.e., the whole halakic-ethical structure of Judaism; and culminates in the doctrine of last things, the redemption of history and the renewal of creation.

VI. *The Existential Risk*

In doing this, the theologian's own suppositions and pre-suppositions will have been called into question. He will have been called upon to affirm or refuse. He will have had to take the risk, to put his own relation to the Tradition in jeopardy. Where he is able to say yes, he will say it with humility; where he must say no, he will say it with candor and with courage.

One needs to remind himself over and over again of this, the situation of his study. It is not cut off from the community, but only in its midst that one can learn, affirm, refuse. Nor can this be done in isolation from the rest of one's self. He who faces the Tradition, he who enters into this crucial conversation with it, does not come to it unencumbered;

he is not merely the sensitive plate of a camera recording all
that it sees. He chooses and refuses, says yes and no, out of
the situation in which he stands. It is within and through his
own life that the stuff of learning becomes Torah. His standing within the community confronts him with the Tradition
he must affirm or refuse. The community's standing within
the world, its meeting with the variety of the world's thought,
sets the situation in which he affirms or refuses. But our own
contemporary theologians, with few exceptions, do not move
from within the Tradition outward to meet the world's
thought and subdue it. The modern Jewish thinker most
often begins not entirely outside and not entirely within, in a
dynamic situation in which the relationship among the fields
of his existence is ever in motion, ever changing, ever forming new constellations and clusters of meaning. Torah is
always becoming, for he is always becoming. He is always
becoming, for Torah is always becoming.

VII. *The Philosophic Challenge*

Recognizing this, we can ask ourselves some questions about
the various ways in which this encounter occurs. It is clear
that there is always an incommensurable quality rooted in
the uniqueness of each person; it is equally clear that as creatures bound by time and space, as finite beings, we are
involved in finite possibilities. Indeed, the limits at any one
time seem rather narrow. Yet though the options may be
few, they are real.

In addition to, or perhaps because of, the limitations we
impose upon the relevance of the whole Tradition, we break
off the crucial and constructive conversation between the
Tradition and the world. Our limitations inhibit any truly
creative confrontation; in fact, the limitation is the acceptance
of the world's judgment upon the Tradition. But more than
this, the vitality of the option toward which the liberal movement turned its understanding of even this truncated Tradi-

tion has faded. Only Hermann Cohen dared anything like a grand confrontation of the Tradition against what was for a time at least the vigorous option of neo-Kantian thought. But it has not been this option that has in our day faced the Tradition, to become its dynamic partner in the becoming discussed above. Rather, the Tradition has been faced by that revolutionary break with rationalist philosophy that originated with the late Schelling, found its early Christian theological expression in Kierkegaard, and flowered in Nietzsche, Bergson, and what has loosely been named the existentialist school. Indeed, this later meeting has provided the basis for almost the entire development of European theology, Christian and Jewish, during the last half-century. Few other options have been offered; few other philosophic positions have existed that have been ready and willing to enter into conversation with the Tradition. On the American Jewish scene only one notable confrontation took place, that between the Tradition and the pragmatic instrumentalism of Dewey— a particularly American form of existentialism. But its full impact was vitiated by the transformation of the Tradition's ontological affirmations into sociological functions. For the most part we have been unable or unready first, to relinquish our limited view of the Tradition, and second, to enter into the conversation at all. We have assumed an anti-intellectual stance that dismisses theology as at best a luxury, at worst, sheer drivel. Hence the present task of the theologian.

"Existentialist" theologians have made it evident that one theologizes from one's situation. But it has become ever more apparent to me that merely to stay with this necessary subjectivity is ultimately to defeat oneself. As theologian my subjectivity is confronted by the stuff of the Tradition, and I am called upon to thrust myself into it in learning; in Rosenzweig's words, "to rivet oneself to the chain of the Tradition as the latest link." But this thrusting, this transforming of "stuff" to Torah—the living word of God— does not take place (and here I paraphrase Rosenzweig), because I wish it, but because I have the capacity for it. Whence the capacity? To ask this question is not to dismiss but to honor subjectivity by recognizing it as the legitimate source of the theologian's task, without making it his goal.

It was in answer to just this question that Moses Maimonides wrote to his pupil, R. Joseph ibn Aknin, in the letter that serves as the Introduction to the *Moreh Nebukhim*, "I perceived that you had acquired some knowledge in these matters [metaphysics] from others, and that you were perplexed and bewildered; yet you sought to find out a solution to your difficulty. I urged you to desist from this pursuit, and enjoined you to continue your studies systematically; for my object was that the truth shall present itself in connected order, and that you should not hit upon it by mere chance." How was the disciple, how was the teacher himself to affirm within the sphere of human reason, the truth of Torah? The question is not bookish, for the language it uses carries us into the human situation as defined by modern existentialist thought: "He is lost in perplexity and anxiety . . . he would be left with those errors which give rise to fear and anxiety, constant grief and great perplexity." The whole of the *Guide of the Perplexed* was the answer laid out in terms then accessible to human reason. It sought to give the perplexed the capacity to affirm.

The task of the contemporary theologian is the same. He must acquire the capacity for affirming and must affirm what he has the capacity to affirm. "I do not presume to think," wrote Maimonides, in clear recognition of human limitation, "that this treatise settles every doubt." But that he had to grapple with doubt, in the very terms that doubt presented itself, was for him indisputable.

VIII. *The Theologian's Task*

The theologian is then concerned with the question of what makes it possible for him to affirm the Tradition and what makes it possible for the Tradition to be affirmed by him, not as abstract, disembodied spirit, but for and by him as *this* living man at *this* point and place in history. It is Tradition, this Tradition in its scandalous particularity and not in abstract general principles, that he struggles to affirm. Once we recognize the double nature of our task, we have escaped from mere subjectivity on the one hand and sheer objectivity on the other. But again we need to remind ourselves, our recognition insists, that there is no *a priori* way of affirmation. At the same time that Maimonides worked through the architectonic rationalist structure that made it possible for him and his disciples to affirm the Tradition, the speculative mystics were engaged in the exploration of quite another world, seeking the same end, the affirmation of the dogmas. Liberalism has consistently refused to recognize the intellectual achievement of speculative mysticism, of *Kabbalah*, and to understand it as a valid mode of theological construction. I make no claim for it in our present situation, but at the same time I do not accept the liberal bias of *a priori* denial.

The central concern of the theologian is not how the problem has been dealt with before (although he must know how), but what are the tools at hand in his present situation as he looks toward the future. Are they those that have proved so valuable for European theologians—the *Existenzphilosophie* of Heidegger, Jaspers, and others? Are they those that are beginning to emerge within the English philosophic scene, as linguistic analysis moves away from its earlier positions and directs its attention toward areas of human activity previously considered unproductive? Or will the promise of a renewal of the classical philosophic tradition (duly chastened, of course, in the manner of Tillich) develop into a real movement, so that the conversation either broken off in the nineteenth century or generally unproductive in the twentieth may be renewed?

The answer lies not with any official body, not with organizations, commissions and conferences, but in the life of the single one who is in actuality the creative field in which Tradition and world meet and struggle to relate. The answer comes out of the risk he takes. The risk? He dares to say what he dare not say, to do what he dare not do. There is a passage quoted in Buber's *Ten Rungs* that sheds light on this:

> In the Book of Elijah we read: "Everyone of Israel is duty bound to say: When will my works approach the works of my fathers, Abraham, Isaac and Jacob?" How are we to understand this? How could we ever venture to think that we could do what our fathers did?
>
> Just as our fathers invented new ways of serving, each a new service according to his own character: one, the service of love; another, of stern justice; a third, of beauty; so each one of us in his own way should devise something new in the light of the teaching and of service, and do what has not yet been done.

This is the theologian's task, his hope, his bread, his tears, his trust.

JAKOB J. PETUCHOWSKI

The Dialectics of Reason
and Revelation

OURS IS AN AGE when the immanentist view of God, predominant in the nineteenth century, has given way to the recognition that God is God, and man is man. No longer is man himself a part of an impersonal Absolute, a proud manifestation of Universal Spirit. The gulf separating man from God has been made most painfully obvious. Yet it is that very recognition of the gulf which enables the modern Jew to empathize again with the frame of mind of his biblical ancestors. For them, too, God was God, and man, man. For them, too, the ways of God were as distant from man's ways, and God's thoughts from man's thoughts, as were the heavens from the earth (Isa. 55:8-9).

But this biblical attitude would never have become biblical *religion* had not recognition of the existence of this gulf been supplemented by the certainty that it can be bridged, and by the knowledge that, on occasion, the gulf has been bridged. This metaphor must not be misunderstood in the sense of obliterating the boundary lines of two distinct entities: God and man. They never merge, neither by an apotheosis of man nor by an "incarnation" of God. But God, remaining God, makes Himself known to man, who remains man. And God does so, because He takes an interest in man, because He cares, because He loves.

A god who does not care, and who does not make himself known, is a god whose existence is of no particular religious relevance. More than that: such a god is the antithesis of the God of biblical and Rabbinic Judaism, to such an extent that "Epicurean" becomes the technical term for "heretic" in the literature of the Rabbis.[1] Now, the real Epicureans did not deny the existence of the gods; they merely negated the view that the gods took an interest in human affairs. But, from the Jewish point of view, this is itself a form of atheism, an assertion that "there is no justice and no Judge."[2] What distinguishes the God of the Bible from the gods of the Epicureans is precisely the fact that our God makes Himself known to man. In the language of theology, this fact is called "Revelation."

The language of theology, however, speaks in the accents of the theologian's own age, and the meaning of "Revelation," affirmed by a given theologian, need not necessarily coincide with the meaning of "Revelation" to biblical man. For the Protestant Schleiermacher, "Every original and new communication of the universe to man is a revelation. . . . Every intuition and every original feeling proceeds from revelation."[3] For the Jewish liberal Abraham Geiger, "Revelation" had resolved itself into the "peculiar Jewish *genius* for religion,"[4] even as Kaufmann Kohler was to speak of the Jews' "peculiar religious bent," and the "unique insight into the moral nature of the Deity" on the part of the Jewish people's "leading spirits."[5]

The language of the Bible itself is more direct. Here we read that "the Lord appeared" to certain people,[6] that "God spoke" certain words to individuals[7] and to Israel as a whole,[8] that "the Lord met" a man,[9] and that the Lord "sent" His servants, the prophets.[10] Indeed, apart from the fact that later Judaism—and Christianity—identified the Bible as a whole with the word of God, there are numerous biblical passages which themselves purport to represent the actual content of divine revelations.[11]

Basically, then, "Revelation," as seen in the Bible itself, is of two kinds: it is a "vision" or "sight," [12] and it is "the Word of the Lord" [13] or "Torah," divine guidance.[14] Rabbinic Judaism was, therefore, quite faithful to its biblical prototype when, instead of using an ambiguous term like "Revelation," it spoke, as the occasions demanded, either of *gilluy shekhinah* (the revealing of God's presence) or of *mattan torah* (the giving of divine guidance).[15] Max Kadushin is wrong, however, to deduce from a differentiation between *aspects* of "Revelation" that Rabbinic Judaism lacked an awareness of "Revelation" as such.[16]

According to biblical teaching, then, God makes Himself known to man, and He also reveals the commandments "which a man shall do and live thereby." [17] Man's knowledge of the "right way," his possession of wisdom and intelligence, come from God.

In the so-called Wisdom Books of the Hebrew Bible, Proverbs, Ecclesiastes, and Job, we meet with another aspect. While, according to Deut. 4:5–6, the Israelites' "wisdom and discernment" consist of the "statutes and ordinances" taught by God, the "wisdom" of the Wisdom Books is something acquired by man through his own efforts. Koheleth applied his mind "to seek and to search out by wisdom all that is done under heaven" (Eccles. 1:13). He said to himself, "I have acquired great wisdom, surpassing all who were over Jerusalem before me; and my mind has had great experience of wisdom and knowledge" (Eccles. 1:16). Though tradition identifies Koheleth with King Solomon, the Solomon of I Kings 3:5–14 acquired his "wise and understanding heart" as a direct, once-and-for-all gift from God, "when the Lord appeared to him" in Gibeon, whereas Koheleth seems to have preferred the trial and error approach to wisdom.

Again, to underline the difference between the "Revelation" approach and the "Wisdom" approach, we may take the prohibition of adultery. Two Hebrew words in Exod. 20:14, lightning-like in their impact, represent the prohibition against illicit sex as part of God's Sinaitic covenant. But the Book of Proverbs expatiates: its whole seventh chapter is devoted to warning the young man against the "loose woman." There is no reference to divine law or categorical imperatives here. The whole *tendenz* of this chapter is that crime does not pay. The lesson of fidelity is learned from experience.

It is clear, therefore, that in biblical Israel, as among other Eastern peoples, "wisdom"—the knowledge of how to live— was there to be had for the asking. Both experience and the teachings of elders helped a man to acquire it. If, then, we take Torah as "Revelation," and "Wisdom" as man's own acquisition, we could read the Bible itself as the first record of the dialectics of Reason and Revelation. But even before the biblical period ended, a synthesis was in the process of being established. After all, if wisdom is the *summum bonum*, it cannot remain unrelated to God; it, too, must be a part of divine revelation. Wisdom was still something that men had to acquire, but no longer through their own efforts alone. It was God's mercy which made possible man's acquisition of wisdom.[18]

In the apocryphal Book of Ben Sira (Ecclesiasticus), of the second century B.C.E., we have the earliest literary evidence of the culmination of this biblical process. Ben Sira repeatedly stresses the *identity* of Torah and wisdom (e.g., 1:26; 15:1b; 19:20). This identity was to remain basic to the Judaism of the Rabbis. Once established, it immediately yielded a concept of Torah which went beyond the written word of the Pentateuch. In other words, God's revelation was not to be confined to the text of the five books of Moses. This, above all, was the bone of contention between Pharisees and Sadducees, the latter denying the revelatory character of anything not actually stated in the written text. The Pharisees, on the other hand, by reason of their broader concept of Torah, were able to bring all of life under the sway of "revealed religion." Here was their sanction for teaching such doctrines as Resurrection, for going beyond the letter of the law to its spirit, and for making innovations demanded by the exigencies of life. Even the kindling of the Hanukkah lights, an institution commemorating the victorious Hasmonean uprising in the second century B.C.E., could be provided with a benediction in which God is praised for "commanding us to kindle the lights of Hanukkah." [19]

The identification of Torah with wisdom made the biblical attributes of Torah and wisdom interchangeable: what the Bible said about wisdom could now be applied to Torah, including the speech of personified Wisdom in Proverbs 8:22ff: "The Lord created me at the beginning of His way, the first of His acts of old. Ages ago I was set up, at the first, before the beginning of the earth." This, together with the Platonic doctrine of ideas and Hellenistic notions of the Logos, which were not unknown in the Palestinian schools—Palestine being part of the Roman-Hellenistic world—enabled the Rabbis to see in the Torah the "blueprint of creation," thus elevating it to the level of a cosmic principle.[20] In still more sophisticated Alexandrian Judaism, where what "the philosophers" taught was taken even more seriously than in Palestine, the story was circulated—long after to be repeated by Church Fathers—that Plato and Aristotle acquired their philosophy by being students of the writings of Moses.[21] And Philo of Alexandria applied himself to reading contemporary philosophical notions out of, and into, the Greek version of the Hebrew Bible.

Common to both the Hellenistic-Jewish and the Palestinian-Pharisaic approaches was a logical corollary of radical monotheism: there can be only *one* source of truth. If, therefore, the teachings of the philosophers make sense, then they must be derivable from the "revealed" documents of truth, i.e., the Torah. The identification of wisdom and Torah precluded any concept of a "twofold truth."

And yet, with revelation thus construed in its most all-embracing sense, the claims of reason were by no means silenced. The very broadening of the Torah concept in Pharisaic Ju-

daism necessitated sustained intellectual endeavor, for it had
to be shown that, whatever Torah had come to mean, its
written source was still the canonized scripture. In other
words, there had to be an acceptable system—or systems—
of "interpretation." Neither the Alexandrian allegorists nor
the Palestinian legalists claimed to be innovators in religion.
Their task was that of "interpretation," and interpretation,
in its turn, must be based on commonly accepted norms or
canons. While the allegorical interpretation of the Alexan-
drians could afford to be quite arbitrary, and was, in any case,
of little influence on the development of "normative" Judaism,
the Palestinian and, later, the Babylonian schools had to proceed more systematically.

At this point we have to mention the "hermeneutic rules,"
such as the *a fortiori* and the word-analogy, seven of which
are said to have been applied by Hillel the Elder (end of the
first century B.C.E.—beginning of the first century C. E.),[22]
and thirteen of which are reported in the name of Rabbi Ishmael (second century C.E.).[23] The influence of Hellenistic
rhetoric upon the formulation of these rabbinic hermeneutic
rules has been asserted by some modern scholars.[24] That this
influence was exerted upon the technical formulation of the
rules, rather than upon the actual application of the norms,
or at least some of them, is obvious, once we realize that the
a fortiori argument figures in the biblical text itself.[25] But
what mainly concerns us here is the fact that a system of
logical methodology was required in order to make the rabbinic concept of Torah viable, and that, to the extent to
which this system incorporated elements of logic and common sense, of induction and of deduction, the documents of
Revelation had to be approached with the tools of Reason.

Equally important is the rabbinic concept of *sebhara* ("common sense" or "reasonable argument").[26] This involved the
application of pure reasoning to the determination of a law
and not the use of a hermeneutic rule in connection with a
scriptural text. A study of the relevant material has led Louis

Jacobs to the conclusion that, in the discussion of the schools, "a law which can be arrived at by a process of reasoning (*sebhara*) requires no Scriptural warrant, but enjoys of itself full Scriptural authority." [27]

Basic to the role of *sebhara* is the consideration that human reason is capable of arriving at certain truths; therefore, such truths did not have to be stated specifically in the Scriptures. What is more, rabbinic literature even affirms that there are laws in the Bible which man would have arrived at by logic in any case. Among these laws it lists the prohibitions against robbery, immorality, idolatry, blasphemy, and murder.[28] In other words, it is clearly assumed that unaided human reason would have coincided with the divine law, making the revelation of at least these five laws unnecessary. Medieval Jewish philosophy, as we shall have occasion to see, addressed itself to this very problem, since, after all, an "unnecessary" revelation would hardly fit into the Jewish concept of Torah. It is suggestive, however, that all five of the above-mentioned laws are included among the Seven Laws of the Sons of Noah,[29] and are therefore deemed to be part of the primordial divine revelation to the ancestors of the whole human race. Thus it is not a question of "unaided" human reason, after all, but of a "natural religion" of which the foundations were laid by God Himself. Nor must we leave out of account the implicit presupposition that, with God as man's Creator, human reason itself is God's gift to man. The first intermediary benediction of the daily *Amidah* (which was "The Prayer" to the Rabbis) reads as follows:

> Thou favorest man with knowledge,
> and teachest mortals understanding.
> O favor us with knowledge, understanding and discernment
> from Thee.
> Blessed art Thou, O Lord, gracious Giver of knowledge.[30]

How consistently this presupposition was held can be seen also from the rabbinic requirement that, upon seeing a Gen-

tile(!) sage, the following benediction is to be recited:
"Blessed be He Who hath imparted of His wisdom to His
creatures." [31]

Within such a system, of course, there was hardly room
for real dialectics of Reason and Revelation. In the final analysis, all that the proper exercise of Reason was able to
achieve was to explicate the contents of the written documents of Revelation, or to arrive, independently, at conclusions already found in the sacred text.

It is in this connection that mention must be made of a
well-known Talmudic story, found in b. *Baba Metzi'a* 59b.
Here we read that a number of Rabbis engaged in the discussion of a legal minutia. The majority reached one decision,
Rabbi Eliezer another. A number of miracles occurred in
response to Rabbi Eliezer's appeal for supernatural support
of his position. Finally, in response to a last frantic appeal
by Rabbi Eliezer, a voice came from heaven and proclaimed
that the law accorded with Rabbi Eliezer's decision. Where-
upon Rabbi Joshua arose and exclaimed, "It is not in heaven"
—a statement explained by the Talmud to mean that, once
the Torah had been revealed at Sinai, no further supernatural
interference was needed in determining a law, but the principle of human decision by majority rule, itself derived from
Exod. 23:2, must be followed in all cases.

This story, at first sight, creates the impression that Reason
is being championed against Revelation. It is in this sense that
Erich Fromm quotes the story, pointing out that "it empha-
sizes the autonomy of man's reason with which even the
supernatural voices from heaven cannot interfere." [32] However, Fromm has failed to notice that the side of Reason, in
this story, is represented by a rabbinical interpretation of a
biblical text. Walter Kaufmann is therefore absolutely justified in objecting to Fromm's interpretation, on the ground
that "no appeal to miracles is tolerated, and decisions must be
based on arguments—but these arguments must be based on

citations and interpretations of an absolutely authoritative text, and no critical questions about the text are allowed any more than an appeal to other books or independent observation." [33] Indeed, this story might well be used to illustrate that, in rabbinic Judaism, the role assigned to Reason was wholly *within* the framework of revealed religion.

It could not have been different. The legalists whom we encounter as the champions of Reason used rational methods for the classification of laws, and reasonable criteria for adapting the biblical provisions to the ever changing circumstances of life. But in reality, and this fact has until quite recently been ignored, the savants themselves were "pneumatic" personalities, mystics whose true source of enlightenment lay in religious experience.[34] Men who were accustomed to *gilluy shekhinah* (the revelation of God's Presence) in their own time [35] would not doubt the veracity of traditions which spoke of similar revelations in ages past, and, in particular, of the revelatory sequence of Exodus—Red Sea—Sinai.

This is not to say that the Rabbis were unaware of the fact that, on so-called rational grounds, a given provision of the Torah might be seriously questioned. But those "rational" grounds were identified with the quibblings of the Gentiles, and with the promptings of man's own "evil inclination." [36] Their own certainty of the *fact* of Revelation made all such "disparaging thoughts" completely irrelevant.

Disparaging thoughts—but not thought as such. There were, indeed, some differences of opinion among the Rabbis as to the legitimacy of man's attempt to fathom the "reasons for the commandments." [37] Yet the rationalistic approach to this subject so prevalent in medieval Jewish philosophy has its roots in the rabbinic period. Even those Rabbis who disparaged the attempt to find "reasons for the commandments" did not deny the fact that each commandment may have its reason. They merely doubted man's ability to find it, or preferred to accept the whole legislation of the Torah in terms of "radical obedience." "The divine law itself," as Jacob B. Agus summarizes that position, "may be nonrational and amoral, though not antirational and immoral." [38]

For the Rabbis, the Revelation of the Torah was the basic datum. Reason functioned in an auxiliary capacity. It could trace the implications of a given law. It could bring various details under a general classification. It could even parallel, to a certain extent, the contents of the documents of Revelation —though, as we have seen, such findings of apparently "un-aided" Reason were themselves deemed to have been part of the primordial Revelation to the "sons of Noah." Reason, moreover, was at liberty to picture for itself the "how" and "when" of Revelation. In the light of misunderstandings which were to plague the nineteenth and twentieth centuries, it is important to emphasize this fact, to note that it was not the Mosaic but the divine authorship of the Torah which was a matter of dogmatic affirmation for the Rabbis.[39] Schools of thought differed on how the Torah as a literary document came into existence—whether it was all written down as one unit, or whether it came into being in instalments.[40] Such subsidiary questions were not thought to affect the basic issues. The only serious objection which was reckoned with was the outright denial of the revealed character of the Torah. Yet such an objection automatically placed the objector beyond the pale.[41]

But if, in the Palestinian and Babylonian schools, Reason could be assigned an auxiliary function, this simple solution was no longer adequate when, by way of Moslem philosophy, Jews were once more confronted by the rationalistic heritage of Greece. Saadya Gaon (892-942) had to reckon with Reason, together with sense perception and inferential knowledge, as legitimate "sources of truth and certainty." [42] This, of course, poses the problem of the very need for Revelation, and we shall see how Saadya comes to terms with it. One question, though, is really *hors de combat*, and that is the fact of Revelation itself. Saadya, after all, and his successors in medieval Jewish philosophy, operated within a definite Jewish framework, which itself was based on the Sinaitic Revelation. That is why Saadya adds to the above three "sources of truth and certainty" a fourth one: "the truth of reliable Tradition." [43] If, then, the written and oral traditions of Judaism are accepted as reliable reports, then the Revelation at Sinai is a *fact*, a fact which philosophizing does not have to establish, but which is itself the starting-point of philosophizing.[44] This same *fact* is asserted by the greatest philosophers, Judah Halevi (1086-1145),[45] and Maimonides (1135-1204).[46]

With Reason and Revelation thus recognized as equally authoritative facts, the *problematik* of medieval Jewish philosophy does not lie in the presence or absence of either one, but in their interrelation. What if the conclusions of Reason and the revelatory text should fail to agree? And, if they are in agreement, why does God use two channels of communication where one would do?

The first problem is solved by denying its real existence. Such contradictions can only be apparent. They arise either through a misunderstanding of the text or through a faulty application of Reason. As the Bible commentator Abraham Ibn Ezra (1092-1167) put it succinctly, "Balanced judgment is the foundation, for the *Torah* was not given to him who is lacking in Reason. And the messenger between a man and his God is man's intelligence." [47] It is this rationalistic approach that leads Maimonides to assert that "those passages in the Bible, which, in their literal sense, contain statements that can be refuted by proof, must and can be interpreted otherwise." [48] Maimonides himself makes use of this principle whenever the anthropomorphic descriptions of God in the Bible conflict with his own more sophisticated notions of the Deity, or whenever he feels compelled to tone down the miraculous element of the biblical narrative. Indeed, he regards it as the primary purpose of his *magnum opus* "to explain certain words occurring in the Bible. Of these, some are homonyms, and ignorant people persist in choosing the wrong meaning. Others are used in a figurative sense, and are understood by such people in their primary sense." [49]

In short, Reason is the final arbiter of the contents of Revelation. But this brings us to the second problem, namely, why is Revelation as such necessary? Here, Saadya gives us a twofold answer. In the first place, the documents of Revelation contain *more* than unaided Reason could give us. In fact, the commandments of the Torah fall into two categories, (*a*) the "laws of Reason" and (*b*) the "laws of Revelation." To the former category belong such laws as regulate human conduct in terms of elementary morality; to the latter belong ritual and ceremonial provisions, at which unaided human Reason would never have arrived. And even the "laws of Reason" are in need of Revelation, for, while unaided Reason could arrive at general principles, their detailed application would never meet with common consent were it not for the specific legislation given by Revelation.[50]

Second, even though the "laws of Reason" are, in theory, accessible to man without Revelation, it would be a very long time before man arrived at those laws. And many of us would never reach this stage, because we lack either the ability or the necessary patience.[51] Consequently, as a kind of short-cut and pedagogical device, God gave us His Revelation. "Even women and children, and people incapable of speculation, now have a perfect religion, and are able to attain unto it." Revelation, therefore, becomes, with Lessing (1729-1781) a stage in the "education of the human race."

The door was thus opened to a complete identification of the conclusions of Reason with the contents of Revelation, and, by and large, this is the direction in which rationalistic Jewish philosophy moved in the Middle Ages. But, as Julius Guttmann has pointed out, when it came to details, the identification of Reason and Revelation could be carried out only with difficulty. After all, the cold metaphysics inherited from antiquity remained foreign to the personal character of biblical and talmudic religion.[52]

What is involved here is the fundamental problem of whether the Bible is primarily a textbook of metaphysics, or whether it is not first and foremost a book of religion. That it lends itself to metaphysical *interpretations* we have already seen. But does metaphysics exhaust the content of biblical religion? Could the Bible possibly be addressed to something other than man's *mind?* Maimonides would have answered the first question in the affirmative, and the second in the negative.

But the answer of Maimonides is not the only possible one. In the thought of Judah Halevi we find a dialectical approach to Reason and Revelation, which, while maintaining that there is nothing in Judaism that contradicts Reason,[53] insists that Reason is unable to comprehend God.[54] For, according to Halevi,[55] there is a difference between the "God of Aristotle" and the "God of Abraham." Rational speculation leads us to the former, but only the latter is actually *experienced* by the worshipper. Although, as we have already seen, Halevi sets much store by the reported fact of the Sinaitic Revelation, it is religious experience as such, the existential certainty of the presence of God, which is the real basis of Halevi's approach to our problem. Judaism, for him, is not the sum total of metaphysical doctrines, but a matter of heredity and environment, of history and biology, of a divinely instituted cult the purpose of which is to enable Israel to experience God ever anew. Of course, correct belief and right moral conduct have their rightful place within this system, too, but they do not exhaust it. Nor, do they, in and by themselves, produce it. God's interference in history, and God's Revelation, do.[56]

It is not the purpose of this presentation to give a full description of medieval Jewish philosophy, or even a more or less detailed account of the systems of Halevi and Maimonides. It suffices for us to look upon the two last-named thinkers as representatives of the two different ways in which the Jewish Middle Ages were able to come to terms with the problem of Revelation and Reason. For a better understanding of the radical break which was to occur in modern times, it is well for us to bear in mind what the different schools of medieval thought did hold in common.

First of all, there was the acceptance of the *fact* of the Sinaitic Revelation, the *datum* which was the starting point of Jewish philosophizing. As late as the eighteenth century, Moses Mendelssohn, in his *Jerusalem*, was still to maintain the historical fact of the Sinaitic Revelation, even though for him the event was one in which legislation only, and not doctrine, was revealed.

This brings us to the second point: Revelation, as understood by the medieval philosophers, had content. God revealed *something*, and this something consisted of laws, of metaphysical truths and correct beliefs. And this was so even in those cases where Revelation might merely confirm something at which human Reason had already arrived.

Third, the acceptance of the fact and content of Revelation did not bind the medieval thinkers to an acceptance of the literal meaning of the biblical account of that Revelation. Thus Maimonides, taking his stand on a talmudic passage (b. *Makkoth* 24a) which claimed that the people assembled at Sinai heard only the first two of the Ten Commandments directly from God, while the rest were mediated by Moses, insisted that the principles of the existence of God and of His unity (which is what the first two of the Ten Commandments meant to Maimonides) are principles which can be arrived at through *reasoning*, for "whatever can be established by proof is known to the prophet in the same way as to any other person. . . . These two principles were not known through prophecy alone." That is to say, "hearing the commandments directly from God" means to Maimonides that the ideas which they express are wholly accessible to human Reason.[57] All the other commandments were transmitted by Moses, which, Maimonides explains, means that the people heard a sound which was unintelligible to them but which Moses interpreted in terms of the commandments. Medieval Jewish thought stressed this "sound," or "voice," which the people perceived at Sinai. Rejecting any anthropomorphic notions of God, it was inconceivable to those thinkers that God should have spoken to Israel in the same way in which one man speaks to another. What Israel heard was not God speaking in human language at all, but a specially "created voice," or a "shaping of the air into the form of letters which would indicate to the prophet or to the people the matters which God wanted to let them know." [58] Even the reference to the tables of stone which "were the work of God" (Exodus 32: 16) is understood by Maimonides as an indication that the tables were of *natural*, rather than of artificial, origin; "for all natural things are called 'the works of the Lord.' " [59]

This kind of interpretation leads us to a fourth and final point, the conclusion that there could be no real conflict between Reason and Revelation. Thinkers might differ in their estimate of the powers of unaided Reason. Some, like Judah Halevi, might deny Reason's ability to fathom that which is the real concern of Revelation. But, as we have seen, even Halevi denies that that which Revelation has over and above Reason is *anti*-rational. The ancient identification of wisdom with Torah, effected at the close of the biblical period and taken for granted by the Rabbis of the talmudic age, remains operative even here. For the Jew, there can be only one ultimate source of truth, and both Reason and Revelation flow from it.

Satisfactory as this position undoubtedly was to our medieval ancestors, it has an aura of unreality for us in the modern age. Each of the four points which we have singled out has been exposed to a merciless assault. To begin with, the modern rationalistic temper cannot exempt any reported fact from critical investigation. For the thinkers of the Talmud and the Middle Ages, as we have seen, the *fact* of the Sinaitic Revelation was outside the realm of discussion. It was the presupposition on the basis of which further philosophizing took place. It was the *miraculous* fact which did not have to be fitted into any over-all view of the uniformity of natural and historical events. Yet it is precisely the search for uniformities which, in the modern view, is the function of rational inquiry. "It seeks these throughout the world of empirical fact. To come upon the non-uniform, in this view, is not to discover an exception to uniformity but merely one's ignorance; it is, therefore, not an occasion for ceasing to inquire, but rather a spur to further inquiry." [60] Thus, modern inquiry cannot take Tradition's word for the "fact" of Sinai. If that fact is to be accepted at all, it must fit into the over-all view of the historical process. But the moment the Sinaitic Revelation was ousted from its privileged position of being an exception to the rule, it was open to attack from all sides. Deists in the seventeenth and eighteenth centuries, putting their faith in the "religion of reason," and identifying Reason with "natural religion," ruled out all supernatural revelations. Historians and Bible critics of the nineteenth century, mistrustful of "pious forgeries" by priests living centuries after the events they purported to describe, were unable to find any corroborative evidence to establish the truth of the biblical account of the Sinaitic Revelation. On the contrary, they felt sure that the real content of the supposed Revelation was of such a nature as to compel a dating many centuries after the time of Moses.

With this, we have broached the subject of "content." It will be recalled that the medieval thinkers agreed that something was revealed, a position still maintained by Mendelssohn, though he limited it to legislation only. Such a view presupposes a God Who, in one way or another, "speaks" to man, and tells him, in unmistakable terms, what he should believe and what he should do. This kind of God must, of course, be conceived in personal terms—terms which no longer fitted the Absolute or Universal Spirit, in which disguise alone could God be made respectable in nineteenth century philosophy. Such a God does not "speak." He may "manifest" Himself in "the starry heavens above" and even in man's moral conscience. But He certainly does not impart any factual information. Reason alone provides man with the "eternal verities" required for "bliss." Besides, the Bible was now recognized as incorporating evidence of man's slow groping for divine truth, rather than as a transcript of that truth itself. The theory of evolution had come upon the scene, and, without further ado, it was assumed that what holds true in geology and biology must necessarily hold true in the realm of the spirit. There could have been no Revelation of the whole truth right at the beginning of Israel's history. The Jewish reformers who drew up the Pittsburgh Platform in 1885 found "the Bible reflecting the primitive ideas of its own age." [61] Now thinkers spoke in terms of "inspiration," and of the "peculiar Jewish genius for religion" [62]; but "the Book coming down from heaven" [63] had become a myth past credibility.

Another point of agreement among the medieval thinkers was the conviction that the biblical text need not be taken literally. Not only did this notion facilitate the ongoing process of adapting the legal provisions to changing circumstances, but it was also very helpful to the medieval philosophers in averting many possible conflicts between Reason and Revelation. The Catholic church, with its doctrine of tradition, and Rabbinic Judaism, with its doctrine of the oral Torah in the light of which alone the written Torah is to be understood, both provided the necessary dogmatic structure to keep fundamentalism at bay.[64] But for the modern temper, this was too easy a way out. Baruch Spinoza (1632–1677) had already attacked the attempt of Maimonides to harmonize the biblical text with the demands of Reason.[65] And certainly the task which modern biblical scholarship set itself was one of determining the original and pristine meaning of a text, freed even from its biblical "glosses," let alone the interpretations of postbiblical exegetes.

In uncovering the motivation for Spinoza's polemic, we find ourselves in the middle of the attack against the fourth point on which the medieval thinkers had agreed, namely, that there can be no real conflict between Reason and Revelation. Peace between them was possible because, if truth be told, Reason did not have an independent existence, after all. In discussing the role assigned to Reason by Rabbinic Judaism, we noted that Reason was given a function *within* the system of "Revealed Religion." It served as an auxiliary to scriptural interpretation but never as an independent critical principle. While in the Middle Ages Reason was more a power to be reckoned with, it must be remembered that even then Reason's limits were strictly circumscribed. Reason was identified with special philosophical systems, such as Aristotelianism or neo-Platonism. Reason itself became synonymous with *literary* authority, and the resolution of the conflict between Reason and Revelation took the form of effecting a reconciliation between two *literary* traditions. With Spinoza, however, and with other modern thinkers, Reason came into its own; nothing better demonstrates Reason's self-sufficiency than the insistence that its language (and its audience) is quite different from those of the Scriptures. If the Bible spoke naively, and was innocent of metaphysics, that was of little concern to the modern thinker. If anything, its naivety justified the philosopher in turning his back on the documents of the supposed Revelation. The roles had now been completely reversed. While Rabbinic Judaism assigned Reason a role *within* the system of "Revealed Religion," the problem was now to find a place for "Religion Within the Limits of Reason Alone," to quote the title of Kant's treatment of this subject. Reason itself was now regarded as the origin of Religion, and Religion had its justification only to the extent to which Reason acknowledged its contribution to "the moral improvement of men." [66]

In short, with the new independence of Reason, and with its relentless application to all areas, the imposing structure of the medieval compromise was unable to survive into our own time. We see only the ruins, and no longer the structure. Fragments are scattered along the path of our religious search. But fragments do remain, and the question arises whether these fragments could not now be built into a new configuration more appropriate to our age.

Basic to such a new configuration would be the frank admission that there is nothing in the realm of empirical fact which can legitimately be barred to the investigation of Reason. Reason, after all, is and remains, in Ibn Ezra's words, "the messenger between a man and his God." There may be areas beyond Reason's reach, and today we know Reason's limitations much better than did the nineteenth century; but that does not mean that a rational search should not be attempted. To the extent, therefore, to which biblical history and biblical documents are in the realm of empirical fact, they are completely subject to critical investigation. That this may, on occasion, result in upsetting cherished notions of the past is obvious, but inevitable. That, in many instances, our age will have to put a question mark where earlier generations boasted a dogmatic affirmation will be another inescapable result—as will the continuous revision of so-called scientific results themselves. (The most recent trends in biblical scholarship, for example, have recovered a healthy respect for ancient oral traditions.)

But none of this amounts to a denial of Revelation, though it does involve a reformulation of what is meant by Revelation. We now apply our term to a certain *interpretation* given to naked historical data (on which scientific research may shed light). "Revelation," in the words of John Baillie, "is given, not in the form of directly communicated knowledge, but through events occurring in the historical experience of mankind, events which are apprehended by faith as the 'mighty acts' of God, and which therefore engender in the mind of man such reflective knowledge of God as it is given him to possess." [67]

The Exodus from Egypt may serve as an illustration of this. Whatever the detailed events might have been—and to determine them is the function of critical scientific scholarship, not of religion—the central fact remains that ancient

Israel saw the beginning of its history in an escape from Egyptian slavery. But what does this fact *mean?* It could have been recorded as the first strike of the bricklayers' union in history. It might be put down to "population shifts." But ancient Israel itself regarded this bare fact as a "revelation" of God, as a manifestation of the divine author of liberty. And a great deal of the social legislation of the Hebrew Bible is motivated by this particular apprehension of the "mighty acts" of God. Moreover, the sequence of event and legislation is typical of the Jewish understanding of Revelation, and need not be any less compelling today simply because we moderns look upon legislation in terms of man's "response" to the experience of Revelation, rather than of its actual historic "contents." [68]

In fact, today we readily admit that "the Bible is more than the word of God: it is the word of God *and* man; a record of both revelation and response." [69] That is why Revelation, according to Franz Rosenzweig, "is only this: Revelation. The primary content of revelation is revelation itself. 'He came down' (Exodus 19: 20)—this already concludes the revelation; 'He spoke' (Exodus 20: 1) is the beginning of interpretation, and certainly 'I am' (Exodus 20: 2.)" [70] Yet Rosenzweig significantly adds, "But where does this 'interpretation' stop being legitimate? I would never dare to state this in a general sentence; here commences the right of experience to give testimony, positive and negative." [71]

Similarly, Martin Buber maintains that his own belief in Revelation "does not mean that I believe that finished statements about God were handed down from heaven to earth. Rather it means that the human substance is melted by a spiritual fire which visits it, and there now breaks forth from it a word, a statement, which is human in its meaning and form, human conception and human speech, and yet witnesses to Him who stimulated it and to His will." [72]

It might seem, at first sight, that by the ceding of all empirical facts to Reason, the old harmony between Reason and Revelation has been re-established. But the matter is more complicated. As we have seen, in the nineteenth century, Reason had made of God an impersonal Force or Principle, thus by definition ruling out the kind of God Who can reveal Himself to a given person or people. A God Who reveals *Himself* must be a Self, a Person. Many spokesmen for Reason still maintain the nineteenth-century God-concept, and thereby deny the possibility of any divine incursion into history.

This is a dogmatic stand, but one which, as Emil L. Fackenheim has demonstrated elsewhere, does not follow from Kantian critical rationalism.[73] Kant admitted that "rational inquiry must *treat* man as an instance of law and uniformity, as much as any natural object. But he denied that this proves that man *is* an object among objects." Human freedom and personal uniqueness are at least a theoretical possibility, apart from being a moral and practical necessity. We have learned to value the human *individual;* Fackenheim shows a direct line of descent from Kant to Buber's *I and Thou*. He also wonders whether the possibility of an I-Thou experience might not be extended to the possibility of such experiences between the human and the Divine. He adds, however, that while critical rationalism can raise this question, it cannot answer it.

The answer is provided by life itself. Man's ever more urgent need to assert his own individuality, his value as a person, and the corollary recognition of the value of his fellow man's individuality, have shown that all rationally constructed systems of uniformity reach their limit in the face of the *fact* of personality. And the same holds true of the rationally constructed "God-concepts" in the face of the Personality of God. At this point, the modern religious Jew finds himself in accord with Judah Halevi's distinction between the "God of Aristotle" and the "God of Abraham." He speaks in terms of his own experience, and of the experience of the millennial tradition of his people within which he has his being. (How impotent are all theories limiting God's ability to communicate with man when seen in the light of one moment of true prayer! How clumsy the attempt to fit Jewish history into a "rational" pattern, when there is no escape from the fact of the covenant which was made "with him that standeth here with us this day before the Lord our God, and also with him that is not here with us this day!" [74]) This is the position of Revelation in the current stage of the dialectics.

And Reason? It has a twofold task today. In the first place, through its investigations into nature and history, it furnishes us with the data in which faith might apprehend the "mighty acts" of God. Second and no less significantly, Reason is the indispensable yardstick to be used in "interpreting" Revelation. As we have noted, "interpretation" is man's "response" to Revelation, and, being man's, the response is subject to the normative arbitration of Reason. Among the abundant varieties of religious experience, Reason has no small part in deciding whether the word spoken to us emanates from a "prophet of the Lord" or from a "prophet of Baal." Reason will continue to guide us, as it guided the Rabbis of old, when it comes to implementing in our social, vocational, and religious lives the concrete "commandments" which, in the Jewish view, must always result from authentic experiences of Revelation. The reconstruction of Reason may lead to a recovery of Revelation in our time.

EMIL L. FACKENHEIM

The Revealed Morality
of Judaism and Modern Thought
A Confrontation with Kant [1]

Preface: On Jewish Philosophy Today

THIS PREFACE is in the nature of an afterthought, written after the essay itself. Its purpose is to state the method which the essay itself uses, and to clarify the reasons for the use of this method, a clarification which will show that this essay means to fall into the discipline of modern Jewish philosophy.

First, while the essay is throughout concerned with the revealed morality of Judaism, it nowhere categorically affirms the reality of revelation. This is not because I am not prepared to make such an affirmation but rather because, in my view, to do so would transcend the scope of philosophy, Jewish philosophy included. For I hold the affirmation of revelation to presuppose a commitment, which in turn permeates the religious thinking which springs from it. Philosophical thinking, however, both presupposes, and stays with, objective detachment, which is why both a religious commitment and the religious thinking flowing from it are, as such, extraphilosophical. I hasten to add that they are not for that reason antiphilosophical.

This is enough to indicate that the very concept of a Jewish philosophy is gravely problematical. How can thinking be at once truly philosophical and yet essentially Jewish? To say that it must be *essentially* Jewish is to dismiss, as deserving no further thought, that a philosophy might become Jewish by virtue of the accidental Jewish origin of its author. How then can it at once have the objectivity and universality which is required of it as philosophy, and yet be essentially committed to a content which has Jewish particularity? To judge by many contemporary samples of Jewish philosophizing, it must sacrifice either one or the other. If it is a rational endorsement of "values" found in Jewish history and literature, the very endorsement—which, being rational, is universal—makes these values essentially human, because universally valid, thus reducing their Jewishness to a historical accident. But if it remains bound to specifically Jewish goals, such as the survival of Jewish life, this limitation deprives it of the radical detachment and the radical universality required of philosophy. This is not to say, incidentally, that either of these pursuits is useless or illegitimate.

Can there be a Jewish philosophy, then, which is at once genuinely philosophical and yet essentially Jewish? This was possible at least under the special intellectual conditions which prevailed in the Jewish Middle Ages. Jewish philosophy then was the *confrontation between philosophy and Judaism*. This confrontation presupposed that philosophy and Judaism were different from each other and irreducible to each other; that it was necessary to confront them; and that it was possible to confront them in a manner which would compromise neither.

In the Middle Ages, all these conditions were accepted by those who engaged in Jewish philosophy. They accepted, first, the existence of two independent sources of truth, of which one was human reason, and the other a divine revelation embodied in the sacred Jewish Scriptures. On the basis of this fundamental assumption, they accepted these additional ones: that reason and revelation cover at least in part the same ground; that there is at least some apparent conflict between them; and that the conflict is apparent only—that it can be resolved without violence to either reason or Judaism. Without the first and third of these additional assumptions, there would have been no possibility of a Jewish philosophy, and without the second, no necessity for it.

It is noteworthy that, although there was a continuous tradition of Jewish philosophy in the Middle Ages, Jewish philosophy has appeared only sporadically in the modern age, and then unsure of its status. This is no accident. First, it has not been easy—to put it mildly—for modern philosophers to accept revelation as a source of truth, over and above reason itself. Reason, in the modern world, is apt to take itself as autonomous and all-encompassing. It is evident that, on such an assumption, philosophy cannot *confront* Judaism. If taking note of Judaism at all, it can only *absorb* it. Judaism then turns out to be, essentially, a "religion of reason," which is Jewish only by accident.

But even when philosophic reason does not make such radical claims a modern philosophic confrontation with Judaism is beset with difficulties unknown in the Middle Ages. At that time, it was assumed that there was at least one common basis for argument, in principle acceptable to both philosophers and religious believers. Revelation at Sinai—or revelation anywhere else—if actual, was an objective historical fact exactly like any other historical fact. If its acceptance as fact depended on the acceptance of authorities, this was true of *any* historical fact. Judah Halevi could argue, *both* as a philosopher and a believing Jew, that the testimony of the six hundred thousand present at Mt. Sinai could not have been mistaken.

But this view concerning revelation and authority is no longer acceptable either to modern philosophers or to thoughtful modern believers. Modern analysis has disclosed that it is not authority which is the source of faith but rather faith which is the source of acceptance—if any—of authority. An agnostic, had he been present at Mount Sinai, would have heard only the thunder and no voice of God. Revelation, as an objective event of communication, is hearable only to those already listening; and the listening is a listening in faith. This is a view accepted alike by modern philosophers and the best of modern religious thinkers. At any rate, it is my view.

It is on this view that the question arises whether, under modern circumstances, there can be a Jewish philosophy at all. For if that view is correct, then religious thinking—at least Jewish religious thinking vis-à-vis revelation—is from beginning to end *committed* thinking, which stands in dialogical relation to the God of Israel. But, as has been said, philosophical thinking must be from beginning to end *detached* thinking. It may thus seem that there is now no basis for meeting, as there was under medieval assumptions, since revelation is accessible, if at all, only to a commitment which is *ipso facto* non-philosophical. At best there could be only an attempt to show the compatibility of modern reason with a modern acceptance of revelation; and even such an attempt, unlike its medieval precursors, would be more concerned with keeping the two apart than with binding them together.

It is in this precarious situation that the following essay seeks, nevertheless, to contribute to a revival of Jewish philosophy. Although insisting both on the detachment of philosophic thought and on commitment as the condition of the accessibility of revelation, I nevertheless assume that revelation is not *wholly* inaccessible to philosophic reason. Under what conditions can this be possible?

As has already been said, this requires, in the first place, that the philosopher, *qua* philosopher, should suspend judgment as to the actuality of revelation. The essay that follows confronts the revealed morality of Judaism with certain modern philosophical standards of morality. It does not commit itself to the actuality of a revealed morality.

But how, without such a commitment, can there be a philo-

sophical understanding of the *nature* of a revealed morality?
The essay undertakes such an understanding through what
may be called a *sympathetic phenomenological re-enactment.*
This remains bound to the limits of philosophical detachment,
while at the same time seeking a sympathetic understanding
of truths accepted only on the basis of a commitment. Such
an understanding will obviously have certain limits. One cannot, for example, remain a detached philosopher and yet ask—
let alone find an answer to—the authentic Jewish question,
"What does the God of Israel demand of *me?*" At the same
time, it would seem that to deny in principle the possibility
that detached thinking might understand some of the meaning
of committed faith is impossible, for it is to be led to absurd
consequences, such as that unless one shares the faith of a
religious literature it must be wholly unintelligible; or that a
leap from detachment to commitment, if and when it occurs,
must be wholly blind. It would also be to imply that a Jewish
philosophy is impossible in the present age.

The argument for the possibility of such a philosophy, as
presented in this preface, is obviously fragmentary. It is hoped
that the reader may find less fragmentary the example of
Jewish philosophizing given in the following pages.

I

Can a law be at once moral and the will of God? Can one
accept it as at the same time a moral duty and divinely
revealed? Or is, perhaps, a revealed morality, radically considered, nothing less than a contradiction in terms?

At one time, such questions would have seemed preposterous
to uncritical religious believers, and even critically minded
philosophers would have seen no need to ask them. Today,
they have become part of the fabric even of popular religious
thought. This is due, more than to anything else, to the
influence of one single philosopher. Present-day academic
moral philosophy may not pay much attention to Kant; most

popular moral or religious tracts may not so much as mention his name. But on the topic of revealed morality, moral and religious thought at both levels is still much influenced—consciously or unconsciously—by Kant's moral philosophy.

A Jewish philosopher concerned with that topic does not therefore engage in a mere antiquarian academic exercise if he seeks a confrontation of Kant and Judaism; that is if, investigating this topic, he takes Judaism as his example of a revealed morality, and Kant as his main guide in moral philosophy. This is the undertaking of the present essay which, under double guidance, asks whether the moral characteristics of a religious law or commandment must clash with the way in which it is revealed. We say: "must clash." For that a clash is *possible* must be taken for granted, and one need not be either modern or a philosopher to know it. Rabbinic teachers, for example, knew well enough that human behavior falls short of true morality if it is motivated solely by fear of heavenly punishment or the hope of divine reward.[2]

II

Philosophy has always questioned revelation in general and revealed morality in particular. But no philosopher prior to Kant found it necessary to question all revealed morality as being less than truly moral simply by virtue of being revealed. The question whether all revealed morality might be a contradiction in terms is a question which was not asked.

This may be shown by a brief review of the most radical objection to revealed morality made by pre-Kantian philosophy on grounds of morality alone. Theologians often claim that revelation is the sole source of our knowledge of moral law. Philosophy has almost always been forced to reject this claim. For to be obligated to any law, a man must be able to know that law; and to qualify as moral, a law must be universally obligatory. But, on the admission of theologians themselves, revealed moral law is accessible only to those who possess the revealed Scriptures.

It will be noted that this objection by no means amounts to a rejection of revealed morality. It is merely a threat of rejection, unless a certain demand is met. The demand is for an independent, universally human access to moral law, in addition to revelation.

Can Judaism meet this philosophical demand? One's first resort would be to the general Noachidic revelation which, unlike the revelation at Mount Sinai, is given to all men. But this can satisfy the philosopher only if he can exact a further concession. The Noachidic "revelation"—if one chooses to retain this term—must be accessible without a Scripture: for the Noachides have no Scripture. It must be, that is, a universal human capacity; in short, just what the philosopher has called reason all along.

Traditional Judaism may have misgivings about this concession. If pressed, however, it will nevertheless concede. For it must then, itself, distinguish between *moral* revealed laws which, "had they not been written by God, would have had to be written by men," and *non-moral* revealed laws, "to which Satan and the Gentiles object." [3] But if, except for divine action, men would have *had* to write moral law, they must be *able* to write it. And if the Gentiles—who object to non-moral revealed law—do *not* object to moral revealed law they must, in fact, have written or be able to write at least some of it.

This clarifies sufficiently for the present purpose the relation between Jewish revealed morality and philosophical rational morality, as set forth prior to Kant. However loudly and lengthily the two moralities may quarrel about the *content* of moral law, they have no necessary quarrel concerning its *foundations*. The philosopher has no moral reason for objecting in principle to a morality resting on revelation. And the Jewish theologian has no religious reason for objecting in principle to a morality resting on reason. What is more, this mutual tolerance concerning the foundations of morality produces opportunities for settling conflicts concerning its content as well. This is attested to by a long line of Jewish rationalists who believed that, since the same God was the creator of human reason and the giver of the Sinaitic revelation, the discoveries of reason and the teachings of Judaism could be in no genuine conflict.

III

This peaceful coexistence was upset by a thesis advanced by Immanuel Kant, first prominently stated in his *Fundamental Principles of the Metaphysics of Morals* (1785). Kant himself recognized that his thesis was both crucial and revolutionary; he held that previous moral philosophy did not contain it, and that, because of this failure, it had failed as a whole. Kant also recognized the revolutionary implications of his thesis for revealed morality. Indeed, this is a theme to which he kept returning, as if unable to leave it alone.

In a passage exemplary for our purpose Kant writes:

> [If the will is moral] it is not merely subject to law, but subject in such a way that it must also be regarded as imposing the law on itself, and subject to it for that reason only. . . . All past efforts to identify the principle of morality have failed without exception. For while it was seen that man is bound by his duty to laws, it was not seen that he is subject only to his own, albeit at the same time universal legislation, and obligated to act only according to his own, albeit universally legislating will. So long as one thought of man as merely subject to a law, whatever its content, without this law originating in his own will, one had to think of him as impelled to action by something other than himself. The law had to carry with it some interest which induced or impelled him to action. But in this way all labour to discover the supreme ground of duty

was lost beyond recovery. For one could thus never arrive at duty, but merely at the necessity of acting for some interest.[4]

But this, Kant concludes, is at best only an impure morality. An externally compelling or cajoling law must necessarily be heteronomous or impure so far as moral motivation is concerned. To be pure, a moral law must be autonomous, or self-imposed.

We must be sure to grasp the essence of the Kantian thesis. It is by no means the mere assertion—as we have seen, far from new—that in order to be morally obligatory, a law must have a universality enabling all men to know it. Kant would have thought this condition satisfied by those ancient moralists who identified the moral law with the law of the universe, or by their present-day heirs who identify it with the laws of mental health. The essence of the Kantian thesis is that neither of these laws, however universal, can by itself *obligate* a man to obedience; they can do no more than promise happiness or mental health as the reward of obedience, and threaten unhappiness or neurosis as the punishment of defiance. This is because both laws confront man only from without. They are not imposed on man by man himself. A law which cannot unconditionally obligate may be prudent, wise, or beneficial. It cannot be moral.

According to Kant, then, there may be much that can induce us or force us to obey. But no law in heaven or on earth can obligate us to obey unless we *accept ourselves* as obligated to obey. And unless we can accept ourselves as obligated we cannot *be* obligated. Once clearly identified, the Kantian thesis seems very nearly irresistible.

It poses, however, an unprecedented challenge to every revealed morality, regardless of content, and simply by virtue of its being revealed. *If in order to be moral a law must be self-imposed, not imposed from without, then how can a law given or imposed by God have genuine moral qualities?* Pre-

Kantian moral philosophy, as was seen, could accept revealed morality conditionally. Kant's moral philosophy threatens it radically. It does so because revelation is either a gift to man from without—the gift of a God *other* than man—or else it is not revelation at all.

IV

According to one widely popular interpretation of Kant's thesis, the will, in imposing moral law on itself, *creates* that law. Moral law is the collective creation of the human spirit; and only because it is such a creation is it moral at all. In rising to the life of morality, man actively transforms his own being in the light of ideals which are themselves a creative human product. All true morality is creative simply by virtue of being truly moral. And all passive submission, no matter to whom or what, is less than truly moral simply *because* it is passive submission.

Philosophers who accept this version of the Kantian thesis must reject in principle all revealed morality, radically, unequivocally, and immediately. To them, such a morality must be at worst a mere passive submission to the whims of an alien Deity. Even at best, it is just a creative morality which fails to recognize itself for what it is, for it mistakes its own creation for a passively received gift. And by virtue of this mistake it still falls short in some measure of the ideal morality.

But it is a matter of great importance that this version of the Kantian thesis is decidedly not Kant's own.[5] Kant does not assert that the human spirit creates moral law; he emphatically denies it. And his denial dramatizes his conviction—often stated by Kant himself but frequently overlooked by his interpreters—that in order to impose moral law on himself, man need be neither its individual nor collective creator. He need be capable only of *appropriating* a law, which in fact he has *not* created, *as though* he had created it. The attacks of "creative morality" philosophies on revealed morality, whatever their merits, we may thus ignore.

Unlike these, Kant's own doctrine does not rule out revealed morality from the start. For if the moral will need only appropriate, and not create, moral law, why might it not be *prima facie* possible for it to appropriate a law given by God? This, however, seems possible only *prima facie;* while not ruling out revealed morality from the start, Kant's doctrine deeply threatens it in the end. Indeed, this threat may be described as far more dangerous than that of "creative morality" philosophies. These latter—which reject revealed morality on the basis of criteria external to it—invite a like treatment from the defenders of revealed morality. This is not true of Kant, who takes revealed morality in its own right with a considerable degree of seriousness before he questions it radically.

Kant does not rule out revealed morality from the start; his moral will does not create moral law. Yet he threatens that morality in the end: for his moral will must act as though it were the creator of moral law. This Kantian assertion confronts the believer in a revealed morality with a grave dilemma: *Either he concedes that the will can and must impose the God-given law upon itself; but then its God-givenness becomes irrelevant in the process of self-imposition and appropriation; or else he insists that the God-givenness of the law does not and cannot at any point become irrelevant; but then the will cannot impose the law on itself—it can only submit to it for such non-moral reasons as trust in divine promise or fear of divine threats.*[6]

Kant himself perceives this dilemma with the utmost clarity; only for him it is not a dilemma. In his view, the religious man must choose between what Kant terms, respectively, "theological morality" and "moral theology." But to choose moral theology is to gain everything and to lose nothing.

The religious man chooses theological morality when he

accepts laws as moral because they are the will of God. In so doing he not only submits to an alien law, but he submits to it because it is alien. Hence he cannot impose that law upon himself; and he can obey it—if he does obey it—because of its external sanctions only.[7] "Theological morality" is, and must be, heteronomous morality.

The religious man can rise above this only if he embraces "moral theology." He must not accept laws as moral because they are the will of God, but he must ascribe laws to God because they are intrinsically moral, and known to be so, quite apart from the will of God. It is because the will is capable of recognizing their intrinsic morality that it can impose laws upon itself, thus achieving moral autonomy. But this achievement is bought at a price. In imposing moral laws on itself, the will need not and, indeed, cannot pay heed to their God-givenness. The same act which appropriates the God-given moral law reduces its God-givenness to irrelevance.

One might therefore well ask why Kant's religious man, when achieving moral autonomy, should still *be* a religious man. Why should he end up with "moral theology" rather than with morality pure and simple? What necessity is there for ascribing the moral law to divine authorship, and what is the function of this ascription? This is a question of some complexity. But so long as we move in a purely moral context—asking ourselves what our duty is and why we should do it—the question does not arise at all. In that context, the question of the authorship of the moral law may be, or possibly even must be, left open. Kant writes:

> The veiled goddess before whom we bend our knees is the moral law within us . . . To be sure, we hear her voice and clearly understand her commandments, but are, in hearing them, in doubt as to who is speaking: whether man, in the self-sufficient power of his own reason, or Another, whose nature is unknown, and who speaks to man through the medium of his reason. Perhaps we would do better to refrain even from inquiring. For such a question is merely specula-

tive, and our duty remains the same, whatever the source from which it issues.[8]

V

Such, then, is the challenge of Kant to revealed morality. The student who in its light considers the revealed morality of Judaism makes two extraordinary discoveries. One is that this morality cannot be classified as either autonomous or heteronomous in the Kantian sense. The other is that, in the nearly two hundred years since the Kantian doctrine first appeared to challenge them, Jewish religious thinkers have noticed this fact but rarely, and, when they have noticed it, only dimly.

Apologetic tendencies have marred at least all the standard Jewish responses to the Kantian challenge. Thus, orthodox thinkers can certainly never have forgotten that, according to a central traditional Jewish doctrine, the commandments are not truly performed until they are performed for their own sake. Yet when faced with the Kantian challenge they have tended to behave as though they had indeed forgotten that Jewish doctrine. Rightly concerned to rescue the divine Law-giver from irrelevance, they have been prone to argue that, but for the divine sanctions behind the commandments, the latter would remain universally and necessarily unperformed. They should have insisted that the revealed morality of Judaism is not heteronomous. What they did insist all too often was that all human morality must be so. But thereby they not only put forward a false doctrine but pleaded Judaism guilty to a mistaken charge.

Liberal responses to Kant have suffered even more gravely from apologetic bias. While orthodox thinkers argued that the morality of Judaism is revealed but heteronomous, their liberal colleagues have often acted as though it were autonomous but not revealed. They would have prophets and rabbis speak with the Kantian voice of self-legislating reason.

This can be done in one of two ways; but both are foredoomed to failure. One can say that prophets and rabbis taught an autonomous morality, as it were, unconsciously: for they still gave conscious fealty to a revealing God. But then their morality stood, after all, still in need of liberal purification which finally eliminated the revealing God. Or one can picture prophets and rabbis teaching an autonomous morality for what it is—but this picture is a scandalous distortion of historical fact.

Because of the haste with which they resorted to apologetics, both these standard reactions to Kant failed to bring to light the authentic revealed morality of Judaism, which takes it out of the realm of both autonomous and heteronomous morality. One group of apologists saw that the revealed morality of Judaism is not autonomous, because it stands in an essential relation to a commanding God. The other saw that it is not heteronomous because, bidding man to perform commandments both for their own sake and for the sake of God, it rises above all blandishments and threats. But neither group was able to perceive the essential togetherness of these two elements. And yet the source and life of the revealed morality of Judaism lies precisely in that togetherness; a divine commanding Presence which never dissipates itself into irrelevance, and a human response which freely appropriates what it receives. The Jewish thinker does not respond adequately to the Kantian challenge until he brings this togetherness to philosophical self-consciousness, in order to ask a question which Kant literally forces upon him: *How can man appropriate a God-given law or commandment, accepting and performing it as though it were his own, while yet remaining, in the very act of appropriation, essentially and receptively related to its divine Giver? How can man "morally" obey a law which yet is, and never ceases to be,* essentially revealed? According to Kant, this is clearly impossible. Puzzlement and wonder arise for the Jewish philosopher because—if he is to believe the testimony of both Jewish life and Jewish thought—what Kant thought impossible is real.

VI

We must take care above all lest what is essential in this remarkable togetherness slip from notice. This would happen if one were to attend now to the divine commanding Presence in its otherness, and then to the human response in its power of free appropriation, but not to the two together. This togetherness is essential. In displaying it, we shall find that it exists in Judaism from its beginnings and throughout its history. Only in periods of spiritual decay can the one element seem capable of existence without the other. And this *is* the decay. With the exception of such periods, there is no age in the spiritual history of Judaism so "primitive" as to manifest—in the style of "theological morality"—only a divine commanding Presence but "not yet" an act of human appropriation. Nor is there an age "advanced" enough to manifest—in the style of "moral theology"—only a free human appropriation but "no longer" a commanding God who can be present in all His otherness.

At no moment in the spiritual history of Judaism is the otherness of the divine commanding Presence so starkly disclosed as in that pristine one in which the Divine, first reaching out to the human, calls it to His service. For in that moment there are as yet no specified commandments but only a still unspecified divine commanding Presence. Abraham is commanded to go to another country without being told of the country, nor of the purpose which his migration is to serve. Prophets are called as messengers, without as yet being given a specific message. Israel as a whole is challenged, knowing as yet no more of the challenge than that it is divine. In the pristine moment, the divine commanding Presence does not communicate a finite content which the human recipient

might appraise and appropriate in the light of familiar standards. On the contrary, it calls into question all familiar
content, and, indeed, all standards. Whatever may be true of
subsequent history, there can be, at any rate, no mistaking
this initial voice for one already familiar, such as conscience,
reason, or "spiritual creativity." [9]

It may therefore seem that, whatever the nature of the
human response to this pristine challenge, it cannot, at any
rate, be free appropriation. There can certainly be no appropriation of specific commandments in the light of commen-
surate human standards; for there are as yet no such commandments. And how could there be an appropriation of the
unspecified divine commanding Presence itself, when in the
pristine moment it discloses itself as wholly other than
human? It may thus seem that, if there is human freedom at
all in the pristine moment, it can at most be only heteronomous freedom; the kind, that is, which is conditioned by
fear or hope.

And yet a freedom of this sort could not survive the touch
of the divine Presence. Such freedom might survive, perhaps,
in moments of divine distance which, giving rise only to finite
fear or hope, could leave room, as it were, for a freedom
conditioned by them. But a fear or hope produced by the
touch of divine Presence would of necessity be an absolute
Fear or Hope; and as such it would of necessity overwhelm
the freedom conditioned by them. If in relation to God man
is capable of heteronomous freedom only, then the event of
divine Presence would reduce him, while that event lasts, to
a will-less tool of a blind fate.

Such a reduction is indeed the primordial experience of
some religions. But it is not the primordial experience of
Judaism. For here the Divine manifests Itself as *commanding*,
and in order to do so it requires real human freedom. And
since the Divine is *Presence* as well as commanding, the
required human freedom cannot be merely conditional; it
must be unconditional and absolute. Finally, this unconditional

and absolute freedom must be more even than the freedom to accept or reject, for their own sake and on their own merit, specific commandments: There are as yet no such commandments. The freedom required in the pristine moment of the divine commanding Presence, then, is nothing less than *the freedom to accept or reject the divine commanding Presence as a whole, and for its own sake—that is, for no other reason than that it* is *that Presence.* It is such freedom that the prophet displays when he responds, "Here I am, send me"; or the people as a whole, when they respond, "we shall do and hearken." [10]

This pristine human freedom of choice is not autonomous. Without the Other, man might have the self-sufficient power for all kinds of choice, but the power of choice to accept or reject the divine commanding Presence he would not have. How could he accept God, unless God had become present to him, for him to accept? How could he reject Him, unless He had become present to him, for him to reject? The divine commanding Presence, then, may be said to *give* man choosing power. It may even be said to *force* the actual choice upon him. For in being present, It *singles out;* and in singling out It rules out every escape from the choice into some spurious third alternative.

And yet this pristine choice most decidedly *is* a choice. The divine commanding Presence may force the choice on singled-out man. It does not force him to choose God, and the choice itself (as was seen) is not heteronomous; for it accepts or rejects the divine commanding Presence for no other reason than that it *is* that Presence. But this entails the momentous consequence that, *if and when a man chooses to accept the divine commanding Presence, he does nothing less than accept the divine Will as his own.*

But how is this humanly possible? We have already asked this question, in a general form. But it may now be given a sharper form which states in full clarity what is at stake: *How can man, in the very moment which starkly discloses*

*the gap between him and God, presume to bridge that gap,
by accepting God's will simply because it is God's, thus
making it his own? How can man presume to act out of
love for the sake of God?* It is perhaps no wonder that a
philosopher, when first coming upon this decisive question,
should shrink from it in thought. Even prophets shrank from
it, when first confronted with it in life.[11]

VII

It may therefore seem prudent for a philosopher to suspend if not to avoid that question, by turning from the pristine moment which initiates the revealed morality of Judaism,
to the developed life of that morality itself. Here revelation
has become a system of specified laws and commandments;
and at least insofar as those are moral in nature they possess
in Judaism undoubted permanence and undoubted intrinsic
value.[12] A Jeremiah may believe that whereas in one situation
God demands resistance to the enemy, in another He demands
submission.[13] But one cannot conceive of him as saying that
concerning justice or love and injustice or hatred. Just how
moral law can assume permanence and intrinsic value within
the framework of a revealed morality is indeed a deep and
weighty question, which requires treatment in its own right.[14]
The fact of its doing so, in Judaism at any rate, can be in
no serious doubt.

This may suggest to the philosopher that, once permanent
law of intrinsic value has made its appearance in Judaism, the
divine commanding Presence of the pristine moment has
vanished into an irrelevant past. What could be the function
of His Presence? If it contradicted moral standards already
in human possession, its voice would surely have to be
rejected, as a voice of temptation. And if it confirmed these
standards, it would only tell what is already known. In short,
once revelation has become specified as a system of laws, new
and revealing immediacy is either false or superfluous.[15]

If this were the full truth of the matter, then revealed moral law in Judaism would allow of only two human responses: One obeys it for its own sake, by recognizing and appropriating its intrinsic value. Then, however, one obeys it for its own sake *only*, and the divine Giver of the law becomes irrelevant in the process of appropriation, and so does the revealed quality of the law itself. Or one obeys it *because* it is revealed. But then one could not obey it either for God's sake or for its own; not the former because the Divine, having lost commanding presence—immediacy—after the rise of law, would have reduced itself to the mere external sanction behind the law; and not the latter, because the law would then need such sanctions. In short, one would be driven back to the Kantian alternative between a "moral theology" which is essentially unrevealed, and a "theological morality" which is less than fully moral.

But must the divine Presence pass into irrelevance once revealed moral law has appeared? To ask this question is to recognize that the Kantian alternative contains a hidden premise. This premise, to be sure, is hard to reject, but Judaism implicitly rejects it. According to the testimony of Jewish life and teaching, the divine commanding Presence does *not* pass into irrelevance once moral law has assumed permanence and intrinsic value. The Torah is given whenever men are ready to receive it,[16] and the act of receiving Torah culminates in the confrontation with its Giver. The prophet, to be sure, has a specific message; yet the words "thus saith the Lord" are not an empty preamble but an essential part of the message itself. Kant holds that, mediating between man and God, moral law rules out or renders irrelevant an immediate divine commanding Presence. Judaism affirms that, despite the mediating function of the revealed moral law, the Divine is still present in commanding immediacy. The Kantian premise is that moral law is a *bar* between man and its divine Giver. The premise of Judaism is that it is a *bridge*.

How can the law be a bridge? Only by making a most

startling demand. For Kant, all morality, including religious
morality, demands a two-term relationship between man and
his human neighbor. The revealed morality of Judaism
demands a three-term relationship, nothing less than a relationship involving man, his human neighbor, and God Himself. If it demanded a human relationship only, then the God
in Whose name it was demanded would indeed reduce Himself to mere external sanction behind the demand. The startling claim of the revealed morality of Judaism is, however,
that God Himself enters into the relationship. He confronts
man with the demand to turn to his human neighbor, and
in doing so, turn back to God Himself. Micah's celebrated
summary of the commandments does more than list three
commandments which exist side by side. It states an internally
related whole. For there is no humble walking before God
unless it manifests itself in justice and mercy to the human
neighbor. And there can be only fragmentary justice and
mercy unless they culminate in humility before God. Here
lies the heart and core of Jewish morality.[17]

What human response is adequate to this divine demand?
The response remains fragmentary until the commandments
are performed, on the one hand, for *their* sake, and on the
other for *God's* sake. And each of these must point to the
other.

Moral commandments, to be moral, must be performed for
their sake. For unless so performed they do not realize a
three-term relationship which takes the human neighbor in
his own right seriously; they function merely within an
attempted two-term relation between man and God. We
say "attempted." For such a relationship is rejected by God
Himself. It is God Himself Who bids man to take his neighbor
in his own right seriously. To obey God, man accepts both
his neighbor, and the commandment concerning him, as pos-
sessing intrinsic value. He performs the commandment for
its own sake.

And yet the commandment remains fragmentary if performed for its own sake *alone*. For if such performance discloses the human neighbor, and ourselves, too, as beings of intrinsic value, it is ultimately *because the divine commanding Presence so discloses them*. This is why, even if beginning with the acceptance of the disclosure only, a man is finally led to confront the divine Discloser; why performance of the commandment for *its* sake points to its performance for *God's* sake. Both are certainly part of Jewish teaching. And they exist not contingently side by side, but in an internal and necessary relation. God is not barred from direct human access by the intrinsic value of man, or by the intrinsic value of the commandment which relates to man. On the contrary, *He discloses Himself through all intrinsic value, as its ultimate Source*. And the man who accepts this disclosure acts for the sake of God. In the hour of his martyrdom, Rabbi Akiba knew that the love of God is not one commandment side by side to others. It is the life of all.[18]

The territory in which we have sought philosophic refuge from the decisive but bewildering question raised by the pristine moment of divine commanding Presence, while no doubt safer, is by no means absolutely safe, if by "safety" is meant the comfortable distance, and hence the irrelevance, of the Divine. We first saw that in the pristine moment of divine commanding Presence there is already the possibility of free human appropriation, and we have now seen that, once human freedom can appropriate specific laws and commandments endowed with permanence and intrinsic value, the divine commanding Presence will still confront it. Divine commanding Presence and appropriating human freedom still point to each other. And the philosophical question raised by their togetherness can no longer be suspended or avoided. In the light of the foregoing, we may reformulate that question, to read as follows: *how can man presume to participate in a three-term relationship which involves not only his human neighbor but also God Himself? How can he—as he must, in order to participate in such a relationship—act out*

*of love for the sake of God, when God is God while man
is only man?* In Kantian language, what is the condition of
the possibility of such action?

VIII

It is a testimony to Kant's genius as a religious thinker
that he should not have wholly ignored this question. He
even supplied it with an answer. But Kant's answer is not
and cannot be the Jewish answer. Instead, we come to a final
parting of ways.

Kant writes:

> The virtuous man fears God without being afraid of Him.
> This is because he is not worried lest he himself might wish
> to resist Him or His commandments. God is awe-inspiring
> to him because such resistance, while unthinkable in his
> own case, is not in itself impossible.[19]

For Kant's virtuous man, it is "unthinkable" that he might
not will the will of God. For a prophet when first singled
out, it is unthinkable how he *could* will it. To fear God at all,
Kant's virtuous man must imagine himself as willing what
he is in fact incapable of willing. The rabbis need no such
strategy in order to stand in fear of God. Their impossible
possibility is not the fear but rather the love of God.[20] For
Kant, the oneness of the human with the divine will is automatic once virtue is achieved. For prophets and rabbis, such
oneness is very far from automatic even for the virtuous man,
and, in a sense, for him least of all. For prophets and rabbis,
there is a radical gulf between God, Who is God, and man,
who is only human. How then is a oneness of wills possible
at all?

It is possible if God Himself has made it possible. Man
can appropriate divine commandments if they are handed
over for human appropriation. He can live by the Torah in
the love and for the sake of God, if the Torah itself is a gift

of divine love, making such a life a human possibility. He can participate in a three-term relationship which involves God Himself if God, Who in His power does not need man, in His love nevertheless chooses to need him.

The belief in the reality of such a divine love is as pervasive in Judaism as is the belief in revealed law itself. For here divine commandment and divine love are not only coeval, they are inseparable. The Torah manifests love in the very act of manifesting commandment; for in commanding *humans* rather than angels, it accepts these humans in their humanity.[21] Hence in accepting the Torah, man can at the same time accept himself as accepted by God in his humanity. This is why to attempt to perform the commandments, and to do so both for their sake and for the sake of God, is not to attempt the humanly impossible. At least in principle, the commandments *can* be performed in joy.[22]

This belief in divine love manifest in the divine commandment is present in Judaism from its pristine beginnings and throughout its history. From its beginnings: having first shrunk from the divine commanding Presence, the prophet ends up accepting it because he has experienced the divine love which makes acceptance possible.[23] Throughout its history: our daily prayer renders thanks for the divine love in which God has given the commandments.

If this faith permeates Jewish life so universally and so obviously, one may well ask why Jewish thought, when confronted with the Kantian challenge, should have failed to bring it clearly to philosophical self-consciousness. Had it done so, it would not have accepted so meekly the terms of the Kantian dilemma, between a morality which, because genuinely moral, cannot be essentially revealed, and a morality which, because essentially revealed, must be less than truly moral. It would have repudiated this dilemma, recognizing— and clearly stating—that, if divine love is manifest in the revealed commandments, the dilemma does not arise.

Perhaps it is not far-fetched to identify as the cause of

failure, in the case of non-Jewish philosophers like Kant, an ancient prejudice against Judaism bolstered by ignorance of Judaism; and, in the case of Jewish philosophers, uncritically assimilated reliance on non-Jewish modes of philosophical thought.

An ancient prejudice contrasts Jewish law with Christian love; and this is only slightly modified by the concession that love "evolves" in later stages of Judaism as well. Against this prejudice, it is by no means enough to insist that divine love is as ancient in Judaism as is divine commandment. For such love might still be confined, in Pelagian style, to the remission of sins which strict justice would condemn; and this would still leave law itself prior to love, and in itself loveless. In Judaism the primordial manifestation of divine love is not subsequent to but *in* the commandments; primordial human joy is not in a future subsequent to the life of the commandments but in that life itself.

Now it is precisely this teaching which Paul either could not comprehend or could not accept. Paul did not merely assert that the commandments cannot be performed wholly, which to the rabbis was not new. He asserted that they cannot be performed at all. This was because, while accepting one aspect of Jewish teaching he did not accept the other. He saw man commanded to act for God's sake, by a God incommensurate with all things human. But he did not see, or was personally unable to experience, the divine love which, handing the commandments over for human appropriation, makes their performance a human possibility. Hence he thought man was obligated to do the humanly impossible.

Kant's moral philosophy may be regarded, among many other things, as a protest against this Pauline conclusion. It rightly insisted that man can be morally obligated to do only what he is able to do, and hence that, if an unbridged gap exists between the human and the Divine, divine commandments cannot be moral commandments. It also properly refused to divorce the Divine from the moral. But this compelled it to deny the gap between the Divine and the human. And the result was that the divine will become a moral redundancy.[24] In all this, Kant's anti-Pauline protest shares one assumption with Paul's own position; the denial of divine love manifest in the God-given commandment. From the standpoint of the revealed morality of Judaism, Kant may therefore be viewed as the nemesis of a tradition which begins with Paul.

IX

Throughout our essay, the term "Judaism" has meant classical Judaism which finds literary expression in the Hebrew Bible and in rabbinic literature. Re-enacting this Judaism in thought, we have rejected the Kantian dilemma between a morality which, if autonomous, is not essentially revealed, and, if essentially revealed, must necessarily be heteronomous. But can the Jewish philosopher of today do more than give a phenomenological re-enactment of the classical faith? Can he accept it himself? It is all too obvious that faith in a divine love manifest in revealed commandments, always under much pressure in life, is subject to pressures of the gravest kind not only in modern life but in the realm of modern thought as well.

This is a question for separate inquiry, the results of which one cannot anticipate. One can only be certain that the Jewish philosopher who conducts it must not, at any rate, surrender quickly to modern pressures. For if there is anything that makes him a *Jewish* philosopher, it is precisely the duty to confront, and take seriously, his own Jewish tradition. He would fail in his duty if he were ever to forget that his ancestors could often live by the belief that "when the Torah came into the world, freedom came into the world." [25]

MONFORD HARRIS

Israel: The Uniqueness of Jewish History

I

EVER SINCE the beginning of political emancipation and rationalist "Enlightenment," Jews have been faced with a task of self-understanding that is probably unique in their history and unique in human history. Since the modern period, Jews have been asking themselves: Are Jews Jewish by virtue of being adherents of a religion, members of a race, participants of a culture, or citizens of a nationality group? It is possible that this question was raised in the Maccabean period, but it was not faced again until the beginning of modern times. It seems without parallel in history that a group rich in historical experiences and memories should suddenly be confronted with the embarrassing task of self-definition.

It is not accidental that this issue of self-understanding became problematic in the modern period. It is the high mark of the modern period in Jewish history that the Jew begins to look at himself through non-Jewish eyes and consequently feels compelled to understand himself only through universal categories. One of the curious paradoxes of Jewish history is the rich cultural creativity of the modern Hebrew renaissance, which came into existence as a result of a group of literary artists and brilliant masters of the Hebrew language

who looked upon Jewish existence as fitting into universal
categories such as nationality, culture, and folk. Inheriting
the eighteenth century tradition of the *Measfim*, the nineteenth and twentieth century shapers of the modern Jewish
mind and modern Jewish existence whose contribution has
been rich and vital were, paradoxically, viewing Jewish existence with categories derived from non-Jewish historical experiences. There was in their thinking a certain reductivism.
The ancient and medieval Jewish certainty (which we aim
to pursue in this study) was given up by them in the attempt
to reduce Jewish existence to the common, universally apprehended category of a nationality group with a specific
culture.

What seemed so clear and certain during the last two
centuries is now no longer. We can now see the inner contradiction of their view; but even more significant is that
their view does not truly clarify Jewish existence. They had
absolutized eastern European Jewish existence in their time
as typical of all times and of all places. Despite their brilliant creativity and despite their many critical insights, they
remained essentially precritical. With naiveté born of a
revolutionary acceptance of modern categories of thought,
they had prejudged the Jewish understanding of Jewish
existence.

The inadequacy of their understanding of Jewish existence
has been made clear to us by the three most important events
of the twentieth century: the development of American
Jewry, the decimation of European Jewry, and the creation
of the state of Israel.

American Jewry, despite its celebration of a 300-year anni-
versary, is for all intents and purposes, less than a hundred
years old. There are yet among us remnants of essentially
European movements: Eastern European Yiddishist movements, European-formulated Zionist tendencies, and European-
created religious movements. But these, less and less viable on
the American scene, have been displaced by the growth

of Jewish denominationalism, a denominationalism incipient
in the European environment but really developed in all its
exotic richness in America, the land par excellence of *religious*
denominationalism. About our Jewish denominationalism there
is a certain churchlike sectarianism. To many Jews, being a
Jew in America appears to mean synagogue membership.

Despite all its one-sidedness, however, and despite all its
historical artificiality, the dominant Jewish view of Jewishness, that it has something to do with religious affirmation, gives us a vantage point from which to survey the
meaning of Jewishness. The eastern European ideologies of
the nineteenth and early twentieth century, which played a
great role in Jewish historical existence, are no longer richly
creative and viable for American Jewry. There is an archaic
quality about even the best of the East European writers like
Ahad Ha'Am and Dubnow. In America it is simply not true
to our existence to view us as a separate cultural or nationality
group with its own language, national costumes and customs,
and separate political aspirations comparable to the self-deter-
mination of minority nationalities. There are some Jews in
America who still take this view seriously but their numbers
are rapidly growing smaller.

The destruction of European Jewry in the twentieth century, the most terrifying event in all of Jewish existence,
plays its role in Jewish understanding of Jewishness. This
destruction necessitated a shift in Jewish self-understanding.
Negatively, it destroyed the existential matrix of the *Haskalah* ideologists; but other shifts necessarily took place. Two
are worthy of note. First, and foremost, we have begun to
realize that despite the differences in ideology growing out
of the *sitz-im-leben* of the two Jewries, European and American, we are members of one people. Despite all the verbalized
humanitarianism of the (demonic) twentieth century, their
loss is our loss only. No one else really cares. In this growing
awareness we have learned that we were deeply, metaphysically, as it were, related to them. The destruction has served

as a shock of recognition in helping us American Jews redis-
cover ourselves as Jews. Never again will a Western Jew be
able to use the smug, assimilated term of "Americans (or
Englishmen, or Germans) of Mosaic persuasion." It is true
that we have not become saints, but our smug modernism
about the twentieth century as the messianic age has been
shattered. One other, less tangible, change has taken place.
In the nineteenth and early twentieth centuries eastern European Jewry, both the leaders and the masses, considered
American Jews as world Jewry's *Yishuvniks.* We were considered Jewish heathens, living on the heath, the periphery
of Jewish life—indifferent and irresponsible. With the decimation of European Jewry, we are filled with a new sense
of obligation and responsibility. It would be fatuous to assume
that every American Jew feels this, but it would be equally
wrong to ignore the fact that slowly but surely American
Jewry is beginning to come of age, has rediscovered its past,
both ancient and immediate, and its flesh-and-blood kinship
with world Jewry.

The third most important event in the life of twentieth
century Jewry is the establishment of the state of Israel. This
paper is an exploration of the theological underpinning of
Zionist ideology, and the theological momentum on which
world Jewry's affirmation of the state coasts.

American Jewry is deeply committed to the state of
Israel; of this there can be no doubt. Yet this creates surprising problems, for the gulf of separation between American
and Israeli Jewry is vast. Politically, our loyalty here is to
the United States and their loyalty is to the state of Israel.
Our language, even as seen through the eyes of the most
optimistic American Hebraist, is and will remain English.
Their language is and will remain Hebrew. Our life here
develops in its cultural manifestations as indigenously American, as eastern European Jewish life was indigenously eastern
European. Just as the thirteenth century Pietists of Germany
were indigenous to their time and place, just as Sholom

Aleichem and the life he conveniently represents were indigenous to his time and place, so American Jewish life is developing its Jewish life style. Israeli Jewry will develop its life style. We are already aware of all this in our frequently voiced concern for "cultural bridges." There are and will continue to be all kinds of barriers between us. All aspects of our cultural life will be different, cultural in the high aesthetic sense of the term and in the everyday sociological-anthropological sense of the term which includes mores and folkways.

What then is the common basis of our existence? In what sense are we and will we continue to be Jews? What will be the common denominator of our existence? Historical experiences, the development of an American Jewry, the decimation of European Jewry, the establishment of Israeli Jewry, have pointed out the insufficiency of nineteenth century ideologies of Jewish existence. These have brought us to a critical analysis of the *Haskalah*–emancipation period categories of Jewish existence. They have enabled us to see the complexities of Jewish existence afresh, to see through the precritical, naive modernism of nineteenth century Jewish thinkers; they have enabled us to see that the formulations of the last century and a half are non-Jewish categories of understanding which cannot come to grips with Jewish existence.

II

The only category of Jewish existence that makes sense and serves to clarify its uniqueness is the classical category of covenantal peoplehood. Until the modern period this was the basic premise of Jewish self-understanding. While it is true that the actualities of Jewish life still are based in a functional way on this classical category, our conscious formulations of Jewishness have given it up. In attempting to arrive at a new awareness of the meaning and importance of the classical category of covenantal existence I shall briefly review the inadequacies of the modernist alternatives.

That Jewishness is to be understood as a racial category in the rigorous physiological sense of that term is hardly maintained by anyone. Perhaps Hitler's racism sounded the death knell for this category. Empirically, it is not tenable. There are Jews who represent each of the three major races and their subgroups. Even to say that Abraham was a Semite, a member of a Caucasian subgroup, is meaningless; for it takes the Biblical account of his genealogy, as a descendant of Shem, out of context and imposes on it nineteenth century cultural-racial categories. There never was a constant Jewish physiology-physiognomy. A basic rule, embodied even in the most modern Jewish ideologies, denies the racial explanation of Jewishness: A non-Jew by virtue of personal decision and certain specific acts can become a Jew. If Jewishness were a racial category this could not possibly happen. A Caucasian, for example, can never by personal decision become a Negro.

That Jews are to be understood as a nation has been seriously and consistently maintained by some Jewish thinkers since the beginnings of Jewish emancipation. They have been aided and abetted by the establishment of the third commonwealth, the modern state of Israel. No one would deny that the modern state of Israel is a nation. But to maintain that Jewishness is finally to be understood in terms of nation is to deny important empirical data. If nation is understood as a group having a common government, common language, and common territory, then for close to 2,000 years Jews have not been a nation. How is Jewishness, from the destruction of the second commonwealth to the establishment of the third commonwealth, to be explained; since in that period the Jews did not have a common language (Hebrew is not the diurnal language of the overwhelming majority of Jews and was not for the last 2,000 years), government, or territory which they inhabited?

The second empirical embarrassment to the category of

nation as an explanation of Jewish existence is the fact that
most Jews still do not live, and do not plan to live, in the
state of Israel. Yet they are Jews. An Israeli like Ben-Gurion
may challenge the authenticity of Diaspora Jewry, but he
does not deny that there is the empirically ascertainable phenomenon of American Jewry. We are not denying that at
given times and places, e.g., in the first and second common-
wealths and for the segment of Jews comprising the third
commonwealth, Jews have been and are a nation. We do
deny that the category of nation is a viable understanding
of Jewishness, clarifying the meaning of Jewishness at all
times and places, serving as common denominator for the
various Jewries down the ages to our own time, and connect-
ing us to Jewish existence in the future. The emancipation
category of the Jews as a nationality group having in common historical memories, a language, and aspirations for
national independence may have been true for eastern European Jewry. But these characteristics are theirs only from a
period beginning around the time of the First World War.
What is true of that time and place certainly does not
characterize all Jewry at all times and in all places. There
is no evidence to indicate that nationality can explain the
medieval Jew, or contemporary American Jewishness, or the
Jews of Arabia before their destruction by Mohammed.

The Jews as a cultural group is another category of emancipation-era thinking which also does not explain Jewishness.
The appeal of this category, based on seeming empirical veri-
fiability, is due to two factors: American Jewry's primarily
eastern European origin, and therefore homogeneous cultural
life, and Jewish life in the state of Israel, which is in the
process of developing a homogeneous cultural life. American
Jewry still has both a nostalgia for that eastern European
past and a sense of genuine joy at the promise of the state of
Israel's future.

Yet the category of culture does not serve to define or
clarify Jewishness. Culture, either connoting the creation of

great aesthetic forms or as connoting folkways and daily life styles, cannot explain Jewish existence. For while it is true that a given group of Jews living together in a given territory for any length of time will develop its own cultural life, in both connotations of the term "culture," it is also true that "culture" does not describe Jewish existence at all times and all places. The Arabic-Jewish tribes until Mohammed developed a cultural life very much like that of their Arabic neighbors. In the high sense of culture they wrote and enjoyed Arabic poetry, for example. And in the sociological sense of culture theirs was similar to surrounding Arabic culture. They lived in tents, went on raiding forays, and generally lived the life of Arabic bedouin. What would an eastern European *shtetel* Jew or a modern, middle-class American Jew have in common with them? Certainly not culture!

While the foregoing categories of Jewishness have their protagonists in the American Jewish community, none of them is taken as seriously as that of Jewishness as a religion. This understanding of Jewishness is equally fallacious. It is obvious that some of the most loyal Jews in American Jewry make no religious affirmation at all; and while one may criticize their rejection of Judaism, one cannot deny their Jewishness. Neither can one ignore the fact that some of the most intensely loyal and creative Jewish movements of the nineteenth and twentieth centuries have been radically atheistic in their orientation. Their Jewishness cannot be denied. Furthermore, it is no secret that a significant segment of Israeli Jewry is indifferent or antagonistic to Judaism as a religious affirmation. Yet their Jewishness cannot be denied. Religiously, the *Chazon Ish* and Ben-Gurion had absolutely nothing in common; yet they are both Jews. The American Council for Judaism, passionate defender of Jewishness as a pure "religious" category, has easily betrayed itself by operating with other than "religious" categories. It was discovered some years ago that a Jew applying for membership informed the organization that he was an atheist. Nevertheless, he was accepted by the Council as a Jewish member.

Each of the categories whose inadequacy we have attempted to demonstrate does have applicability; each is true, but in a very limited way. Numerically, most Jews are Caucasian. At times, Jews make up a nationality, nation, culture. Historically speaking, Jewishness has been involved with a religious affirmation. But ever since the beginning of modern Jewish history, vast numbers of Jews have denied the validity of any religious claim. Yet they are Jews. Jewishness as religious affirmation has a limited truth but it does not account for the secular Jew whose Jewishness cannot possibly be denied, even by the American Council for Judaism.

One solution to the problem would be to take all the partially true categories and put them together as complementary explanations for Jewishness. But this method does not allow for an understanding of what brings all the disparate phenomena into a unity that makes Jews Jews.

The current definitions of Jewishness derive from emancipation-era experiences. Until that time Jews knew very well what Jewishness was. Emancipation-era Jewishness is involved with understanding itself through universally valid categories, and in this process authentic Jewish understanding of Jewishness is rejected. The Jewish understanding of Jewishness had become too particular and parochial for modern premises. It would be well to reflect on what this implies.

The "scandal of particularity," one of the most consistent themes of Western culture, made no serious inroads on Jewish thinking about Jewishness until the beginning of the modern period. The "scandal of particularity" implies that to be true an idea must be universally true. It is a scandal or stumbling block for philosophy as an enterprise of universal ideas to deal with particular truths. Truth for the whole philosophical tradition is, by definition, universal. Until the modern period Jewish thinking about Jewishness had by and large been unconcerned by the scandal of particularity. But emancipation-era thinking, with its assimilationist orientation, has tried to understand Jewish existence with categories that are universally valid. The task confronting us, therefore, is not the simple one of a "post-*Haskalah*" theological analysis, but a radical break with a century and a half of a specific historical orientation. It necessitates a historico-theological analysis.

Having rejected the various modern understandings of Jewish existence, and having come to an awareness of the scandal of particularity, the major modern stumbling block to apprehending the classical Jewish view of Jewishness, I shall turn to an examination of covenantal Jewish existence.

III

Darwin-oriented moderns have tended to read Genesis as a book dealing with primitive notions of astronomy, biology, and zoölogy. Darwin himself saw Genesis this way; always in the back of his mind was the fundamentalist Christian view of Genesis. Darwin and moderns generally have assumed that the fundamentalist Christian view is the authentic biblical view.[1] The moderns, both Christian fundamentalists and Darwinians, did not know that the main event in Genesis, *from Genesis' point of view*, was the creation of the Hebrew people. The crux of Genesis is chapter 12, where God reveals Himself to Abram with the offer that he will be made into a great nation if he will go to the land that God shows him. From chapter 12 throughout Genesis, everything is involved with the coming into being of this people. The barrenness of the matriarchs, the binding of Isaac, the problems of Jacob, the career of Joseph, all these are part of the story of the coming into existence of the Hebrew people. Everything else in Genesis is subservient to this theme. Genesis is not an introduction to primitive astronomy or geology, but the story of the promise to Abraham, and, despite all stumbling blocks, the first stage of the fulfilling of the promise. For Genesis, the most important creation of God is the creation of the Hebrew people.

In the biblical tradition other nations come into being in a natural way,[2] but the nation whose existence God promises comes into being after much storm and stress. Sarah, the matriarch, is barren all the years that a woman is normally fertile. No such problem besets Abraham's brother and sister-in-law. The story of Lot and his daughters after the destruction of Sodom and Gomorrah also functions to point up the barrenness of the matriarch. The binding of Isaac points up all the difficulties in the coming into existence of God's creation among the nations. Abraham, in giving up his native land and father's house for the promise of being a mighty nation, was giving up his past and present for a promised future. All the years of waiting for an heir seemed to imply that there would never be an heir, that the promise of the future would never be fulfilled. Finally, against the normal ways of the world, the old matriarch bears a child. It would seem that that for which Abraham had given up his past had finally been fulfilled, when he is asked to give up this, too. He is asked, therefore, to give up the promise, the promise for which he had initially given up his past: his native land and his father's house. The story of the binding of Isaac is to be understood as another link in the coming into existence of the Hebrew people.

So, too, is the barrenness of the other matriarchs to be understood. So, too, the theme of (potential) extramarital relationships of Sarah and Rebekah is developed because of the theme of the stumbling blocks to be surmounted, the dangers that threaten to interfere, and the coming into existence of this people. The potential extramarital relationships of the first two matriarchs are repeated with the next two matriarchs and in the stories dealing with Dinah and the son of Hamor, Judah and Tamar, Joseph and Potiphar's wife.

All these separate stories are linked together by one con-

sideration. Sterility-fertility and illicit sexual temptations seem
to interfere with God's promise; but ultimately God's promise triumphs and the Hebrew people comes into being.

Exodus continues this theme. Exod. 1:12, in telling us that
"the more the Egyptians afflicted them, the more they multiplied and the more they spread abroad," is carrying out
the theme of Genesis about the coming into existence of the
Hebrew people.

This people comes into existence through God's providence.
Its coming into existence is not simply a biological event; it
is also an historical event. *Genesis'* emphasis is the sheer
biology of the birth of the Hebrew people. Exodus deals
with its historic existence. Genesis is the story of the coming
into existence of a biological family; Exodus is the story
of the coming into existence of a historic people. One cannot
make a sharp distinction between biological family and historic people, for the biological family of Genesis becomes
the historic people of Exodus; but there is a distinction, difficult as it may be for us moderns to grasp. At the center of
life there is no longer a couple, a patriarch-matriarch, and the
central problem is no longer one of reproduction. There
are a number of tribes which in some sense constitute a
people. But this people is lorded over by Pharaoh. The story
of the exodus from Egypt, then, is the story of redemption
in the history of a people. This "redeeming" is done by a
power higher than Pharoah's. In asserting His power over
the power that seems to control them, this higher power
acquires possession of this people. He is now their Lord for
He has asserted His sovereignty over them; they are His
people for He has acquired them from Pharaoh. There are
then two parties involved with each other, God and people.
He is their Lord; they are His people.

This is the classical view of the "election of Israel," the
idea of the "chosen people." From the early days of political
emancipation to our very own day, the idea of the Jews
as "chosen people" has been eclipsed. Yet it is so central to

classical Jewish thought that it could not be wholly surrendered. It was, consequently, reinterpreted.

One way of dealing with it was to say that each people had its own characteristic talent or genius: the Greeks had a genius for beauty (or philosophy, or science), the Romans for law, the Jews for religion. There are many hidden premises underlying this assumption that make it extremely debatable and finally absurd. For our purpose, one of its most serious weaknesses is that if the Jews had a talent for religion the Biblical story should have been a picture of Israel's complete and constant trust in God, its abiding faithfulness to God's word. There would have been no temptations to idolatry, no need for denouncing prophets, no stiff-neckedness.

Another and related modern way of reinterpreting the idea of the chosen people, is to say that the Jews are the "choosing people." Since the day of the Nazi idea of the master race it has been said that the idea of the "chosen" people is ethically untenable, and that it is better to understand the Jews as the choosing people; i.e., the Jews were the only people in antiquity to recognize the true God. Precisely that which it tries to avoid is what this notion falls prey to. To say the Jews are the choosing people is to assert a position of such arrogance as to violate the canons of good manners, let alone ethical considerations. To assert that only *our* ancestors were wise enough, good enough, to make the right choice and that all other nations lacked either the wisdom or the sensitivity to do so is on a par with Nazi racism.

The idea of the chosen people is a deflation of all claims to inherent wisdom, sensitivity, or ethical greatness. It asserts that the choice, the election, comes from God, and it is not due to Israel's inherent merit. Both explicitly and implicitly the Bible is extremely critical of the Jews. The Jews are not pictured as ethically and morally superior to all other nations; they are pictured as failures. Z. Adar in his *Biblical Narrative* [3] sums this up: "If ever at any time there was a great action, it is the act of God in creating the world, and if

ever at any time there was a great failure, it is God's failure
with the people of Israel, for this failure cancels the value
of the Creator's great act."

The concept of the chosen people, one of the controlling
assumptions of the Bible and the Talmud, is not the Nazi
notion of a master race. It is in diametric opposition to it.
The modern, naive understanding of the Jews as a choosing
people is closer to the Nazi image. The biblical-talmudic
tradition sees the radical sinfulness of the Jews, not a superior
nation making the right choice among the gods. The One
God makes an insignificant and stubborn people His choice
for the covenant.[4]

This covenant was first made with the patriarchs and reaf-
firmed throughout the Pentateuch. Its terms are that God
will be their God and that the Jewish people will be His
people. The covenant, once accepted by both parties, remains
for all time.

The universal God Who has created all and is Lord of
all has a covenant with one particular people. This people
comes into existence by virtue of his covenant. That is the
people's uniqueness. It is different from the other people's
in that its coming into being is an act of providence. God
does not cease to be the Lord of all. For the nations, however,
His sovereignty is by and large an unrecognized sovereignty.
He, the Lord of all history, has brought out the Philistines
from Caphtor and the Arameans from Kir (Amos 9:7); but
these nations do not know of God's sovereignty in their
history. Only the Jews know of God's role in the life of the
nations and in their own historic existence, because God has
told them.

The covenant made for all time means that all future generations are included in the covenant. Being born into this
covenantal people makes one a member of the covenant.
Berith is election. This is very difficult for moderns to understand, let alone accept. It is our modern orientation that sees
every human being as an "accidental collocation of atoms," [5]

the birth of every person as purely adventitious. From the classical Jewish perspective, being born to a Jewish mother is a divine act of election.

But Jewishness is not a racial category which excludes all those born out of the racial group. A non-Jew by an act of decision can become a Jew.[6] It would not be amiss to point out that King David, who is the ancestor of the Messiah, was the descendant of Ruth and Tamar, both non-Jews by birth. All down the ages there have been converts to Judaism. The Talmud considers these to be "like a new-born child." And they are called "children of Abraham *our* Father."

The ancient Jew and the medieval Jew took seriously the notion of Israel's uniqueness. The lust to be like unto the nations, which Samuel had to face when the Hebrews wanted a king (I Samuel 8:5) is an indication that they were aware of the fact that they were *not* like unto the nations. There is no record in antiquity of any other group of people so concerned with being like unto the nations. Only ancient Israel, in spite of all its rebelliousness, is aware of its difference which it wishes to transcend, in a way that only strengthens the difference.

The medieval Jew took his uniqueness seriously. The idea of the covenant is consciously held by him. It is only from the beginning of the modern period, when terms and their ideas become dissipated, that we have the development of terms like "Germans of the Mosaic persuasion," the Jews as "minority people," Americans of "Jewish descent." Despite the modern conceptualizations we still, in many ways, depend on the conceptions of the covenant. When an orthodox institution names its medical school after Einstein, an *apikoros* (unbeliever) even from the standpoint of other Jewish denominations, we still affirm the covenantal assumption, "An Israelite even though he has sinned is still an Israelite." The many Jewish jokes about the apostate whose Jewishness is still so apparent are part of this deep awareness that the covenant is affirmed for all time. The dynamic of Zionism, as this paper shall explore, is only possible on the basis of covenantal solidarity. On what other grounds can we explain American Jewry's vital interest in Israel and Israeli Jewry? What does Ben-Gurion, a man whose early formative years were spent in eastern Europe—a man who is basically a chastened but doctrinaire nineteenth century socialist, attracted by classical culture, essentially atheistic—what does he have in common with the average American Jew, born and reared in America, committed to capitalism, with practically no ideological sophistication, for whom socialism is a "bad" word, who is "religious" in a purely middle-class and conventional way? Yet there is a profound connection between these two Jews. None of the universal categories—race, nation, nationality, or religion—can account for this involvement. It is accountable only on the basis of covenantal solidarity throughout Jewish history. While twentieth century Jewry no longer uses covenantal terms and has lost its conscious awareness of its self-understanding, it does, nevertheless, operate with the ideas of the Covenant.

The classical view of Covenantal existence as the basic meaning of Jewishness has always been that the Jew who rejects the Covenant is still a Jew. The atheistic Jew of our time (and perhaps this is the dominant type of our time) who may reject the covenant on the grounds that there was (or is) no God with whom a covenant was made, is still claimed by the covenant as a member of that covenant. The covenant made by God with the ancestors stands for all time, with all Jews.

IV

We, the people of the covenant, what are we like?

The earliest sustained record of our people's historic existence is our Bible. There are two interrelated basic elements in the Bible's view of the Jewish people: There is an intense, deep love for this people together with continual criticism. Perhaps the medieval argument most frequently advanced for the validity of the revelation of the Torah, that so many eyewitnesses at Sinai constitute proof of the revelation, is really not so strong an argument as another, non-philosophical argument: So highly critical a document could not be merely the production of the people criticized. No national literature contemporary with the Bible is so severely critical of its people as the Bible is. This people is criticized from a vantage point outside itself. To assume that so deep a criticism came from the very depths of the spirit of this people is fallacious for two reasons. As we indicated, no contemporary national literature has so critical a view of its producers. In terms of this alone, disregarding other crucial differences, the difference between the Bible and other contemporary non-Jewish literature is a difference not of degree, but of kind. This basic difference cannot be explained by viewing the Bible simply as a collection of national literary treasures. It can be understood best, as the Bible itself demands, from a vantage point outside the collective life of the people.

A second reason for rejecting the assumption that the Bible's sustained criticism of the people is but a record of the people's own inner critical evaluation is the contradiction resulting from this assumption: Any given people having such a clear and deep sense of self-criticism would, on the strength and vigor of that criticism, be able to cast out the impurities that provoked it. Their self-criticism would then finally cancel itself out, for the people would have purified themselves and then any critical statements would be nothing more than an artificial pose, or false humility, which, in the nature of the case, neither genuine criticism nor a purified people would manifest. But transformation never happens in the Bible. The people never do anything about the criticism. We believe, therefore, that this rigorous, sustained criticism in the Bible of the Jewish people, a criticism never artificial but an aspect of Biblical realism, a criticism rooted in a source outside the people, points to the validity of the biblical claim that it is *not* the cultural product of the Jewish people but is God's revelation both of Himself and of them to this people.[7] He revealed Himself to them because of His great love for this people, and He also criticized them because He loves them, for His criticism is one aspect of His love.

Criticism of the people is voiced in various ways in almost every book of the Bible. But there is one concept which serves as both criticism and description, the idea of the Jewish people as a stiff-necked people. This term is used explicitly a dozen and a half times in our Bible but is implicit throughout. "Stiff-necked" is both a descriptive term and an evaluative analysis.

The Bible never analyzes theoretically or abstractly this characteristic quality of the Jewish people, for this is not the Bible's way. But I think it is correct to say that one of the many implications of the narrative portions of the Bible is that the Bible views the Jewish people as basically stubborn.

It is worthwhile to reflect on something implied above. The Bible's view of any serious issue has authentic quality. Even if one were forced to conclude that the Bible's entire world-view is not tenable, one would be forced, nevertheless, to note its rootedness in the real world of men and events. It is not an artificial book like *The Book of Mormon*. Its views of Jewish history and Jewish destiny, even if one were to argue against their tenability, are based on the factual and the real. The biblical writers never sound like spinners of fairy tales.

We believe, then, that the Bible's view of the Jewish people's stiff-neckedness or stubbornness is a valid view, describing a basic quality of the people. It may be unpleasant, but it is still true that the Jewish people are stubborn. This stubbornness so criticized by the Bible remains a constant in Jewish existence, constant to this very day. Yet curiously enough, in the postbiblical literature one does not again hear this kind of indictment. The standard medieval commentaries never elaborate, at the appropriate passages, on this charge. The reason for this shift in postbiblical literature has important implications; I think that here is one of the most important clues for understanding the theological significance of the role of Pharisaic Judaism. But now I shall attend to only one aspect of postbiblical silence on Jewish stiff-neckedness: The Jewish people is still, in the vast postbiblical period, the same people. It is still a stiff-necked, stubborn people; but this quality now functions in a radically different way.

In the biblical period the Jew was humble before the nations and stubborn before God; in the postbiblical period stubbornness exists in relationship to the nations.

We were avid assimilationists in the biblical period; in spite of all the miracles during the exodus, we were tempted again and again to worship the gods of the nations and we stubbornly resisted the God of Israel. In the postbiblical period the overwhelming majority of the Jews are not tempted by idolatry. The dialectic of stiff-neckedness clarifies the most striking phenomenon of Jewish history; the nation that was disloyal to its God in the biblical period, the time of miracles and the prophets, is faithful to God in the postbiblical period, when miracles have ceased and prophecy is silent. The constant is the nature of the people. When God is vocal and would have the Jews conform to His law, they stubbornly reject Him. When the nations are vocal and would have them conform to pagan laws, the Jews reject them. The assimilating idolaters of the biblical period become the Hasidim and Maccabees of the hellenic period.

It is for this reason that the midrashic and medieval commentators do not take up afresh and extend the biblical denunciation of stiff-neckedness. The people remain stubborn and stiff-necked, but this quality has positive value now, for it is directed on God's behalf against the pagans.

Those professional leaders who, prior to the recent outbreaks of anti-Semitism in Europe and America, lamented the possible disappearance of our people in America when the goad of anti-Semitism no longer existed, were not only inept in their judgment of general society but were saying, essentially, that they lack faith in God's eternal covenant with us. In this sense, they assimilated the Christian view of the Jews, for they thought our covenant had grown old and weak. Furthermore, they showed no real understanding of the nature of our people. These professional prophets in our postprophetic age, forgetting the Pharisaic observation that after the age of prophecy prophecy has been given to fools, forgot what the true prophets knew so well and what the masses also knew: We are a stiff-necked nation who will live, humanly speaking, by virtue of our cantankerousness and contumaciousness.

V

This basic Jewish stiff-neckedness furnishes the very dynamic of all modern Jewish secularism. Modern Jewish secularism is so much part of our life that we take it for granted, but it is an amazing phenomenon. Zionism and modern Hebrew are its twin products. Zionism and modern Hebrew literature and speech were not produced by the religious Jews. Zionism coasted on religious beliefs, but the Zionist thinkers and doers were not religious. The most creative Zionists, the thinkers and the colonizers, were secularists. And this is true, too, of Eliezer ben Yehudah and the great Hebrew writers. Not one of the major writers was committed to a religious affirmation.

The two tremendous achievements, modern Hebrew literature and Zionism, are historically unique. It has been pointed out that the state of Israel is without historical parallel, for it is the only mother country created by her colonials. And the same thing can be said of modern Hebrew speech and secular literature. The language of the literate and devout became transmuted into living speech, speech sometimes illiterate and very frequently impious, for the first time.

Bahya ibn Pakudah, in answer to the question which he raises in *Duties of the Heart*, "Why have miracles ceased?" answers that miracles have not ceased, for the greatest miracle is the continued existence of the Jewish people. I suggest that the creation of the modern Jewish state and modern Hebrew literature are miracles. This has been said before, but without much awareness of its implications. Without discussing the biblical view of regularity in creation and allied problems, we can say that, for the Bible, miracles are God's wondrous signs in great historic junctures of his abiding love for Israel; signs of life which might be hoped for, but could never be predicted. Who in the early modern period could have believed that the most assimilatory period in the last 2,000 years would see the rise of Hebrew literature and speech and a Jewish state? Not one Zionist thinker was born in the land. Not one of the *creators* of modern Hebrew literature spoke Hebrew as his mother tongue. For a religious Jew these are signs of God's abiding love, and the growing question is, what will we do with these gifts? For the religious Jew these are wondrous signs in one more sense: they are signs that Jewish stiff-neckedness is as strong as ever.

Dr. Ignaz Maybaum in his *Jewish Existence* [8] points out that Zionist thinking and Zionist activities were deeply shaped by German romanticism, and he argues that Zionism is therefore an aspect of Jewish assimilationism and a break away from the most genuine aspects of Jewish faith. Theological analysis cannot stop here. Dr. Maybaum has himself added very brilliantly: "Jewish history in its entirety is a commentary on the Bible and enables us to understand the Bible and ourselves." [9]

This brief statement has far-reaching theological significance, and could serve as a profound evaluation of Jewish history, an evaluation which is one of the most necessary enterprises for contemporary Jewish theology. It may be true that German romanticism furnishes the source for much in Zionism, but to know only this is to know half of the story. The other half is what Jewish existence makes of the facts, how Jewish stubbornness uses history for its own purposes. For if Jewish history is an extended commentary on the Bible, then the source of an idea does not indicate how the idea will be used.

What romantic, non-Jewish Zionism created is taken over by the Jewish people, not only those confined to the state of Israel, and used in its own stiff-necked way, for its own existence. It is true that Eliezer ben Yehudah was a secularist, but without his secular stubbornness contemporary Jewish scholarship would have been unthinkable. And we believe that Israeli Jewish scholarship has great contributions to make to Jewish religious thinking. Such milestones of scholarship as the work of Kaufmann and Cassuto, which help us to understand the Bible on its own terms, will yet revolutionize Biblical studies and theological thinking. Jewish Biblical scholarship in America depends directly and indirectly on both Israeli scholarship and the renaissance of Hebrew speech and literature.

The American Council for Judaism, so devout in its rejection of secular nationalism on behalf of a "purified" Jewish religiosity, has been rejected by every serious religious thinker in our time, whether liberal or traditional. Rabbi Elmer Berger will be little more than a forgotten footnote in Jewish covenantal existence, despite his "religious" concern, yet Theodore Herzl will remain an important figure whenever and wherever Jews think and reflect on Jewish life in the twentieth century.

Let us see, at least briefly, why this is so. Zionism has never, insofar as we know, received any serious sustained theological analysis. On the one hand it has, if only on occasion, been dismissed as a sort of false messianism; and it does have this danger. On the other hand it has been too easily accommodated into modern religious thought and life.

Let us begin with the following assumption: An ideological position which becomes an overwhelming concern in the life of the Jewish people and a factor in its *actual* history is an important area for theological analysis; since the life of the Jewish people is the central interest for a Jewish theology. This ceases to be so only for a Jewish theology misshapen by a foreign frame of reference. We also assume that any serious event in the life of the Jewish people has earlier roots and can be clarified on the basis of an earlier set of assumptions, since Jewish history is a commentary on the Bible.

This, too, is of crucial theological significance. For it implies two important points: that the Jewish people are a historical continuum and that the revelation to the Jews (and their exploration of the meaning of that revelation) is a revelation of God's dealing with them in history, what He grants them and what He demands of them. God is, therefore, concerned not only with their past but also with their future. Therefore, whatever happens to this people has roots in its past, for it is a historical continuum and what happens in its future is already implied in God's revelation.

Jewish theology first approaches the question of Zionism by asking why there was such an overwhelming response to it. Even its detractors were passionate about it. And why, since the establishment of the Jewish state, have Jews so overwhelmingly and joyfully accepted Israel?

To understand the Jewish response to Zionism and the establishment of the state of Israel, let us turn to a biblical text. "The sceptre shall not depart from Judah, nor the ruler's staff from between his feet, until Shiloh comes (Gen. 49:10)," [10] is on the surface a rather innocuous verse. Its original meaning—or at least the meaning of "until Shiloh comes"—is a problem. One thing, however, is certain: for close to 2,000 years this has been a highly significant text. Both in personal confrontation with Jews and in numerous books and tracts, Christians have claimed that this verse is crucial, that it validates the Christian claim in opposition to Judaism.

The Christian argument can be stated quite briefly. Gen. 49:10 meant, in a very prophetic way, that the Jews would have national autonomy until the Messiah came and that once the Messiah came the Jews would lose this autonomy. After Jesus' coming the Jews lost their autonomy. This "proves" that Jesus was the Messiah. The Jews shared the prophetic view of Gen. 49:10 but they argued, in various ways, that the Jews still had autonomy and that this proved that the Messiah had not yet come. Therefore, Jesus was not the Messiah. Because of this basic "religious" concern, the Babylonian exilarchate was so important for early medieval Jewry. The Spanish-Jewish quest for the Chazars was based, essentially, on this concern: to show that some place in the world a group of Jews still had autonomy. So, too, the very late medieval concern in eastern Europe to perpetuate the "Council of Four Lands" was based on the desire to show the world that an important measure of autonomy remained to the Jews.

A number of other examples might be cited; e.g., the medieval Jewish interest in the ten lost tribes; but these will do. For two thousand years, until the period of Emancipation, Gen. 49:10 has been the battle cry. Stated negatively, the Jewish position has been that Jesus is not the Messiah, for Jewish autonomy still exists. Stated positively, the Jewish position has been that God maintains His Covenant with His people and this is proved by the fact that we still have our historical existence as a people that lives autonomously by its *own* laws somewhere.

This is the outline of the debate about Gen. 49:10; but I must assert that this has been a highly serious, highly charged issue. For medieval Jews and Christians this verse was part of understanding the most serious act in one's life, one's ultimate faith, which shaped everyday existence. The Jews, in rejecting the Christian claim, were not simply rejecting one set of philosophical principles in favor of another. They were fighting for their existence as a people and they did this because of their loyalty to God. We must remember that it was not easy to be a medieval Jew.

Their attempt to show that *some place* the Jews had autonomy was at the very inner core of medieval Jewish existence. Gen. 49:10 did not furnish the original dynamic of the Jewish attitude. Gen. 49:10 was the rubric and frame of reference for the whole large issue. Curiously enough, the medieval Jew was only concerned to show that Jewish autonomy existed *some place*. All Jews did not move to Babylonia, in spite of their knowledge that Babylonian Jewry had autonomy. Hasdai ibn Shaprut, who established contact with the Chazars, did not go to that "Jewish state"; it was enough for him to know that Jews had sovereignty somewhere else. Neither did all Jews in eastern Europe relocate their communities so they could live under the aegis of the Council of Four Lands.

Zionism, as hope and fulfillment, is to be understood as just one more landmark, though the most important, in the concern summed up in the Jewish understanding of Gen. 49:10. It is true that the days of the Messiah have not come; we are still in exile; but neither is our people in its historical existence rejected by God, for some place we do have autonomy. The contention that Zionism, as hope and finally as actualization, is really rooted in the Jewish concern converging on Gen. 49:10 clarifies what remains, otherwise, extremely enigmatic. On the one hand, once the establishment of Israel was a fact, the overwhelming majority of anti-Zionists and non-Zionists accepted the state. This turnabout was not sheer opportunism, for they now realized that the state of Israel has some positive meaning, though they did not really know what it is, that merited their loyalty. Yet, on the other hand, as is embarrassingly well known, the overwhelming proportion of Zionists did not settle in the state of Israel. This contradiction is understandable once we see Zionism's roots in Gen. 49:10.

Just as the medieval Jews who were concerned to discover Jewish autonomy somewhere in the world and yet, once the autonomy was found, did not go to the particular place but realized that their problem was solved, so, too, Zionists all over the world remained outside once the state was established. Their Zionism had been (and is) no hypocrisy, no self-deception. Their position was a reaffirmation of the Jewish understanding of Gen. 49:10. It is a theologico-historical necessity that Jews have autonomy somewhere; though all Jews need not go to that place, they are concerned with its survival.

Our analysis of Zionism as another landmark in the Jewish concern rooted in Gen. 49:10 clarifies another problem. Modern Zionism had always argued that the Jewish state was important because it would solve the problem of anti-Semitism, for it would destroy the image of the Jew as a wanderer and pariah. Today we know Zionism has only complicated the issue, for the anti-Semite's cry now is either "Go back to Israel," or "Zionism has started all the trouble; it is an international plot." This is hindsight on our part. But looking back at early modern Zionists we ask: Could they really believe that Zionism would bury anti-Semitism? Was it not apparent even in the nineteenth century that a small state was but a pawn for the big powers, and that worldwide anti-Semitism could destroy even a Jewish state; as a matter of fact, could destroy the Jews even more effectively if we were all gathered into one small state? The founders of Zionism were astute political men; what were they really saying? This, too, is clarified on the basis of Gen. 49:10. What they really meant was what the medieval Jew knew consciously. We Jews now have an answer to the anti-Semite: We are not fossils in providential history, for we demonstrate once again that the sceptre has not departed from us; we still have autonomy; the Messiah has not come; God has not ejected us from the stage of history. What the early Zionists meant, therefore, was that the objective situa-

tion which furnishes ammunition for the anti-Semite's claim
will be transformed by the Jewish state. Once again, the
Jews will be able to disprove the Christian interpretation of
Gen. 49:10.

I do not mean to imply that the early Zionist thinkers
consciously operated in terms of this analysis; but these are
the assumptions they operated with, consciously or not.

If this analysis is valid, we must account for the exception
presented by the American Council for Judaism. First let us
admit that since they are Jews, even if they themselves deny
the realities of covenantal *peoplehood*, they are bone of our
bone, flesh of our flesh. As a segment of Jewry, though a
tiny segment, they are characterized by sheer stiff-neckedness,
and they use this stiff-neckedness in their own way. We could
show that their roots extend even to the biblical period, that
they are the modern Tobiades, in direct lineage of the pre-
Maccabeean hellenizers—but this would take us far afield.
Unlike the Jewish secularists who in their basic dynamic
operate with classical Jewish concerns, the American Council breaks with all Jewish assumptions. For the American
Council, religion is a highly individualistic affair; it is a
kind of privatized culture of individual piety. It has no roots,
therefore, in historical existence and this means that vast areas
of human life have no religious meaning. Ultimately, this leads
to idolatry.

For them the religious man cultivates his own garden,
ignoring all other human enterprises. This is a form of idolatry, for it implies that God is Lord only of one personal
plot; and like all idolatry it is self-centered, selfish. Despite
its vaunted concern for the ethical it is by virtue of its underlying presuppositions unethical, since the really ethical is
always involved with politics and all historical existence. Once
there is a radical break between religion and politics there is a
break between religion and the ethical. Religion becomes a
mystery cult, ahistorical, unworldly. And in this sense the
religion of the American Council for Judaism is a subtle,

refined sort of Gnosticism, interested only in personal, meta-physical salvation for which it is willing to damn the world.

The American Council for Judaism represents a radical break with the basic assumptions which Judaism and Christianity both share. Both Judaism and Christianity took Gen. 49:10 seriously; their disagreement was only in how it is to be applied. But both took it seriously, for not to take it seriously is to imply that God does not act in history. To say that God does not act in history is to imply that only other powers act in history, that there is a vast area controlled by other powers. This denies God's ultimate sovereignty, and for both Judaism and Christianity this constitutes idolatry.

The leaders of the American Council for Judaism, despite their putative piety, will be totally forgotten and will leave no mark on Jewish historical existence, while people like Theodore Herzl, despite his secularism, will never be forgotten. For Theodore Herzl, a convenient example of the secular, nationalist Jew, was in the hands of the most crucial elements of Jewish faith.

VI

In the biblical view, the conquering pagan nation is the rod of God's anger, God's weapon against the people's stiff-neckedness. But in the postbiblical period, stubbornness became meritorious defiance of the nations. The contemporary loyal Jewish secularist, in his great contribution to Jewish existence, is asserting Jewish stubbornness against the nations of the world. He, as a secularist, does not express his loyalty to the God of Israel but, to the extent that his active loyalty affirms Jewish existence, he is the instrument of God's covenant love. To the extent that the secularist has contributed to our historical existence, and his contribution has been immense, he has demonstrated that our historical covenant with God still exists. His affirmation, as a secularist, denies

God's existence, but his act as a Jew validates our existence and, in Western culture at least, gives witness to God.

The touchstone of Jewish faithfulness is the concept of the covenant. Crucial for the covenant is the continuity of the generations, for this guarantees historical existence. And the continuity of the generations has been strengthened by the secular yet loyal Jew. He is a weak link in the chain in Jewish existence because he is corroded by secularism; yet a weak link is better than no link at all. The weak links are still used by God, the Lord of all history. A weak link can still connect the strong link of the forefathers to the potentially strong links of the descendants; the authentic Jew is a stubborn man, stubborn enough to use his father's weak link as a connection with the strong link of his forefathers.

When the state of Israel came into existence, the nations of the world reacted in various ways, as is well known. What is not well known is the Christian reaction to this event. At least one Jewish scholar was approached by Catholic theologians who were trying to understand the theological significance of the Third Commonwealth against the Christian reading of Gen. 49:10. The Catholic church's biblical exegesis was shocked by an event in Jewish history, for to the Christian theologian, blind to the autonomous richness of medieval Jewish existence but alert to the realities of the twentieth century, a state came into being which according to some fundamental Christian assumptions could *not* come into existence.[11] God's covenant with this people still exists evidently in the concrete, physical world. And a good deal of human toil that went into the building of the state was performed by secularist Jews.

These secular Jews strengthened our covenantal existence so that even Christian theologians were shocked. But we who hold that the covenant remains for all time also know that God makes use of those who deny Him. The secular Jew in his stubborn attachment to the covenantal people, although he has no understanding of the covenant and therefore denies our sonship in the process of denying God's Fatherhood, is, nevertheless, one of the builders in Jewish life, if we recall the *Midrash* which implies that sometimes sons are not builders and sometimes builders are not sons.

The secular Jew has contributed to our existence in the twentieth century. Whatever his religious ideology is, his Jewish stiff-neckedness operated to strengthen our existence as a people in the historical world. The religious Jew, the only one who can make sense of our unique existence in the historic world, our existence as a people, must understand the secular Jew even better than the secularist understands himself. For at best the secular Jew sees himself as an impersonal mite among other historic forces. The religious Jew, however, supremely concerned with our people's historic destiny as witness to God (for without our witness God would not be God, to recall the *Midrash*), sees the stubborn, secular Jew as the balm of God's love.

God sent us the rod of His anger when our stubbornness was directed against Him, and it is He Who sent us builders when the sons, enervated by ideological struggles, often more self-centered than pious, failed. All Israel, each Jew whose stiff-neckedness is directed to our existence, bears a share of Jewishness in this world.

In the nineteenth century, the great century of Jewish secularism, *Ramataim Zophim*, a hasidic anthology-commentary to *Seder Eliahu*, was composed by a Hasid named Samuel. Samuel evinces a deep concern for the secularist Jew. He raised the question, "Why is it first stated in *Sanhedrin* 'all Israel has a share in the world to come' and yet subsequently it is said of some 'these are the ones that do not have a share in the world to come [certain infamous personalities such as Ahab and some who deny the pentateuchal basis of resurrection]'? The answer is: they do not have a share in the world to come, on the basis of their own affirmation; but, included among all Israel, they do have a share; therefore, the Mishnah begins, 'all Israel.' "

The secular Jew, because of the limitations of his secularism, does not understand this. But we who do affirm the covenant he shares with us know that Jewish existence, spaning time, place, and culture, gives us through the covenant a common destiny to witness to God's Fatherhood. His *hesed*, covenant-love, is over all Israel.

The Individual and
the Community in Jewish Prayer

THE FORMS of communal prayer vary greatly among the religions of mankind. From the formulas accompanying stylized dances to spontaneous shouts and cheers, from quiet utterance at a local shrine to mass pilgrimage and recitation, the patterns differ almost without limit. Though Judaism and its daughter religions may hold similar, biblical views of God, man, and the worshipping community, yet the character of their divine services too may fall anywhere between widely placed poles. Thus the Quaker service has no set liturgy or ritual. The Friends meet at an appointed time and wait in silence for the Inner Light to move them to speak or pray. Whether much is said or little, whether emotion overflows or an unruffled calm is broken occasionally by a simple declaration, makes no difference. The meeting has served its function.

Near the other pole stands the Roman Catholic mass. Here all is ordered by God through the tradition of the church. The number, style and color of the vestments for this occasion, the specific psalms and prayers and their sequence, the very gestures of the officiant all are a fixed part of the only authorized pattern of formally required communal worship.

Each religious group shapes and justifies its service in terms of its faith. The Friends believe God works within the individual. For them, unless they are prompted by an active sense of God's presence within, all words are futile, all gestures in His direction meaningless. Better to sit silently and wait in openness for His stirrings in us than to assault Him or demand His gracious presence. Here, the group plays no special role in man's relation to Him. It is the useful instrument of mutual help and joint labor, but the Quakers have little doctrine of "the church." They work and pray together as little more than an aggregation of individuals faithful to the working of the Inner Light in each of them as in others of previous generations.

The Roman Catholic church, in substantial contrast, knows and encourages personal piety, but it knows, too, that this must be channeled through the church. The church is no human invention, no mere social instrumentality. God established the church. He did so that through it men might receive His grace and serve His will. The mass is the service He founded, the medium of His love and the honoring of His will. No private service of the heart, as valuable as it may be, can take the place of the church's celebration of the mass, nor is the worshipper's personal participation required for its effect. The mass is God's sacrament and fulfils its function not because of its subjective effect on those attending or on those performing it, but from God's action in it.

Where, within the broad spectrum of the possibilities of communal prayer, does Jewish worship fall? And what are the religious commitments which gave it this form?

Jewish faith affirms the existence of a living relationship between God and all men, not just the Jews. The covenant God made with Noah and his descendants after the flood is its classic expression. Noah stands for Everyman, since with him God begins history once again. With the previous wickedness washed away, man receives another opportunity and mandate to serve God in righteousness. In the covenant relationship, God gives man some commandments by which to live (most versions say seven) and God, in turn, promises never to bring another flood to destroy mankind. Since that day men may have wilfully rejected or quietly ignored that pact. No matter; the Noahide covenant remains and, the Jew believes, provides a continuing possibility that non-Jews like Jethro or Balaam may truly know God, that there may be righteous men among the nations who will share in the world to come.

What prayer may mean to all men, as a Jew sees it, can be derived from this fundamental understanding. The covenant with Noah established the reality of man's relation to the one, true God. This gives man the basis, perhaps the right, to worship God. More, a real relationship between man, the creature, and God, the creator, would of itself require man to serve God in worship. So the Jewish tradition regularly understood that one of the Noahide commandments was the worship of God, not of idols. (Not without significance is the fact that the covenant with Noah is made when Noah offers a sacrifice.) It may perhaps be unfair to see in the prohibition against idolatry a mandate to worship God, or in the practice of sacrifice the beginnings of prayer. Whether the act of sacrifice was or was not early accompanied by private prayer is not relevant here. In Noah, Melchizedek, Jethro, and Balaam there is an early biblical tradition that non-Jews might truly worship God, a tradition which the rabbis centuries later formalized and symbolized in their concept of the covenant of Noah. As prayer accompanied sacrifice in biblical time and gradually established itself as a separate and legitimate means of Jewish worship, so it is safe to assume a similar legitimacy for the righteous non-Jew. (Solomon's dedication prayer beseeching God's attention to such non-Jewish prayers is a unique biblical indication. There are a number of positive rabbinic expressions.)

Another aspect of the general view may be derived from the view that all men, not just Jews, were created in the image of God. Man is enough like God to know God exists, to understand what God wants of him, to stand in a covenant with Him, and, thus, to worship Him. Man, because he is in essence like God, can and should communicate with his Creator, the Master of the universe in which man lives.

This is a belief about all men and, at the same time, about each man individually. From it, as prayer becomes ever more significant in Judaism, follows an emphasis on the individual. Our earliest information about Jewish prayer services (again foregoing hypotheses concerning the Temple sacrifices and the personal prayers mentioned in the Bible) comes from the first century of the Common Era. In these sources the Jewish prayer service is already determinedly individualistic. Nothing happens in the service which the man who has come to pray does not himself bring about. The fixed order of the prayers, the leadership of respected figures, the communion with neighbors, the special room devoted to the worship of God—all these may help. They may be invaluable to the individual, even humanly indispensable. They remain means, instruments, accessories. They cannot take the place of the individual's own action, his turning to God in attentive respect.

The rabbis called this indispensable personal element of prayer *kavanah*. They debated to what extent the unlearned and the ill-at-ease, the simple-minded and the confused, must have *kavanah* if their service was to fulfil the commandment to pray. Realistic as always, they might reduce the requirement to a heartfelt "Amen" ("so be it" or even "that is what I too mean to say") to the leader's prayer; or to the first sentence of the Sh'ma; or perhaps even to its last word, ". . . One!" Still, these were the *limits*. They were the extremes to which they were willing to go to make regular prayer possible for real men in real history. But beyond this minimum of individual devotion even their realism could not force them to go. Ultimately the Jewish view of prayer involves an act of the will, a turning of the self. Normally, *kavanah*, personal involvement and projection, was the standard and the hope of Jewish worship.

Thus, the Jewish service, unlike the Catholic mass, is never sacramental. God does not so much work through the proper recitation of the liturgy as in free response to it. The Jewish service is precisely a prayer service, an order of petitions, praises, thanksgivings, and acknowledgments which men created for God. Its essential characteristic is address, not persons, acts, or places. Anyone may lead a Jewish service, and Jewish ordination is not required to qualify or consecrate one for this role. No objects are used in the service, though a prayer book will help one to remember the order and wording of the prayers. The service may be held in any reasonably appropriate place. While ten men are required for the full form of worship, the multiplication of one by ten does not suddenly alter their religious significance as individuals; it only makes them formally representative of their community. As far as their worship is concerned, they still depend upon the personal efforts of those present. Unless the congregants pray, regardless of rabbi, cantor, synagogue, or the number present, they have not achieved Judaism's purpose in directing them to assemble for prayer.

The point is important not only as a matter of comparison, but because it is vital in understanding the contemporary ineffectiveness of Jewish worship. The contemporary synagogue in its eagerness to have aesthetically appealing services has largely forgotten the role of the individual worshipper.

Nineteenth century Jewry, as it emerged from the ghetto into western culture, properly saw the need for a change in the atmosphere of congregational prayer. Jews could not accept the aesthetic and social conventions of their neighbors in their daily lives without similarly modifying the style and tone of their worship services.

Such cultural adaptation was not new in the history of Jewish prayer. The elegant structures and exalted stance of Spanish Jewish poetry had displaced the intricate word play and learned allusions of the original poets of the Holy Land, only in turn to be succeeded in central and eastern Europe by a more fervent, free-flowing diction. Now modern Europe approached things spiritual with dignity, reserve, quiet, and solemnity, and so these qualities, under the heading of "decorum," were transferred to the synagogue. As against its ghetto forebear, today's synagogue displays the sobriety and reserve that are the contemporary conventions of attention. In this tone, the modern Jew recognized cultural clues to what is important and significant. Thus the decorous style of the modern service does indeed prepare him as a citizen of this culture for the worship of God. And if personal attention and concentration are crucial to Jewish worship, then surely such an emotional setting will eliminate what modern men consider distracting. This much, and it is important, may be said for the movement to dignify Jewish worship.

After decades of experience, the time has surely come to acknowledge that there has been a loss as well. Insistence on an orderly service has nearly eliminated the active role of the individual worshipper, largely by concentrating the effective conduct of the service in the hands of professional prayer-leaders, the rabbi or the cantor. Worshippers are expected to be quiet about their prayer. They must not disturb those around them by raising their voices, crying their grief, or otherwise putting their deeply felt emotion into expression. Rather, they must conform their needs to the congregation's volume, velocity, and emotional level. They are expected to be self-contained—the exact opposite of prayer, which is honest expression from man out to God.

The rabbi and cantor, without anyone's saying a word but with that firmness that culture knows how to impose, are set different limits. They are expected to be more emotional, more personal, as they lead and interpret the prayers. In part, this is because in a group searching for dignity, they can be counted on to do so more effectively. That is to say, the reading of the rabbi and the singing of the cantor will have few, if any, mistakes. They will not hesitate, mispronounce, change keys, lose tone, or become confused. Rather, their renditions can be relied on to be pleasing to the ear, to add beauty to the service. They are aesthetically dependable.

The trained officiant is emotionally dependable as well. True, the range of expression he is permitted is far greater than the congregation's. His knowledge and experience have equipped him not only to show feeling but, more important, never while doing so, to transgress the proper social limits. With the worshipper repressed, the beautiful, safe release provided by the rabbi or the cantor now dominates the service.

What began as a necessary, useful alteration of Jewish worship has therefore created its own evils, undermining the very foundations of Jewish prayer. Under the guise of decorum the worshipper has been aesthetically cowed and emotionally neutralized. This is not to say that beautiful music, meaningfully rendered, cannot uplift and exalt the individual congregant. The long tradition of Jewish song and chant, going back further than that of the prayer texts themselves, speaks eloquently of music's religious value. Likewise the hoary record of men valued as leaders of congregational prayer, men who for their ability to express their fellows' will in prayer were highly honored, testifies to the virtue of pious and consecrated leadership in worship. The problem is not what good leadership can add, but what it has tended to supplant.

Without individuals investing their thoughts and emotions, their full attention, their devoted selves, in prayer, the Jewish service has lost its meaning. Whenever one "listens to" the rabbi or cantor, more in peaceful enjoyment than in identification and common meaning, the crucial distinction between the synagogue and the recital hall has been transgressed. Once started on this passive way, the congregation will always find it easier to shift its prayer responsibilities to those whom it has hired to pray for it. They do it so nicely, so dependably. They should really be allowed to do it all—which is but one step from having them do it alone, without benefit of congregants, not just participating but even attending.

The rabbi and the cantor must be masters of their craft if they are to lead their congregants, yet they must use their talents to stimulate, not replace individual participation if they are to keep their services Jewish at their core.

Jewish worship is by belief and practice uncompromisingly individualistic, and its future depends upon the increasing ability of individual Jews to participate in the service and fulfil its expectations.

These general views of prayer in Judaism should not blind us to the fact that the Jewish service is far from a Quaker meeting. Judaism may base its understanding of prayer on the individual man's relation to God, but it refuses to stop there. Judaism does not think of man abstracted from his relation to mankind. It does appreciate the meaning of the individual in isolation, but holds him, the single one, in unremitting importance, against a background of society and history. For the Jew, man is a social and historical creature. Hence his prayer should properly be a communal, comradely affair. Public worship is a universal human need and, also, a specifically Jewish requirement.

A religion which denied the worth of history might well consider private prayer superior to group prayer. But Judaism's basic view of the universe is historical. The Bible knows man almost from his creation as a child of history. Man's sin began and still powers the movement of events. But history is no senseless, chance succession. There is a God who rules over time. History has a purpose and a goal—that era when God's rule will be fully established by its manifestation in lives of justice, peace, and love. God's kingdom-to-be is not a private matter between one individual and God. It must be accomplished with all men and be manifest in all lives, or it is unworthy of the Lord of the universe. The individual man cannot understand himself, cannot properly know his own life's purpose unless he sees it within the context of all mankind and all of history. Isolated from his fellows he isolates himself from God's social goals.

To want to pray, but only alone and only for oneself, seems therefore to make too much of self, too little of God. Judaism commends communal prayer because God cares for all as he cares for each one, because, while God is the God of each private individual, He is the God of *all* individuals as well. The single self is indispensable. Without any *one*, mankind is incomplete. So too, without *all other selves*, equally precious to God, the single self loses its context and hence its final significance. Man cannot find himself only in others, but he also cannot find himself without them. If prayer is supposed to open man to the truth of his existence it must begin with self but it must reach out to all mankind.

Judaism values communal worship not for its specific Jewish purposes alone, but for all men. Group prayer, by confronting us with others, by asking us to link our prayers to theirs, reminds us immediately and directly that it is never enough to pray for ourselves alone. Speaking as "we," the individual discovers, acknowledges, articulates the needs, desires, hopes, which he, though one man, shares with all men because he is not only a private self but a member of humanity. Besides, when we are conscious of those with whom we stand, what we may have wanted to pray by ourselves is generally made less selfish, more humble, and therefore more appropriate for utterance before God. There before us is the newly bereaved young widower with his three small children. Near him stand the white-haired man who, close to the age of retirement, suddenly faces bankruptcy; the beautiful young woman who has just come from the hospital after the removal of a breast; the quiet mother whose consultation with the school psychologist was deeply disturbing. When we join *them* in prayer, when we must, to say "we," link ourselves with them, we, and our prayer, are refined; and often exalted far beyond our own means, for *they are praying now*, lifting us, helping us, with their "we," even as they silently reach out to the congregation for compassion and understanding.

The joy of others similarly affects our worship. We are

buoyed up by the happiness of the new grandparents offering their heartfelt thanks, the engaged couple who will be married this Sunday, the newly appointed vice-president of his firm, the recently honored community worker. Their joy infuses us so that what might have been a nagging, niggling, whine of prayer can as a proper "we" become worthy of God's attention. Indeed, the dynamism, the momentum, the upreach of a congregation truly at prayer, takes the individual from the commonplace, the humdrum, the depression of his daily routine, and projects him and his prayer far beyond himself. The joy of congregational worship is that together, by a mathematical miracle, individuals transcend the selves they were before the service began. And prayer does so, not against the worshipper's intimate individuality, but by calling him, on the most personal and private level, to do all he can, to lead and lift, to bear and support, all those with whom he stands.

Social worship is a sharp spur to ethical sensitivity as well as to enthusiasm. To stand together as equals before God with the man we dislike, the woman who has cut us, the boors who repel us, the intellects who snub us, the neighbors we do not trust, the fools we cannot bear, to say with them in some bond of unity, "we," is to shake our self-righteousness and expand the breadth of our conscience. Much of what we must pray to God is what we share with them in belief, thanksgiving, and petition. And He hears us as one with them. How can we now see them as enemies, adversaries? How can we prevent our prayer from charging us with a new sense of responsibility, not for our immediate synagogue neighbors alone, but for those of our city, our nation, and our world? Here, form and content join in happy harmony. The social context of praying makes immediately practical the ethical imperatives of the prayers themselves. Learning to pray the communal "we" is the first active step in fulfilling every prayer for righteousness and justice. The act of praying together itself commands us; therefore we know it to be commanded.

Nor should these general comments end without a practical word about personal frailty. The individual, when he is his own standard, will pray when he feels he needs to. Prayer then, finds its occasion and its value in response to his private moods and feelings. What happens under those circumstances to regular prayer with respect to frequency, intensity, and unselfish content is a commonplace of modern versions of religiosity. The man who objects that he cannot pray on schedule often does not pray at all. And when, in this hectic world, he finally allows a conscious desire to pray to take priority over all the important things he should be doing now, he finds he does not have the knack. Obviously prayer in response to the inspiration of a moment has a unique significance, one well worthy of cherishing. But it is a supplement to, not a substitute for, regular public worship—and the acquired habit of turning to God in prayer is readily transferred from the congregational to the private situation.

Where the individual operates by delicious surprise, the community prays by fixed rule. There are two reasons for this. The practical one is: everyone will know when to assemble. The theological one is equally simple. By virtue of devotion to its prophets and saints, the community is less concerned with man's momentary mood than with God's constant presence. If God is real, if He is truly God, men should speak to Him, seek Him, commune with Him regularly—anything less can only be considered folly. And as there is no time when He is not God, when the universe is free of His rule or when men are released from His commandments, so there is no time when men may ignore Him with impunity. On God's side, there is no time when prayer is undesirable. Prayer needs to be as regular, as continual, as much a part of living, as is man's continuing dependence on God. Individuals tend to forget or overlook this. Forgetting is their defense against God's ruling their lives. The community has a better memory.

Some religions have pressed this faith to its logical limit and encouraged their adherents to call on God at every moment, generally by ceaselessly repeating His name. Judaism has avoided this rather mechanical, inhuman pattern. God is always ready for prayer, but man is not. Jewish prayer is directed to God but springs from man. Hence Judaism, in characteristic practical fashion, has sought a rule appropriate to both the partners, one consistent not just with Jewish doctrine but with its goal, to live in history for God's sake. Congregational Jewish services each day are limited to three: morning, afternoon, and evening, with the latter two most often held at twilight and thus combined, as it were, into one service. These regular assemblies remind the Jew, particularly when he attends, but even when he does not, that he should be praying at least twice a day. Is it not true that, left to the promptings of his own heart, he will not arrive at even so modest a standard? Modest that is, if God is God . . .

Much of the conflict between private and group prayer is really that issue. The Synagogue, the Congregation of Israel, knows God is real. That knowledge is what created and sustains it. That is why it has prescribed appropriate regularity for its worship. The individual has his doubts and his weakness—besides, he is busy. When he believes, and when he remembers, and when he has strength, he will pray. Abraham Heschel's analysis is correct. The problem of prayer is not prayer. The problem of prayer is God. *If* God is real, men should pray—regularly. So says the distant, detached, defensive modern individual. The Synagogue says rather, *since* God is real, let us meet to worship Him at least twice each day.

Thus, the doctrine of God and man-in-general that inheres in Jewish faith leads it to command group prayer for religious, ethical, and practical reasons. That is a purely uni-

versal judgment, applicable to all men alike. Like much of
Judaism's universal content, it is implicit in traditional sources
and only rarely explicit. Still, it is part of Judaism and the
background which sets off specifically Jewish needs for
communal prayer.

The Jew as man, as sharer in the covenant of Noah, is,
like all men, enjoined to worship with others. But the Jew
shares in the Covenant of Sinai as well—that is what constitutes him a Jew, not just a man—and thus a special necessity
for communal prayer acts upon him.

This distinction, being critical to the issue of private versus
group prayer in Judaism, demands particular elucidation. To
put it bluntly, can Jewishness ever adequately be defined in
purely personal terms? (Secular or semi-secular but still non-
theistic descriptions of the Jews are beyond discussion here.
In discussing Jewish worship it is of course the Jew known
to the synagogue and prayer book who alone is relevant.) Is
being Jewish something that operates privately and so can be
expressed in a life of relative isolation? Is Jewish faith only
something between each single one and his God alone, so
that living one's Judaism does not essentially involve a
community?

In part, the answer to these questions must be "Yes." To
deny the personal element in the Jew's relationship with God
is to deny Judaism's fundamental view of man-in-general, that
he is created in God's image, that he can and should know
and serve God. But in larger part, to say that Judaism is
merely a religion of individuals requires an emphatic "No."
The Judaism of the Bible, the rabbis, the philosophers, the
mystics, the Judaism of almost every modern Jewish thinker,
and decisively the Judaism of every Jewish prayer book,
avers that Judaism is the religion of a people, a folk, a community. "The Jews" are a social entity in their own right,
not merely an aggregation of believers. The individual Jew
shares in the religion called Judaism as a member of that
people-folk-community. His Jewishness, as personally as he

may and should feel it, as privately as he may believe and
practice it, is not his by virtue of individual discovery or
creation, but by his membership in the Household, the Congregation, the Children of Israel. He brings his will, his assent,
his reinterpretation to a relationship which God established
with this community. He participates in what may, for purposes of corrective exaggeration, be called a group faith,
a social religion.

How strange that sounds in a day when men are accustomed to speak of religion as a highly private matter, something each person should decide for himself. This all-pervad-
ing personalism (akin to what sociologists have described as
"privatism") stems from several sources. One is surely a
reaction to the power of the state. Let it legislate in every
area, but let it not require of good and faithful citizens any
set religious practice or creed. Another motive derives from
a rejection of intolerance and fanaticism. Which religion is
truest, or what practices within that religion one should follow, should ultimately be a matter for each person to decide
himself. Compulsion, lay or clerical, being told what one must
do by friend or relative, seems an infringement of freedom
and a denial of personal responsibility. For most Americans,
the practical content of their religion is consciously regulated
by selection and choice. In the end, they follow only their
heart or conscience, a standard particularly precious to modern Jews since it legitimizes their deviation from traditional
Jewish law.

Judaism, as the faith of a people, does not deny the individual's right to freedom and judgment. It grants extraordinary
liberty to the individual in matters of belief. Today, even in
practice, through several organized interpretations of Jewish
observance, all of them dynamic, all seeking to make place
for personal interpretation, the role of the individual has
been safeguarded and amplified. And the practice and tradition of individuality, one Jew over against other Jews, is
legendary.

Nonetheless, religion for the Jew, as the tradition understands it, is not primarily a personal but a communal matter. The Torah was not given to Moses as an individual possession to share with others of a similar mind, but to the Jewish people as a whole. Again and again Moses is commanded, "Speak to the Israelite people and say to them . . ." The Bible is the history of this folk who found God and joined their destiny to Him. Its concern with individuals is almost exclusively for those who influenced the life and character of their folk. (The personal side cannot be absent, as the wondrous Book of Psalms, among other examples, makes clear.) The covenant of Noah was made with all mankind, and through it each man has a relation to God. The Covenant at Sinai was made with Israel, the Jewish people, and thus each Jew, as a Jew, shares this unique Jewish relation to God as an inheritor of his people's Covenant.

A religion founded on individual decision might one day find that, through laziness or inattention, few people cared. Where the individual is everything, history and its long-term movement means little or nothing; certainly little more than the history of the individual. Judaism takes the other view. Its God is the righteous Lord of creation who demands and assures that the history He made possible will end in free acceptance of His rule. The sweep is cosmic, the scope all-embracing. Judaism is primarily a religion of history, of God's will for mankind, of human destiny entire, and it envisions Israel's role and the individual's worth against that background. For it remains true, in all the grandeur of this purpose, that there is no history without individuals, no Kingdom of God among men unless He is acknowledged in single souls. Again the individual is indispensable—but against this measure not sufficient or ultimate.

Because its range stretches the limits of finitude, Judaism cannot be satisfied to be a religion whose continuity depends on private human decision. Without an endurance as patient and inexorable as time itself, Judaism's hope to transform and redeem history might be destroyed. As the religion of a people, Judaism counterpoises to the individual will-to-be-a-Jew social processes whereby the folk itself continues from generation to generation. History and literature, language and land, custom and folkways, all provide historical momentum. Thus too, the Jew enters the Covenant on entering the people, by birth, not by decision (though one not born a Jew may, paradoxically enough, take the latter route). One born a Jew may spurn or be indifferent to his people's historic character and toil—but his individual repudiation or indifference cannot change the record of history, nor the imperatives it creates for those born into the Jewish people. The Covenant of Sinai transcends the individual Jew, as it encompasses him. (The people, too, might as a whole deny its past. Today this is not hypothetical speculation. But Jewish faith includes faith in Israel as it is based on faith in God.)

Judaism is a folk religion because this best suits its religious goals. Jewish peoplehood is an indispensable part of Jewish religious thought and Jewish religious practice. A specifically *Jewish* religious life, as contrasted to that of Noahide man-in-general, means, therefore, life in and with the Jewish people, the Covenant community.

Jewish worship is, classically, communal in character. Its Jewishness derives not from the external facts that Hebrew is used, traditional texts are recited, or Jewish symbols are displayed. It is Jewish because it is born out of the Covenant at Sinai and articulates Israel's bond with its God. The special language, texts, symbols all stem from this root relationship. Jewish worship, then, is the people of Israel, assembled before its God out of continuing loyalty to their Covenant, to acknowledge, praise, and petition Him. The group may be small; traditionally as few as ten are acceptable for a full public service. When at least ten Jews congregate to pray, they constitute the Covenant folk in miniature. They represent all Israel, past and present, here and everywhere. Not ten or more individuals, but the Covenant people itself now confronts its God. The man who prays in the synagogue prays as a participant in a Jewish history which continues into the living present, and his prayers, therefore, express the needs of the community in which he stands. Jewish law is clear. The individual Jew should seek to pray with a congregation. But if he cannot (that great phrase without which nothing could endure in history) then he may pray alone. Even alone, he should pray the congregational service (with some deletions), preferably at the time the congregation is praying. For a Jew, one's individuality is connected with being one (*sic!*) of the Jewish people, sharer in a mutual Covenant with God.

The Jewish prayerbook, the *siddur*, speaks out of this particular situation of the people of Israel gathered yet again to meet its God, to renew their ancient pact and beseech His current help. That is why most of its prayers are in the plural. They speak of "us," of "our," of "we." This plural should be taken with full seriousness, in all its useful ambiguity. "We" may only mean "I," put in a rather formal, or editorial plural—important, since without "me" there is no meaningful prayer. "We" may mean "this group with whom I am now praying" and therefore I and my neighbors. It surely also means "this congregation or community," those who should be here but may not be, those with whom we share our Jewish hopes, labors, and anxieties. It means all of these—but including these, and embracing them, it means primarily "We, the people of Israel, the folk of the Covenant . . ." Now what might have been a tiny, almost selfish "we" has risen from our cosy group in its familiar associations to embrace all of history in loyalty and obedience to its Master. Through this great Jewish "we" the individual "I" has found an incomparable dignity and an immeasurable worth. This is the boon which worship as a member of the Covenant people freely bestows.

And this too is the source of the special problem of

Jewish prayer today. With some good fortune, modern man may be able to admit that he has faith, that he believes in God. He may even be able to overcome his embarrassment enough to learn to pray to Him. But this is personal religion, *his* God, met on *his* terms and in response to *his* needs. These prayers are intimate indeed, else they could not arise. The *siddur* asks him to pray to Israel's God of the Covenant— and to make Israel's Covenant-based prayers his prayers. What a gap to bridge, what a chasm to cross! If the problem of prayer-in-general is God, then the problem of *Jewish* prayer is *Israel*. To pray as one of this historic people, identifying oneself with its membership and its mission, that is the demand made of modern Jewish man by the *siddur*.

Contrast this challenge with the tone of much else of today's society. Modern America is unthinkable without the thoroughgoing commitment to please the consumer and satisfy his individual needs. Banks say they will be his friend; automobile companies seek to give him status; cigarette makers almost openly promise to enhance his sexuality; politicians mold themselves to the image he desires. Millions of dollars and countless hours of creative research are expended each year in an effort to lay bare the individual's current dissatisfactions, to reach him on a level he can enjoy, and to fulfil his remaining unfulfilments. Moreover, many now promise him that there are no risks involved; no charge will be made until he has received the first gratifications, or, if not satisfied, he may have his money back, or even double. Modern man is trained to the consumer role. He waits patiently, even in boredom. The seller must please him—or else.

Many a religious institution has sought to meet modern man on this level, to "sell" its wares, to appeal to the religious "market" in terms of the benefits its services provide. Attending group worship keeps families together, soothes housewives' nerves, and decreases managerial ulcers or coronaries. Religion permeates deeper, affects distressed areas speedier, brings longer lasting comfort.

These claims are not unwarranted. Religion can and has changed men's lives for the good, and what it offers is so poorly known that it needs the techniques of public relations to reach the unaffiliated. That is not the issue here. When a religious institution renounces its knowledge and tradition of the holy as its basic criterion of activity, particularly its wor- ship, when consciously or unconsciously its new goal is the American pattern of pleasing the consumer, it has begun its own self-destruction. It has made the congregant/consumer, not God, the focus of its concern—and while the service of God does not require ignoring man's desires, it is clear where the real priorities lie. The worship of the synagogue and the content of the prayer book reflect *God's* pre-eminence and see the needs of the individual fused with those of his religious community, the Jewish people.

The gap between Jewish prayer and American consumer logic as it applies to religion can be clarified by noting its effects. A man finally decides to come to a service. He has been told for so long that it will be good for him that he decides to give it a try. He waits for something to happen. Perhaps the music soothes him a little, the quiet is assuaging, the prayers are comforting, and the sermon is not only under- standable but even somewhat inspiring. Some consumers are satisfied with such rewards. Most are not, which is why attendance at worship is poor. They frankly find more than an occasional visit, for reasons of sociability or habit, unsatis- fying. As they say, they don't "feel anything special." Nothing unique "happens" to them that cannot be duplicated in more palpable or less demanding form. Religion really does not "do anything" for them. It doesn't "produce" when given a try.

From this general experience, the consumer-logic inevit- ably concludes: the fault is with the institution, in this case the synagogue, and its prayer book in particular. To get people to services today, the deduction follows, they must have a religion which fits in with their immediate way of life. Thus it is foolish to use a prayer book written centuries ago, in a remote poetic style, about vague generalities that largely fail to express contemporary experience. A few of the old prayers or practices should be retained for emotional or symbolic reasons (the new modernity knows that emotions are important), but the only successful service today would be one that embodied and articulated the very present needs of those praying.

This suggestion runs into great difficulty whenever men seek to put it into practice. Most free and unregimented liturgies (Methodist, Baptist—even the patterns of Quaker meetings or Jewish youths' "creative" services), when they continue from week to week and month to month, fall into a standard format and a regular style. Spontaneity is not easily regularized. Moreover, the personal needs of the congregants are not easy to discover in depth nor to express in a fresh and appealing way. As a result, attempts at a personalized service generally end up a mixture of the customary and the creative, with both the traditionalists and the individualists unhappy with the results.

Why not, however, utilize modern technology to follow this theory to its logical conclusion? No rabbi or committee, regardless of assistance or library resources, could be as effective in identifying the inner needs of worshippers at one given moment and creating a service from modern and ancient materials, verbal and musical, to express them, as a properly stocked and programed computer. The possibilities both in diagnosing needs and responding to them in varied format are exhilarating. A check list of moods and emotions could be provided to each prospective worshipper to determine his individual situation or, if that is too superficial, some sort of religious inkblots which would allow him to project his depth desires. Each Friday before sundown, the worshipper phones the computer and, according to a prearranged code, feeds it his need-data as of the present moment. Thus he knows that tonight's service will reflect his personal situation, and, having also participated in its creation, is very likely to attend. On its part, the computer is a model of rabbinic openness, gratefully and patiently accepting all calls with understanding; perhaps, by simple wiring modifications, even several at one time!

The creation of the service is speedy but to the highest standards. Experts in religious worship have previously programed the machine with the most varied possible patterns of effective religious services, as well as a feedback device which limits the frequency of their repetition. At a given time before the service, to keep the need-data as current as possible, the computer devises the evening's service. First, it mathematically determines the exact proportion of moods which will be present. Then it draws from its memory section from the entire range of literature, perhaps worldwide as well as Jewish, selections appropriate to the needs. These, according to a pattern effective for the night's goal, it structures into a service. The next chore is typing and duplicating (printing, in more affluent congregations), the computer efficiently making only as many copies as there have been calls, plus extras based on experience at this time of the year, with this weather, with such and such competitive activities going on, as to how many others will come. A truly sophisticated installation would provide for evaluation, registering the congregation's response to this service and including such responses as part of its guidance for the future. Thus, so to speak, the computer could *learn to create* ever more effective services.

One more of the many other values of this system must be mentioned: help with preaching. Surely the sermon, too, should speak to authentic congregational situations. Hence the computer might guide the preacher in his choice of text or approach. Better yet, the energetic preacher will stock his computer with a variety of sermons (again based on the computer's memory and analysis of previous congregational need patterns and reactions), and the computer, while selecting materials for this service, could also select the sermon most appropriate to it. What is more, the electronic brain could be relied upon to keep the manuscript, if not the delivery, down to a length carefully adjusted to the congregation's, not the preacher's, needs.

What is satire here will one day be attempted in all seriousness. Those who are committed to the religion of individual needs should obviously do what they can to make their faith function better.

Judaism has traditionally sought the standard of its practice and the chief guide of its observance in another direction. What it cannot do, what it believes no religion can hope to do and still be worthy of ultimate concern, is to make the individual worshipper the final measure of the value of the synagogue in general or the Jewish service in particular. When every judgment is based on whether the prayer book moves him personally, whether the ceremonies satisfy his intimate longings, the question must inevitably also arise whether God also adequately serves him. Now, the essential blasphemy of this position becomes clear. When religion abandons itself to consumers and makes them its judge, it has created a new and false god in place of the One and Only God. And this false and fickle god of the public will betray its "religious" leaders and institutions today as in its various guises it has in the past.

This does not mean that religion cannot *in part* be evaluated by how it responds to the human situation or to deny that every religion must in significant *part* meet man on his own level. The sin lies in making this the exclusive or even dominant goal. Man does have needs but, if one may dare to say it, so does God—rather, man's needs are best met in terms of God's will, His law, His purposes. Religion is more God's commands than man's desires, God's goals than man's dreams, God's presence than man's existence, though both are critical. Man fulfils himself in serving God, not in pursuit of anything he ever was or in his imperfection might, without God, imagine himself to be. This is what Jewish tradition implicitly understood as it sought to relate each man through the community and its discipline to God, and thus to his fullest self. The synagogue and its communal worship are built on that premise. If the modern Jew is to learn to pray as a Jew, and not just as man-in-general, he does not need a better prayerbook but a better theology, not a different form of worship but a deeper belief.

Or, perhaps, he needs to be helped to realize what in the depths of his soul he somehow still does believe, that he is both individual *and* Jew, single one *and* member of the Covenant folk. Then perhaps he can reach beyond the shallow self-centeredness that characterizes so much of modern man's life and that is responsible for its pervasive subsurface anxiety, and learn to say ever more wholeheartedly the "we" that must always begin with and lead back to the self, the "we" that reaches out beyond the individual, beyond neighbors, beyond the congregation, to embrace all the people of Israel (and through the people of Israel, all mankind), and to affirm with such a "we" this one Jew's place among his people before its God. Then, in sum, he will pray *as a Jew*, and praying as a Jew will know what his life of prayer can mean to him as a private self.

It is a paradoxical faith that produces the pattern and structures of Jewish worship. Each individual can and should pray for himself—but a Jew prays as one of the Covenant people. Jewish prayer is simultaneously individual and communal, and the *siddur* is Judaism's living response to the demands of this faith.

ARNOLD JACOB WOLF

Psychoanalysis and the Temperaments of Man

PSYCHOANALYSIS is widely thought of as a "Jewish science." Indeed, Freud took pains to avert just such a notion,[1] though he himself was, of course, the chief reason for it.[2] The enemies of depth psychology still dismiss it as peculiarly relevant to Jews; its friends note with gratification the biblical roots of the new wisdom. Not only are many practitioners of the art, like the very first analyst, Jews by descent if not conviction, but there is a widespread conviction that the method, the spirit, and even the conclusions of psychoanalysis are para-Judaic.

The Jewishness of Freud himself is debatable only by unnecessarily reductive definition. His ancestry and the impact of his ancestry upon his deepest feelings are clearly and profoundly Jewish.[3] His affinity for the Jewish style both mystical[4] and rationalist[5] is unmistakable. His newly emphasized prudishness together with his pioneering honesty in sexual matters is Talmudic.[6] His blend of strict scientific method with visionary dreams, his awareness of the ultimate power of the past along with an open future of incredible novelty, asceticism along with personal physical emancipation, are all Jewish by that stylistic measure which also measures the man.

To his fiancée, Freud promised that "something of the core

of the essence of this meaningful and life-affirming Judaism will not be absent from our home," [7] and he meant by the promise not only "to appreciate every pleasure" but to stand bravely against any danger which his insight would earn him. Says Ernst Simon, perhaps his most cogent Jewish commentator, "To profess belief in a new theory called for a certain degree of readiness to accept a position of solitary opposition—a position with which no one is more familiar than a Jew." [8] "I have often felt," Freud admitted to his Martha, "as though I had inherited all the defiance and the passions with which our ancestors defended their Temple." [9]

The essence of Freud's accomplishment was his recovery of paradox. His antiquarian interest in Moses, the Bible, and classical Hellenism served the purpose of creating new super-historical persons. His own blend of the ascetic (he ceased having sexual relations with his beloved wife when he was about forty-one) [10] with the permissive, the suspicious with the wholly accepting, his hatred of idols combined with a love of truth—all reveal the paradoxical man whose life work was the rebuilding of questions for a world where everything seemed about to be answered. Freud managed to make everything suspect by insisting that in the great human antinomies both sides were right. As Kant had shattered philosophical dogmatism in principle, Freud now made paradox the measurable essence of concrete human existence.

A dream, the stuff on which he found our lives are truly made, is both manifest and latent. And our selves, too, have both a visible and an invisible aspect. We both are and are not what we seem to be. We are both superficial, in the strictest sense, and profound beyond his time's imagining. We are both really sick and potentially well, and insight into our own illness is our health.

We are constrained by *ananke*, the dread reality which is a world we never made. But we are also open to the pleasures of our body-spirit which only we can wholly take away from ourselves. Our illness is precisely interminable, but treatment is finite and men recover from neurosis. We live necessarily in dread of what we fear and what we are, but we can also hope to become what we are not. We are the victims of an endless chain of circumstance which determines our most intimate choices, but therapy itself implies the power to break free. On each small issue Freud is pessimistic, realistic, bound. But with an optimism so long-range and touching that we must call it messianic, Freud breaks free of ultimate constraint. Today is always difficult, but "optimism was Freud's faith in the day after tomorrow." [11] The power of Death (*Thanatos*, personified and capitalized) is everywhere, but love (*Eros*, a God as well) will not be forever denied. The needs of man are set permanently against the awful power of civilization, but it is out of such conflict that humanity is achieved. If Galileo showed the world we are not masters of the universe and Darwin that we are not masters of the world, Freud proved that we are not masters even of ourselves. We are, rather, the uneasy mediators of everlasting struggle, the victims and inheritors of a liberating and stultifying paradox.

Nowhere is this more clear than in psychoanalytic anthropology. To the question, "Is man good or evil?" Freud gives no simple answer. He has examined clinically the demonic in his most gentle and acquiescent patient. He has seen nobility in "wolf"-men and "rat"-men. He has made forever impossible any absolute distinction between body and spirit, between the beneficent and the corrupted. He has opened to us the greatest paradox of all—ourselves. In 1932 Freud wrote, "I have told you that psychoanalysis began as a therapeutic procedure, but it is not in that light that I wanted to recommend it to your interest, but because of the information it gives us about that which is of the greatest importance to mankind, namely, his own nature, and because of the connections it has shown to exist between the most various of his activities." [12] The proper study of analysis is man.

Philip Rieff is right in reminding us that "although he

[Freud] was not a believing Jew, he remained a psychological one," for "grey, grim despair" was only half his knowing. "Freud was his own ideal Jew." [13] He foundered on the paradoxical God of Judaism, but he had rediscovered the Jewish doctrine of man. This is the point of Lionel Trilling's beautiful essay on "Freud and the Crisis of Our Culture": the divided self, against a coercive and repressive world, is the key to literature as it is to life. "In the relation in which Freud stands to it, literature is dedicated to the conception of the self," [14] and for the secularized Jew (Trilling, Freud) "literature" obviously means all the thought of man, our struggle for the self-identity of mankind. Trilling finds in the Viennese parliament, which Mark Twain said was united only in hating the Jews, the paradigm for that non-self from which Freud tried continually to free himself. Against civilization, against the repressions which history and biology impose, the divided self finally discovers its freedom and interprets its own uniqueness.

In another of the liberating interpretations of psychoanalysis which the last decade has produced, Norman O. Brown has acutely discerned the centrality of Freud's doctrine of man.[15] Brown's "eccentric" extrapolations from the Freudian version are beyond our study here, but we accept his interpretation of the Freudian view thus far: the key to Freud is his doctrine of "repression" and the unlocking of the unconscious by a study of illness, dreams, daily psychopathology, and art. What is thus revealed is the split within man, that "animal which represses himself and which creates culture or society in order to repress himself." [16] Religion is the nexus between an understanding of neuroses and an understanding of history. It refracts the objective understanding of man who seeks at once to return to the primal oneness of Eden (or mother) and to ascend toward a messianic kingdom of playful gratification. All of this transmutes humanist notions of morality. It transcends the simplistic view of man as just torn between good and evil, and reveals him as both more complex and more subtle than scientism believes. "The deeper we probe in our study of mental processes," said Freud, "the more we become aware of the richness and complexity of their content." [17]

Man divided is the tragic victim not merely of his bestiality but of his conscience, of the war between "polymorphous perversity," remembered from his childhood, and the structures of objective culture which he has both created and inherited. "We are now led to consider the important possibility of the aggression being unable to find satisfaction in the external world, because it comes up against objective hindrances. It may then perhaps turn back, and increase the amount of self-destructiveness within. We shall see that this actually occurs, and that it is an event of great importance. It would seem that aggression when it is impeded entails serious injury, and that we have to destroy other things and other people, in order not to destroy ourselves, in order to protect ourselves from the tendency to self-destruction. A sad disclosure, it will be agreed, for the Moralist." [18]

Freud is always disgusted by the "Moralist" as by that humanist theologian to whom he would like to be able to say, "Thou shalt not take the Name of the Lord thy God in vain." Both oversimplify and thus betray the image of man. Neither understands what is really at stake or how difficult it is for man to achieve a oneness which reflects the Oneness of God. Both lead to expectations which cannot be fulfilled and which make unchastened man a wolf to man. Both want man to be simply good; and, thus, they help him to violence.

> Why have we ourselves taken so long to bring ourselves to recognize the existence of an aggressive instinct? Why was there so much hesitation in using for our theory facts which lay ready to hand and were familiar to everyone? One would probably meet with but little opposition if one were to ascribe to animals an instinct with such an aim as this. But to introduce it into the human constitution

seems impious; it contradicts too many religious prejudices
and social conventions. No, man must be by nature good,
or at least good-natured. If he occasionally shows himself
to be brutal, violent and cruel, these are only passing dis-
turbances of his emotional life, mostly provoked and perhaps
only the consequence of the ill-adapted social system which
he has so far made for himself.

Unfortunately, the testimony of history and his own
experience do not bear this out, but rather confirm the
judgment that the belief in the "goodness of man's nature"
is one of those unfortunate illusions from which mankind
expects some kind of beautifying or amelioration of their
lot, but which in reality bring only disaster.[19]

It is not religion but "religious prejudice" which suppresses
authentic self-disclosure. It is an anxious and facile optimism
of secularized religiosity (Freud's own, at first?) which hides
the bitter truth about man. And such suppression not only
helps lead to the disaster of returned repression (Fascism,
war, the suicide of man) but obscures the very element of
salvation which lies in man's distress. Against his very will,
Freud is led to reassert the evil that man not only does but is.

In neo-Orthodox Christianity, this is commonly equated
with the notion of original sin. Says Reinhold Niebuhr, "The
two non-religious thinkers of modern times whose estimates
of human nature correspond to those of religious pessimism
were Hobbes and Freud . . . Freud's pessimism derived from
the fact that he regarded the 'ego' or the rational and coherent
self, as an uneasy broker between the pleasure-seeking 'id'
and the 'super-ego' which was the sum total of the social
disciplines in which the self was involved. Freud was, therefore, pessimistic about the course of civilization because he
felt that the increasingly complex disciplines of a cultured
community would repress the id-ego more and more and that
these repressions would result in aggressive tendencies." [20]
For Norman Brown, writing out of an eschatological Christian background, "psychoanalysis would be the science of

original sin." [21] For Paul Tillich, too, there is a direct correlation. H. M. Teibout, Jr., writes, "There are marked similarities between Freud's analysis of human estrangement, as manifested in neurosis and other pathological conditions, and Tillich's analysis of sin." [22]

Niebuhr, among others, finds the hidden Jewish source of the doctrine of original sin: "The concept had no place in Jewish thought. This gives rise to some interpretations which contrast the so-called optimism of Judaism with the pessimism of Christianity. Actually the Jewish doctrine of the evil inclination (*yetzer ha-ra*) which every man has inherited is almost identical with the Christian doctrine of original sin. In fact, Jesus knew nothing of the Pauline doctrine of an inherited sin, but spoke only in terms of the rabbinic doctrine of the evil inclination." [23] Something like a middle ground, too, is discerned by the Catholic existentialist, Alden Fisher: "If this [Freud's] is an image of man which deals a death blow to the pretensions of an optimistic or Cartesian rationalism it is not an image which gives comfort to a pessimistic naturalism. In this respect Freud joins the great tradition of philosophical realism in providing man with a balanced insight into the true human condition." [24] What is this "philosophical realism" if not rabbinic anthropology? While Brown finds its source in Spinoza, I believe we shall be able to disclose more weighty versions of the position which understands sin without assimilating everything to it. It is in classical Jewish teaching that Freud's doctrine of man is both exemplified and enriched. That teaching is parallel to but not precisely the equivalent of "original sin." It is realistic, but its realism is undergirded with sympathy and overarched with hope. It does not submit, as do the Freudian revisionists, to moralizing dismissal and bland avoidance,[25] but, unlike Freud, it does not place man alone in his world. It asserts a tragic split within man, but it does not insist upon the ultimacy of dividedness. It faces up to sin, but without despair.

Freud, writing at the turn of the twentieth century, was

shocked at the evil he found in man. Rabbinic Judaism, after a millennium of going to school with biblical anthropology, is beyond being shocked. And modern Judaism, disciple of both Akiba and Dr. Freud, may succeed to a new understanding of man.

In an important paper, "Eighteen Hundred Years Before Freud: A Re-evaluation of the Term Yetzer Ha-ra," Harris H. Hirschberg attempts to correlate the rabbinic idiom with the Freudian.[26] The Freudian Id, like the *yetzer ha-ra*, the Evil Inclination, of rabbinic literature, is part of man's biologically inherited psychic apparatus. It is tied to the body, driven to seek infinite gratification for its instinctual needs. The Ego, on the other hand, is as Freud himself said, *"anthropos* himself," corresponding to that Good Inclination, *yetzer tov*, which represents the human self struggling for mastery over unconscious libidinal power. Using fear (anxiety) as its method, says Hirschberg, the Good Inclination, like the Ego, checks instinctual wishes which seek to prevent its fulfilment. The *yetzer tov* displaces the *yetzer ha-ra* ("where Id was, shall Ego be"!) and turns it, at a price, into selfhood and social usefulness. Man is told, in the rabbinic literature, not to repress his *yetzer ha-ra*, but to woo it, to sublimate it, to master it. And so Freud sometimes demurely suggests that in manipulating the Id, man becomes more (and more unhappy) than his libido. For both Freud and the rabbis, says Hirschberg, the Id is more than sexuality narrowly conceived, but is explicitly sexual, anyway, and only thus ultimately creative. The constant chastening of man's animality, he finds, is the work of Torah.

We may have reason to modify these parallelisms as we inspect the appropriate rabbinic sources. We shall not, like Hirschberg, succeed in equating what is disparate, but we hope to certify that the Jewish doctrine of man is both instructive and important to post-Freudian thought. By explicating some Rabbinic texts, we shall attempt to understand better the complex phenomenon of man.[27]

The *loci classici* in the Torah from which the term *yetzer* is derived are Gen. 6:5 and 8:21, in the story of Noah. In chapter 6, at the beginning of the story, God looks wistfully upon His creation and is sorry that He made man (or, as we shall see, perhaps the meaning of verse six is that God was instead reconciled to the existence of an imperfect man). In chapter 8 the flood is over, Noah and his family have been saved, and God vows not to destroy the continuities of human history and nature again, even though He still knows that man is evil. Chapter 6, verse 5, may be provisionally translated: "And *Adonai* saw how great was man's evil on earth, and how every *yetzer* (temperament) of his mind was nothing but evil always." (The new Jewish Publication Society translation has: "The Lord saw how great was man's wickedness on earth and how every plan devised by his mind was nothing but evil all the time." This seems to make *yetzer* the product rather than the equipment of human emotion and understanding, which appears to me an error.)

Chapter 8, verse 21, reads "the temperaments of man's mind are evil from his youth," or (N.J.P.S.) "The devisings of man's mind . . ." This verse is important because it reaffirms God's understanding of man even after the cleansing flood waters had passed over him and his world. Despite the promise implied in the rainbow and the irrevocable covenant with mankind, God knows that man's root nature is evil. God is not sentimental nor melioristic. God is the discoverer of the evil *yetzer* in man, because He made it.

The rabbis are moved by the stern description of man's nature put into the Divine mouth by Genesis; they would like to soften it, but they find it difficult to do so. At least eight kinds of interpretation are employed: [28]

1. Only the generation of the flood was so absolutely evil.
2. The generation was evil only with regard to "agricultural" decisions ("evil on earth"), but otherwise unexceptionable.

3. Their sin was that they doubted God's justice.

4. Their sin was that they doubted God's omnipresence.

5. God's punishment "for their own sakes" proved that God did not think they were irredeemable.

6. They were worse than the text seems to say. Not only did they not try to convert their *yetzer ha-ra* into a good temperament, but they actually turned their good self into evil. (Thus "every *yetzer*" was "evil.")

7. Indeed, Rabbi Isaac found the verse directly relevant to each man. The meaning of the verse "evil all the time" (literally "each day") is precisely that the evil *yetzer* conquers every man every day.

8. Against this, others interpret the verse to mean that the generation was evil only by day. But, recalling Mic. 2:1, they remind us that the twelve tribes were also evil "on their beds."

What was God's attitude toward the fact of man's universal (or at least very common) sinfulness? It depends on one's translation of a word in Gen. 6:6.[29] The word can mean either that God "regretted" or "was comforted" in reference to the creation of man. The new J.P.S. translation, and at least one rabbi, prefer the first: "I regret that I created an evil *yetzer* in him, for had I not, he would not have rebelled against me"; but Rabbi Levi translated, "I am reconciled to having made him and set him on earth." The note of divine ambivalence is very characteristic of rabbinic interpretation. God is sorry that the way He made man enables man to sin, but He is also "comforted," as though He knew that man could be man in no other way. Man is both created in the image of God and the only desecrator of that image. To be a man means to be a child of God who, in the "oedipal" period at least, must rebel against his father. Or, to put it another way, the evil *yetzer* is the inevitable fall-out of creation.

The Noah story recapitulates the theme of man's "fall"

earlier in Genesis. Man *is* one who falls. Man's sin changes him from some semiangelic denizen of a more-than-earthly paradise to a worker, a sufferer, hider from God, and parent of children—that is, man with *yetzer ha-ra*. Adam before the expulsion was a superman, a prototype of what in principle we are and, in messianic times, will be. But he was not we. He could not suffer, he could not die, he could not repent. Perhaps there was enough humanity in him to commit one sin, and like any adolescent only thus did he achieve the breakthrough to self-understanding. In his fall was his true creation.

All this is perfectly clear in the story of the generation of the flood. God did not (could not?) change man's nature to sinlessness, even by destroying all but the best. The Noah that emerged from the Ark was still (or, was now) a drunkard and a sinner. God knew that. He was "sorry," but He was also "reconciled." The man with whom He was to deal was to be irrevocably human. Pss. 51:5 ("I was brought forth in sin, and in sin did my mother conceive me") means no more and no less than this to the rabbinic commentators: "Rabbi Aha said, 'Even if one be the most pious of the pious, it is impossible that he should have no streak of sin in him.' " [30] We do not sin, says Buber, *because* Adam sinned, but *as* Adam sinned. We *are* Adam, man, whose *yetzer* is "evil always."

In talmudic literature the most extended, complex, and brilliant formulation of the doctrine of the *yetzers* is found in the Tractate Sukkah, 51b and following. I shall give the text in full, leaving interpretations to follow.

> What is the cause of the mourning [mentioned in the last cited verse]?—Dosa and the Rabbis differ on this point. One explained, the cause is the slaying of Messiah, the son of Joseph, and the other explained, the cause is the slaying of the Evil Inclination.
>
> It is easy for him who explains that the cause is the slaying of Messiah, the son of Joseph, since that well agrees with the Scriptural verse: And they shall look upon me as one

who mourneth for his only son. But according to him who explains the cause to be the slaying of the Evil Inclination, is this (it may be objected) an occasion for mourning? Is it not rather an occasion for rejoicing? Why then should they weep?—Judah expounded: In the time to come the Holy One, blessed be He, will bring the Evil Inclination and slay it in the presence of the righteous and the wicked. To the righteous it will have the appearance of a high hill, and to the wicked it will have the appearance of a lock of hair. Both will weep; the righteous will weep saying, "How were we able to overcome such a high hill!" The wicked also will weep saying "How is it that we were unable to conquer this hair!" And the Holy One, blessed be He, will also marvel together with them as it is said: Thus saith the Lord of Hosts, If it be marvellous in the eyes of the remnant of this people in those days, it shall also be marvellous in My eyes.

Assi stated, the Evil Inclination is at first like the thread of a spider, but ultimately becomes like cart ropes, as it is said: Woe unto them that draw iniquity with cords of vanity, and sin as it were with a cart-rope.

Our Rabbis taught: The Holy One, blessed be He, will say to the Messiah, the son of David (May He reveal himself speedily in our days!), "Ask of me anything, and I will give it to thee," as it is said: I will tell of the decree . . . this day have I begotten thee, ask of me and I will give the nations for thy inheritance. But when he will see that the Messiah the son of Joseph is slain, he will say to Him, "Lord of the Universe, I ask of Thee only the gift of life." "As to life," He would answer him, "Your father David has already prophesied this concerning you," as it is said: He asked life of thee, thou gavest it him (even length of days for ever and ever).

Avira, or as some say, Joshua, son of Levi, made the following exposition: The Evil Inclination has seven names. The Holy One, blessed be He, called it Evil, as it is said: For the imagination of man's heart is evil from his youth. Moses called it the Uncircumcised, as it is said: Circumcise therefore the foreskin of your heart. David called it Unclean, as it is said: Create me a clean heart, O Lord; which implies that there is an unclean one. Solomon called it the Enemy, as it is said: If thine enemy be hungry, give him bread to eat and if he be thirsty give him water to drink. For thou wilt heap coals of fire upon his head, and the Lord will reward thee; (read not, "will reward thee" but "will cause it to be at peace with thee"). Isaiah called it the Stumbling-Block, as it is said: Cast ye up, cast ye up, clear the way, take up the stumbling-block out of the way of my people. Ezekiel called it Stone, as it is said: And I will take away the heart of stone out of your flesh and I will give you a heart of flesh. Joel called it the Hidden One, as it is said: But I will remove far off from you the hidden one.

Our Rabbis taught: But I will remove far off from you the hidden one: refers to the Evil Inclination which is constantly hidden in the heart of man; and will drive him into a land barren and desolate means: to a place where there are no men for him to attack; with his face toward the eastern sea, (implies) that he set his eyes against the First Temple and destroyed it and slew the scholars who were therein; His back part toward the western sea (implies) that he set his eyes against the Second Temple and destroyed it and slew the scholars who were therein. That his foulness may come up and his ill-savour may come up (means): he leaves the other nations in peace and attacks only Israel. Because he hath done great things, Abaye explained: Against scholars more than against anyone else, as was the case when Abaye heard a certain man saying to a woman, "Let us arise early and go our way." "I will," said Abaye, "follow them in order to keep them away from transgression" and he followed them for three parasangs across the meadows. When they parted company he heard them say, "Our company was pleasant, the way was long." "If it were I," said Abaye, "I could not have restrained myself," and so went and leaned in deep anguish against a doorpost. A certain old man came up to him and taught him: The greater the man, the greater his Evil Inclination.

Isaac stated, The (Evil) Inclination of a man grows

stronger within him from day to day, as it is said: Only evil all the day. Simeon, son of Lakish stated: The Evil Inclination of a man grows in strength from day to day and seeks to kill him, as it is said: The wicked watcheth the righteous and seeketh to slay him; and were it not that the Holy One, blessed be He, is his help, he would not be able to withstand it, as it is said: The Lord will not leave him in his hand, nor suffer him to be condemned when he is judged.

The school of Ishmael taught: If this repulsive wretch meets you, drag him to the *Beth Hamidrash*. If he is of stone, he will dissolve, if of iron he will shiver into fragments. "If he is of stone he will dissolve" for it is written: Lo, every one that thirsteth come ye to the water; and it is written: The waters wear the stones. "If he is of iron, he will shiver into fragments," for it is written: Is not my word like fire? Saith the Lord, and like a hammer that breaketh the rock in pieces?

Samuel, son of Nahmani, citing Johanan stated: The Evil Inclination entices man in this world and testifies against him in the world to come, as it is said: He that delicately bringeth up his servant from a child shall have him become a *manon* at the last, for according to the *Atbah* of Hiyya a witness is called *manon*.

Huna pointed out an incongruity: It is written: For the spirit of harlotry caused them to err, but is it not also written: (For the spirit of harlotry) is within them? First it only causes them to err, but ultimately it enters into them. Raba observed: First he is called a passer-by, then he is called a guest, and finally he is called a man, for it is said, And there came a passer-by to the rich man and he spared to take of his own flock and of his own herd, to dress for the guest and then it is written: but took the poor man's lamb and dressed it for the man that came to him.

Johanan remarked: There is a small organ in man which satisfies him when in hunger and makes him hunger when satisfied, as it is said: When they were starved they became full.

> Hana, son of Abba stated: It was said at the schoolhouse, There are four things of which the Holy One, blessed be He, repents that He had created them, and they are the following: Exile, the Chaldeans, the Ishmaelites and the Evil Inclination.

This complicated passage [31] begins with an unmistakably sexual reference. Originally in the Temple, the women sat inside in their own court, while the men were farther out. But this caused levity (*qalut*), so they changed places. But there was still some kind of sexual contact inappropriate to the Temple precincts, so it was finally decided that the women should sit above and invisible to the men. The ruling was based on Zech. 12:12 ff.: "And the land shall mourn, every family apart; the family of the house of David apart and their wives apart.". . . The period of future mourning is messianic; it refers to a time when (according to some) the evil *yetzer* will have no power over man. Even then, men and women will be separated, so obviously there is sanction for separating them in the pre-messianic dispensation.

But if it is messianic time we are describing, then why should the verse speak of mourning at all? Why should "all the families weep" in separation? Perhaps because of the evil days that shall have immediately preceded messianic transmutation (the slaying of the Messiah ben Yosef). But they will weep, too, if the messianic time means the destruction of the *yetzer ha-ra*. For when the *yetzer* is made visible in destruction, each man will be moved. The good man will see his enormous capacity for sin ("like a high mountain"); the evil will discern how little he had to overcome that he could not ("like a lock of hair"). Obviously the "good" man is not less but more capable of sin, if his *yetzer ha-ra* is so much larger.

Or, and now the metaphor becomes more dynamic, the evil tendency is first as thin as a spider's web, but, as one concedes to it, it thickens and its power becomes irresistible.

There follows a description of the ontogeny of the *yetzer*, a kind of seven ages of man.

To God, the *yetzer ha-ra* is just plain *ra*, bad. From the "objective" metaphysical point of view, it is alien, despicable. As the proof-text, Gen. 8:21, which we have examined, implies, God knows how evil is the man that man will always be.

To Moses, the supreme prophet, the type of man's highest possibility but still a sinner, the inclination is the Uncircumcised One. It represents a part of man only accidentally his. It can be removed. To be a Jew means to remove it, at least partly. The *yetzer ha-ra* is the outer layer of flesh and spirit which a man must cut off to find the organ of his redemption. Sin means task.

To David, it is an uncleanness which can be washed (not cut) off, leaving the pure heart that God will make me be. Our messianic hope for a pure heart implies the evil kind of heart we shall, alas, have till then.

Solomon, too, sees his inclination to evil as both inimical and personal. He knows that toward one's enemy the best strategy is kindness. The wise king would not wash away or cut away the enemy within, but feed him, give him to drink, and thus make him amenable to *shalom*, personal integration. The underworld of the spirit is dangerous but can be made more friendly by giving it what it needs (pleasure, "food," libidinal gratification) and thus integrating it with the ego.

For Isaiah, sin is a stumbling-block on man's path. Or, rather, it is the very undergrowth which prevents a path. It is formless, chaotic, directionless. The task of a man is to make a path through the vines and brush of the *yetzer ha-ra* which endangers even "My people."

The rabbis quote Ezekiel's passage on the heart of stone as an equivalent to the Inclination to Evil. The latter is the not-mind, the not-yet-human equipment which is, perhaps, all we have until God at last gives us a self that truly feels and is.

Punning on Joel 2:20's promise that "the northern foe . . . which has done great things" shall be destroyed, the rabbis call that enemy "the hidden one." Man does not know his unconscious self. It is mysterious, subterranean, inaccessible to pure reason, yet inescapable. Its power is greatest against the greatest, as an army attacks only one of similar importance. The ladder of holiness is equivalent to the ladder of potential evil; it was the Hidden Enemy who destroyed the scholars of both Jewish Temples, leaving the simple people alone: it was he who exiled the people of Israel, leaving other nations in peace.

Abaye, a great sage, was dismayed when he saw a plain man walk alone with a woman without sexually approaching her. His agony at the discovery of his own libidinous needs is assuaged when Elijah the prophet, who returns to instruct and some day to redeem, tells him: The greater the man, the greater his *yetzer*. The stuff of human creativity is located in the *yetzer;* the more one is a man, the more he is able to sin, to build, to know, to become. Reality and pleasure stem from the same root and tend toward the same end. Libido should not be denied but exploited. Perhaps that is the secret meaning of Jesus' saying: Love your enemies (Matt. 5:44; cf. Luke 6:27). The Hebrew Bible had not explicitly commended the wooing of the libidinal powers; but the rabbis did, and that may be what Jesus meant to suggest.

Man cannot destroy his enemy, his brother, the Evil Inclination; he should not. He should align himself with the Good Power, which is God's, Who will not suffer His ally to see destruction. The technique suggested is to drag the repulsive but human *yetzer* to synagogue, to school, where his power will diminish. In another rabbinic passage, where a rabbi feels sexual need that cannot be resisted, he is told to go to another city in dark clothes, presumably for anonymous gratification. But a wise commentator suggests that once he wears dark and ugly clothes and goes where he is unknown and unimportant, his lust will diminish and he will not need to vent his sexual need. When the ego is diminished, the id, too, constricts. So here, in synagogue, where God alone is King, his Word will break the pretensions, the ego, and the *yetzer* of man. The Evil Inclination is man's "servant," but a spoiled servant can become a witness against one (for he knows what one really does in the privacy of one's home). The *yetzer* is a necessary servant but a cruel master. He is alien and poor, but if permitted he can become "a man," the whole of the person, the displacer of the ego, the perversion of possibility. The penis exemplifies the potency of the *yetzer*. It effects the transvaluation of all values. It makes the poor man rich, the rich man poor. Sex is, with death, the great leveller. It shows how little we are our own masters. The "small organ" can grow to be a man.

Thus God "regrets" that He created the *yetzer ha-ra*. If, like Exile and the enemies of the Jews, it was inevitable existentially, it is still metaphysically dispensable. God can somewhere make man more than his libido—or what is heaven for?

I have examined this passage at some length because it is important and because it gives us a sense of the meaning certain statements had for the rabbis themselves. Space will not permit such careful explication of other citations, but we have already raised a number of questions and caught something of the flavor of rabbinic anthropology. Now we must turn to more explicit descriptions of the *yetzer ha-ra*.

Another gnomic verse from the Torah is Gen. 4:7, "If you do right, you will be forgiven. If you do not, sin crouches at the door. It wants you, yet you can master it." (New Jewish Publication Society translation: "Surely if you do right, there is uplift. But if you do not do right Sin is the demon at the door Whose urge is toward you, yet you can be his master.") The text seems to mean, whatever else, that sin is a constant threat but not an insuperable one. Man is always capable of evil but he is not himself wholly in the power of evil.

Noting that the word for sin is feminine, but the verb "crouches" masculine, the rabbis infer the incongruity between sin as potency and act.[32] At first sin is weak, feminine; then it becomes strong and masterful. It changes from a spider's web to a strong rope, from a guest to a master. The impulse to sin is deceptive, they say, like Roman dogs who pretend to sleep in front of a bakery. When the shopkeeper naps, the dog dislodges the bread and while the onlookers pick up the loaves, he carries one away. Or, sin is like a weak robber who forces unarmed travelers to pay him, until one comes (Abraham) who sees him for the feeble pretender he is. The Tempter has real power only over the proud, the vain, the blind.

"Hanina said: If your Tempter comes to incite you to levity, cast him down with the words of the Torah . . . And should you argue that he is not in your power, then recall 'His urge is toward you, but you may master him.' " [33] Simon said, "If your Tempter comes to incite you to levity, pleasure him with words of Torah." The *yetzer ha-ra* is dangerously personal and subtle, but the ego is strong and can prevail. The method of choice is the manipulation, instruction, chastening, sublimation of the Tempter. But, as we shall see, the Tempter's real weakness is not always as here assumed.

The verse we are interpreting is also said to prove that the evil impulse is born with man, i.e., "Sin crouches at the door [by which you come into the world]." The rabbis disagree about the exact age of the *yetzer*, but it is not impossible for them to imagine childhood libido, or even embryonic "sin." With brilliant insight, the rabbis date the id from early childhood, reserving ego structures for puberty. Man is the result of growing beyond his unconscious "other" toward selfhood.[34] The verse Gen. 8:21, might be translated: "The devisings of man's mind are evil because of his immaturity" without violating rabbinic understanding. Sin, is, in the most literal sense, regression. To be wicked is to submit to the allurements of early childhood, the old pleasures of Eden's unconscious. To be good is to go on to maturation with a regretful smile at the blandishments of "sin" but a man's work to accomplish.

The state of nature is polymorphously perverse. Childhood's only principle is pleasure. A sinner cannot move beyond the chaotic delights of infancy; he is "hung up" on the satisfaction of his primal wants. For the rabbis this means he is both unchaste and idolatrous. He wants every possible sexual gratification and every possible "god." Indeed, for him, idolatry and unchastity are the same thing: the rebellion against commandment, the refusal to repress.[35]

"Often a man wants to perform a *mitzvah* [good deed commanded by God]. But the *yetzer ha-ra* within him tells him: Why should you be charitable and diminish your possessions? Before you give to others, give to your own children. While the *yetzer tov* tells him: Do the commandment!"[36] The evil impulse resists direction, the expectation to give. Its sin is a kind of permanent anality. It wants to keep everything for itself. It tries to incorporate the world. Having many gods permits it to function as divine arbiter, just as the child is served by many huge powers but remains in fantasy omnipotent. Sexuality, for the unconscious, is chaotic. Everything in the world is subject to cathexis. Everything is crammed into the maw of the id and nothing is distributed. The *yetzer* is childhood telling would-be maturity to keep what it has and to resist all direction that comes from interpersonal encounter. For that reason, sin is described in rabbinic literature as folly. A man who pretends to be a child is only a fool.[37]

We read in the Talmud that childish rage is also idolatry, itself the religion of early childhood.[38] We shall reproduce the passage:

He who rends his garments in his anger, he who breaks his vessels in his anger, and he who scatters his money in his anger, regard him as an idolater, because such are the wiles of the Tempter: Today he says to him, "Do this"; tomorrow he tells him, "Do that," until he bids him, "Go and serve idols," and he goes and serves (them). Abin observed: What verse [suggests this]? "There shall be no strange god in thee; neither shalt thou worship any strange god": who is the strange god that resides in man himself? The Tempter! This holds good only where he does it in order to instill fear in his household, even as Judah pulled the thrums [of his garment;] Aha, son of Jacob broke broken vessels; Shesheth threw brine on his maidservant's head; Abba broke a lid.

For the same reason, it is assumed that non-Jews have a special danger; perhaps (against the passage quoted above) they have a stronger *yetzer*.

It has been taught: Eliezer the Great, said: Why did the Torah warn against [the wronging of] a proselyte in thirty-six, or as others say, in forty-six places? Because he has a strong inclination to evil. What is the meaning of the verse, Thou shalt neither wrong a stranger, nor oppress him; for ye were strangers in the land of Egypt. It has been taught: Nathan said: Do not taunt your neighbor with the blemish you yourself have. And thus the proverb runs: If there is a case of hanging in a man's family record, say not to him, "Hang this fish up for me." [39]

But if the *yetzer* is, like exile, the inevitable fate of man, Jew and non-Jew alike, it cannot be just plain bad. "The Evil *Yetzer*, whatever its nature, is, as is everything else in the universe, a creature of God." [40] We come here upon a deliciously Freudian paradox: the temperament of man which conduces him to evil is itself also profoundly good.

And, behold, it was good: alludes to the creation of man and the Good Inclination; "very" alludes to the Evil Inclination. Is, then, the Evil Inclination "very good"? It is in truth to teach you that were it not for the Evil Inclination, nobody would build a house, marry and beget children.[41]

A wise commentator on this passage (*Tiferet Sion*) reminds us that "very" (more) is a comparative term. There must be two items to compare. What is sinning man more good than? The answer is: himself yesterday. As by using his good impulse, he ascends, so by plumbing his regressive impulse he may be improved. He will enrich his very physical self, and this is necessary to "spiritual" growth. When God saw all that he had made, it was good; through all of it man may ascend to the level of "very good"; man may come nearer to completeness of soul, including that aspect of the soul called body. This notion is dramatically portrayed in the Talmud:

> It was once said: Since this is a time of God's grace, let us pray for mercy from the *yetzer hara*. They prayed for mercy, and he was handed over to them. God said: realize that if you kill him, the world is finished. They put him in jail for three days. Then they looked all over the land of Israel for a fresh egg and could not find it. So they said: What shall we do now, kill him? The world is finished if we do. Shall we beg for half? But they do not give half measures in Heaven. So they put out his eyes and let him go. That is why he no longer is able to get man to commit incest.[42]

Man is continuous physically with the animal world. He depends on its lusts—his own. He can chasten his childish pleasure-seeking but he cannot end it or he ends himself. We have here a more subtle truth than the "good news of damnation." Sin is good not only because it leads to repentance, but because it partakes of the holiness of life. But we have here, too, a grave and dangerous suggestion to which extreme Jewish heretics like Shabbetai Zevi were sometimes to succumb. Ambivalence is not acceptance. To know that sin is "very good" is not to concede that it is metaphysically equivalent to good. To know that we are the enemy is not to surrender to our foe.

The good impulse is a late-comer. The *yetzer, par excellence,* is evil. He is prior in nature and prior to us. But the good temperament, the urge toward selfhood, is human, too. He is the polar opposite, the "poor" stranger in us who wants us for God.

> NOW THERE WAS A LITTLE CITY: the body, AND FEW MEN WITHIN IT: the limbs. AND THERE CAME A GREAT KING AGAINST IT: the Evil Inclination. (Why is it called GREAT? Because it is thirteen years older than the GOOD Inclination.) AND BESIEGED IT, AND BUILT GREAT BULWARKS AGAINST IT: tortuous paths and concealed spots. NOW THERE WAS FOUND IN IT A MAN POOR AND WISE: the Good Inclination. (Why is it called POOR? Because it is not found in all persons, nor do most of them obey it.) AND HE BY HIS WISDOM DELIVERED THE CITY: for whoever obeys the Good Inclination escapes [punishment]. David said: Happy is he who obeys it, as it is written: Happy is he that considereth the poor. YET NO MAN REMEMBERED THAT SAME POOR MAN: the Holy One, blessed be He, said "You have not remembered it, but I will remember it," as it is written; I will take away the stony heart out of your flesh, and I will give you a heart of flesh.[43]

The nature of the good *yetzer* is thus very like the ego of Freud. It is the middleman between the primeval libidinal urge and the commandments given from the superego. It is linked as subject to the id throughout childhood and throughout that lifelong childishness which is the human condition. It seeks to internalize and thus to transcend the dictates of conscience and subvert the paralyzing anxieties of chaotic lust. It seeks to harness the sexual life in the service of the self. It starts poor and yet may become a king.

> The *yetzer hara* is thirteen years older than the *yetzer tov.* From the womb of his mother it accompanies man.

When he violates the Sabbath, it does not protest. He kills
a man, and it does not protest. He moves toward adultery
and it does not protest. When he is thirteen, the good
impulse is born. When he violates the Sabbath, it says to
him, "Fool! God says the violator of the Sabbath will be
put to death." If he kills someone, it says to him: "Fool!
The spiller of man's blood—his blood will be spilled by
man." If he moves toward adultery, it says to him: "Fool!
God says the adulterer will be put to death." When a man
excites himself sexually and moves toward lewdness, all his
limbs obey him, for the evil temperament is king over all
247 limbs. When he moves toward obedience to God's
command, all his limbs grow flaccid, for the evil temperament is king over all 247 of them. The good inclination is
like someone imprisoned, as it is said in Ecclesiastes 4.14:
From a prison he shall go forth a king.[44]

The child does not murder or commit adultery, except in
fantasy. The man who kills—or violates the Sabbath—is playing the child. He grows to a man when he hears, internalizes,
the real word of God. His body would seek gratification in
the way it has known, unless in time it enthrones the prisoned
good. The ego mediates ineluctable anxieties and the ultimate
threat of extinction in order to become ruler in its own house.
"Fear the Lord and the king" (Prov. 24:21) means: Make
God King if you want to rid yourselves of the agonizing
dread the child feels.[45] The rigorous rabbinic limitations on
sexual behavior are not meant to inhibit it, but rather to
free it from infantile fear. Similarly, the *Halakic* Sabbath,
which is essentially pure play, gratifies the child in man and
makes him the child of God. Man will, of necessity, sacrifice
his freedom either to the formless and meaningless permis-
siveness of the id, or to the God who made him and loves
him. The choice is never in Judaism between God and no
God, but rather between God and the gods. For man to
become one, he must come to serve singly the One King.

"A man must bless God for the evil as for the good which
is meant by the verse: 'You shall love the Lord, your God,

with all your heart, with all your soul and with all your might'; 'with all your heart' means with your two inclinations, the *yetzer tov* and the *yetzer ra*." [46] Sometimes that means sublimation. Thus, "when they occupy themselves with Torah and acts of kindness their *yetzer* is mastered by them, not they by their inclination." [47] The greatest of men, like Abraham, were able to turn their libidinal power into pure good. But lesser men, like King David, have no choice but to "kill" it.[48] The angels are less praiseworthy than men, because celestials have no evil urge.[49] But some in order to become men must become angels.

> Simon the Just said: In all my life I have never eaten of any guilt-offerings of a Nazarite except one. On a certain occasion there came up to me one from the South, whom I saw to have a fair complexion with beautiful eyes and a handsome appearance, and his locks were arranged in rows of curls. I asked him: "What cause had you to wish to destroy this lovely hair?" He told me: "Master! I was a shepherd in my native town. I went to fill a trough from the fountain and beheld my reflection in the water. My evil inclination surged up within me and sought to destroy me. So I said to it: "Wretch! Why do you plume yourself on a thing that is not yours? It is of dust, of maggots, and of worms! I undertake to dedicate the locks to heaven and shave them to the glory of heaven!" I bent my head and kissed him and said to him: "May there be many such as you in Israel who perform the pleasure of the Omnipresent. It is of such as you that Scripture said: TO CONSECRATE HIMSELF UNTO THE LORD." [50]

The Nazarites are the type of monastic renunciation in Jewish literature. Their refusal to shave or drink wine is understood as pure repression, and for that repression they are often condemned. But not always. There is also a secret sympathy for the surrender of their parasexual powers. While the Nazarite must bring an offering, because it is a sin against God to renounce licit pleasures, still the very institution of the Nazariteship, to which an entire tractate of the Talmud is dedicated, proves its inevitability. Some men can temper their desires and make them sacred, but some men must take another way. "Joshua, son of Levi, said: He who sacrifices his *yetzer* and confesses over it is considered by Scripture as if he had honored the Holy One, blessed be He, in both worlds." [51] Repression is dangerous, because it produces inevitable neurotic byproducts, but it is preferable to psychotic abandonment of the life process itself. It is because Judaism knows the terrible power of the id that it is both respectful and wary of it. The Nazarite is a kind of failure, but he is a noble one.

The "heart" of man, his inner drives and needs, is very powerful indeed. The rabbis find in scriptural verses warrant for saying that it sees, hears, speaks of itself, walks, falls, stands, rejoices, cries, is troubled and comforted, becomes hard, grows faint, grieves, fears, breaks, rebels, invents, cavils, overflows, devises, goes astray, lusts, is refreshed, is enticed and humbled, is deceitful, trembles, wakes, loves, hates, envies, meditates, receives, arranges, and dies.[52] "It is this feeling of man's comparative helplessness in such a condition which wrung from the Rabbi: 'Woe to me of my [Evil] *Yetzer* and woe to me of my *Yoser* (Creator).'" [53]

As Brown has proved, Freud's theory of instincts is irredeemably death-oriented. What makes man more than his id is simply his ability to get sick.[54] Another word for the unconscious power is *Thanatos*, Death. This "Mythical being" (Freud) is at the root of man's biopsychical nature. The instinctual dualism which underlies that conflict which is life is the war between Love and Death, or as the rabbis put it, between *Torah* and the *Yetzer*. It cannot be resolved this side of Heaven. "The Torah is a stone, and the *Yetzer hara* is a stone. The stone shall watch the stone." [55] And the rabbis know, too, the Freudian name of the Evil Power:

"Resh Lakish said: Satan, the evil impulse and the Angel of death are all one." [56] Man's evil temperament is greater than he; it is one of the metaphysical surds. It is, in the end, his ultimate destruction. Thus one thinks about the *Yetzer* with terror and despair. Sublimation is finally insufficient; repression is evasive but not ultimately effective; death alone atones for all man's sin. Rabbah ben Bar Hana said: "The prophet urges Israel, 'Return and repent! They replied: 'We cannot: the *Yetzer* rules us!' He said to them, 'Curb your desires.' They replied, 'Let his God instruct us.' " [57] Only God can make life out of libido.

And, in the fulness of messianic time, God will. "In this world, they made idols because of the *Yetzer hara*, but in the Time to Come, I will uproot the *Yetzer hara* from them and give them a heart of flesh." [58] The Messianic Age is a biological revolution; not only will the lion lie down with the lamb, but the evil power in man, his id, will be reconstructed! Ezekiel's promise (36.26 ff.) means that God will some day make man constitutionally different. His Kingdom is one in which Death and Love are brothers even under man's skin. Terminable analysis is the gift of grace. Torah, discipline, therapy, all are insufficient without God's transvaluation of our human stuff. It is only in the millennium that real life, without decisive conflict, is possible. The healing of man is a divine act. The dualism which infects and constitutes human biology is transcended only by God's unification of the world. Freud's pessimism is Jewishly penultimate; the final truth is the dialectical unity of opposites in God.

Thus, healing is strictly and precisely "meeting," in Martin Buber's phrase. As dialogue with the therapist and with the world is the essence of psychoanalytic therapy, so is dialogue with God the final act of self-understanding and self-transformation. The divorce of spirit and instinct is a picture of the separation of man and man, of man and God.[59] Psychoanalysis foreshadows redemption.

The Jewish response to man's divided and incompletely autonomous nature is wholly chastened. Despite its detractors and its liberal reductions, Jewish law is neither formalistic nor simply moralizing. There is a profound understanding in Judaism that man cannot be changed by legalisms or by sermonics. The goal of *t'shuvah*, turning, is dynamic; the means, Torah, is likewise personal. The Hebrew for the ten words (not commandments), for instance, may mean not "Thou shalt not murder," but "Thou shalt not become a murderer," and the first of the "commandments" is of course, not a law at all. The instruction to love one's neighbor means, precisely, to act lovingly toward your next one. It is not a counsel of perfection; it is a therapeutic necessity.

The purpose of the *mitzvot*, commands, is to help man turn, to help man become someone he is not, even someone he never can be. God's word enters the divided self of a man and confronts that self with a Model and a Lover. Now, from the "objective," detached observer's point of view, that is, of course, absurd. Dialogue is only real for participants. Freud had a keen insight into the formally absurd relationship of therapist and patient. His ironic treatment of their mutuality shows how subtly he understood its inner implication.[60] The analytic experience is ineffable; so is the confrontation of God and man. To an *apikoros*, an outsider, religious phenomena are nonsense. So, too, the therapeutic moment is objectively incredible. Freud insisted, at the end of his life, that only by analysis and reanalysis could the therapist discover that what he was doing was not useless or worse. Only by the alchemy of transference could a patient find healing. If there is no transference, the analytic procedure is ungainly and impotent. A dialogic act in which man seeks to transcend himself is at once incongruous and indispensable.[61]

What turning produces is not knowledge. Like psychoanalysis, the mechanism of religious insight is pure form. It does not transmute biological man. It does not enrich the intellect or transform his nature. It simply (simply!) modifies and thus somewhat empowers. Whatever truth may emerge about himself from the processes of faith must, like the "truths" of depth psychology, be paradoxical, chaotic, existential. It is in the process of "turning" itself that man is modified, just as the therapeutic experience itself is the only "cure" analysis offers.

The man who turns is both humble and proud. Chastened by confrontation with his self-consciousness and exhausted by the enormously complicated work of making unconscious feelings present to the ego, he has no illusions about the perfectibility of man. He knows that only God could make him an angel or his world a Paradise. But he is also in touch with concern, even with divine concern, and this is a proud gift. By the disciplines of traditional *Halakah* (literally, "way") he invests his tentative spiritual movements with authenticity. With the spontaneous eruption of dialogue, he moves into the presence of God. So, too, in psychoanalysis, the patient humbly accepts more or less arbitrary techniques in service of the unexpected for which no adequate preparation is possible. By narcissistic elaboration of his own symptoms the patient breaks through to the almost wholly other, and thus achieves his own self-transcendence. By a painstaking examination of his own dreams, he discovers in himself the latent universal language of human illness. In bondage to such painful wisdom, man becomes, so far as he ever can, free.

This is all that "turning" promises. The repentance of one Day of Atonement will have to be repeated on the next. Obedience to the law implies a possible and, therefore, a corresponding real disobedience. The presence of God is not only instructive and beneficent; it is also like a flaming fire which sears the soul. Man, under God, remains man. Torah directs but it does not make the *yetzer* disappear. Religion is not magic.

"The reward of a *mitzvah* [commandment] is another mitzvah," say the Fathers of the synagogue. The act of unwinding toward God is an infinitely receding task. Insight produces only and always the hope for new insight. The sins which God forgives are unforgivable. That is why His *metier*, as Heine guessed, is not ours. For us, the problem is never simply to know what is good but to do what is good. And thus an apparently philosophic problem of ethics becomes an existential mystery requiring infinite obedience. Religion absorbs and transfigures the ethical dimension. "You shall be holy men, for I, the Lord your God, am Holy" (Lev. 19:2).

The temperaments of man are sublunar. Only God is the arbiter of eternity. Man is torn, aspiring, passionately in need. But God is One, however passionately concerned. Therapy is a metaphor for faith which, itself, is a metaphor for messianic wholeness. Psychoanalysis looks coolly and pessimistically at every past and present. But it truly foreshadows an incredible healing at last to come. "On that day the Lord shall be One, and His Name shall be One."

ZALMAN M. SCHACHTER

Patterns of Good and Evil

"BEHOLD I SET BEFORE THEE TODAY"

Behold

OF COURSE, one can close his eyes, stop up his ears, and just live.

No! It would not be quite correct for any of us to say, "I live," and make it stick in the active grammatical form. In order to be able to speak in the active form one must be capable of deliberate action. Most of us are passively *lived*, driven and determined by our environment, by our heredity, and by the people around us. Nevertheless one can close his eyes, stop up his ears, and just be lived. This would be far more comfortable than to engage in attempts to live deliberately that at the outset seem doomed to futility.

But there are some of us who cannot close our eyes.

We are aware that we are being called. We are not yet certain whether the voice calling imperatively "Behold!" issues from within or from a nebulous without. Still, the imperative causes us to pay attention, for this voice commands the ear to hear, to heed, to pay attention (*"Sh'ma!"*), or forces a choice inescapably upon us here (*"Hine!"*), or gives us the grace to see a little ahead toward the fork in the road and tells us to look (*"R'eh!"*).

Set before Thee

Life inexorably moves on. It is impossible not to choose in the face of the challenge. If life were to stand still, we could postpone choosing, but with our own life at stake we cannot afford to be objective, to wait for all the evidence to come in. Choosing not to take up the challenge is still a choice as deliberate as the choice to say *yes*. In either case one has to take the responsibility; that is to say, be answerable to someone for the choice made.

The variegated pressures which we face are always before us. Each field of tension in the pattern of challenges is loaded with potentials to which we attach values out of our inner hierarchy.

To choose would be a simple task if only the hierarchy of our values were clearly defined, if the values which are the ultimates of our life did not change their shape and color in the many and terrible contingencies of life. Try as we may to put our values to work within the subjective life-space of the I, they evade our will. As into Zeno's river, we can never step into the same I-stream twice. The co-ordinates shift and are so fluid that "the world is a spinning die, and everything turns and changes; man is turned into an angel, and angel to man; and the head to the foot, and the foot to the head. Thus all things turn and spin and change, this into that and that into this, the topmost to the undermost and the nethermost to the topmost." We are not yet ready to say with Reb Nahman, the author of this quotation, "For at the root all is one, and salvation inheres in the change and return of things." Our consciousness is fluid, our I-stream flows on. If only we could have *one* fixed co-ordinate, according to which we could bring order into our chaotic interior, we might be able to attach values to the gaping potentiality of the fields and the patterns which are before us and of which we are a part.

I Set before Thee

God is the Name which man attaches to the Origin of the voice. Man must do so, because somehow, despite all the confusion between the within and without, the Origin of the voice is "realer than real." Despite the bump of the world's "reality" on our senses, we know that our senses are easily deluded. But this Voice does not speak to the senses and because it does not share the bump of reality-as-we-know-it, we feel it to be the more real.

Even without God, man's predicament is hard enough. Uncommitted man is constantly forced to choose among the clamoring stridencies of loyalty and attachments, which are frequently mutually antagonistic. In the very instant of anticipating one fulfilment, he faces the pain of separation from another loyalty, which he cannot but betray. The stress is too much to bear. The pagan cuts up his life, allotting Sundays to the worship of the sun, Mondays to the worship of the moon, etc. Sunday and Monday are irreconcilably antagonistic to one another. Yet even the pagan lives hermetically sealed in the loyalty of the day, because if man were to pass Sunday by only "sunning" and Monday by only "mooning," he would feel the inherent hostility of both sun and moon as they rip at the wholeness of his being and fragment it. In order to survive, he must, after a quick propitiation of the ruler of the day, set about ignoring him. Once the quick compromise has been made, the pagan has either to tranquilize or to overstimulate himself into oblivion, in order to maintain some vestige of wholeness.

A Jealous God

And at the same time the Voice from that certain uncertain region constantly insists that man consolidate all his holdings, that he be made whole and that he be set free. But if he

rebels successfully against the sun and the moon, he is still
not free. A person's family, his people, his country, his live-
lihood, his friends, will still continue the tug of war for
supremacy, none of them to emerge a final victor. The easiest
way, so it seems, would be to give up the gods and to enter
into the Kingdom of God. However, this cannot be done
with one's outer will, one's instrumental will. If one were to
attempt to enthrone God merely with his outer will, he would
find that he has jumped from the frying pan into the fire.
At least at one's entrance into the kingdom, the Voice is
antagonistic to all other values within man. A jealous God
demands that man "forsake his country, his birthplace and his
father's house."

Today Must Ye Do It

God increases the terror of man's predicament, whose
dread is compounded by anxiety over God's unknowableness.
Pagan deities are predictable; they live in their assigned roles,
they are conditioned to specific functions by their mythic
necessities. Not so God; He obliterates all security that comes
from being able to predict anything about Him. Truly He
is jealous of all the little supports, of the co-ordinates of
comfort into which we would sink for a little bit of rest;
if at this stage we wish to sink into Him, the dread of vertigo
paralyzes us. We dare not yield to a free fall because we are
not really sure that "underneath are the everlasting arms."
The inner will has not yet entered the Kingdom. Since the
outer will is impotent, the temptation for man to plead, "the
heaven is for God and the earth is for men" is immense.
Terrified by the immediacies of today, we would like to do
tomorrow, *mañana*, that which we are challenged to do today.
If one is to take God as the prime co-ordinate for ordering
his inner self, if one is to yield to Him one's inner will, there
is no living "as usual." But neither can living as usual be
sustained if one does not yield his inner will to God.

Before Thy Many Panim

We have already noted that there are many choices "before thee." The "before thee" of this morning is wholly other than the "before thee" of noon. There are times when it seems that one's identity is nothing but a skeleton on which hang a number of ever-changing presents.

"Before thee" also means "before thy many faces." How exact Hebrew is in its vagueness: The word *Panim*—face or faces—is not singular. Many faces, many facets make up the outer self, the *persona*, and the inner self, the *P'nim*. The facets of an individual person, of a corporate person—a community—constantly dance in tune and rhythm with the cacophonous calls that challenge it. It would seem that we confront them all at once, though this is not so. Our predicament is worsened by the fact that "face" nevertheless indicates direction, for our *panim* point to one direction and our back to another.

Our first choice would be to define ourselves, our face, in terms of essence, but our existence precedes our essence, and in our existence there already exists a direction into which our face points. Those slices of life which we already confront are an existent fact. And yet, if one is aware of having a *panim*, then at least there is a possibility of pointing the face into the direction of the Voice and replying to its "*Hine*—Behold" with "*Hineni*—Here I am." To use this possibility is by no means a solution, but it often is the only possible turning toward a solution, for it allows us to turn, to return, to do *T'shuvah*.

Today Is the First Day of the Week

The temptation to escape from history, not to pay for the consumption of yesterday, and not to prepare for tomorrow, is great. If only the statute of limitations were not to exceed twenty-four hours; if only we were not responsible for yesterday and tomorrow; then at least we would have today as a wonderful day to get lost in. On the other hand, the temptation is often very great to pay for all the yesterdays and all the tomorrows today, so that not a minute of today remains, and then today is overwhelmed and crushed by all the yesterdays and the tomorrows. *Today* is a great challenge, for it is the only one and thus unique today, while there are many tomorrows and many which will soon be adding themselves to even more yesterdays.

The yesterdays are determined, the tomorrows will turn into yesterdays and also become determined, but today is brand-new and free. It never happened before and may be altogether different from all other todays we have ever experienced. Today need be determined not by yesterday but instead by the self, which is addressed by the Voice and turns not into a new direction but toward itself. It can be free and can redeem all the yesterdays and shape all the tomorrows. But, if one frees *today* from determination, if one lives in an ahistoric today, one unconnected with yesterday that plans not for tomorrow, or if one pays all yesterday's debts today and is overwhelmed by anxieties for tomorrow, one finds no escape. The debt of an irresponsible today as it turns into yesterday will ultimately have to be paid, crushing all future todays.

Today the Messiah Comes—If Ye Hearken to My Voice

Curiously enough, at the beginning of each day we may tend to say that today can be free, that it can be made manageable, that one can live deliberately in it. At the beginning of each day when the sun is shining one may say, Yes, and at the end of each day say, No, because clouds or no clouds, the sun has set. Unhappy creatures we are, wishing to escape into a wholly spontaneous world, to flee back into the world of child's play. But this is a wish which we cannot fulfil any more, for if we are given a day free from routine, we embrace a routine diversion in order to escape the responsibility of freedom. An adult deliberateness, the spontaneity to be deliberate is responsibility.

But to evaluate all todays as tomorrow-determined yesterdays in a cynical manner also will not do. We all remember momentary snatches of todays; we change direction deliberately, and yet spontaneously. Even if 99 per cent of our experience tended to justify a cynical evaluation, the real experience of the one case out of a hundred in which we lived and achieved freedom is a serious ally to the Voice that speaks to us in unceasing challenge. We claim that we cannot do this every day, that we cannot afford the tremendous inner expense of living deliberately each day. We claim that we do not have enough strength.

How much strength do we have and how much strength do we need? Surely today we do not possess enough strength *forever*, not even enough strength for a year, for a month or a week, but today we do have enough for a today and if we only dare to expend all today's energy today we may rescue this day from a misdetermined in-place-ness with dead yesterdays.

Looking back on such days when we did manage moments spontaneously deliberate, we also know—and this is so humiliating—that our deliberation was not completely our own doing, either that we had "luck" or that we were "blessed." Which word, "luck" or "blessing," do we use? The way in which we shape our inner chaos determines the word.

The Blessing of Failure

Maurice Samuel has given the word *blessing* a new, yet old, meaning. It is not success. Failure can often be a blessing. Did not Jacob, the one who bought, stole, was given (what difference does it make?), finally get the blessing? Was he not the supreme example of a persistent failure?

As we follow his life we see that there appears one success, in itself also a failure, when we see him limping away from the one encounter at which he did prevail. The blessing is that out of the successful failure he received the name Israel.

As infants we are such blessed failures that we can under no circumstances shift for ourselves. The blessing is inherent in our failure, for in the measure in which we are not successful in dealing with our environment, in that measure the blessing of parents becomes apparent.

Blessing—*B'rakha*—is a pouring down, a channeling down of energies, standing pooled above a field in need of irrigation. In order that the *B'rakha* channel may exert its blessed work, the field in need must be below the source. Obviously success cannot command the flow from the pool. If the successful field is too high, it remains dry. The water does not flow upward.

In the choice of today we face both the blessing that failure and humiliation bring and the curse that success brings when it blocks the flow of blessing. In our parable of a field in need of irrigation, the fluid is one that we know—it is water. But in the analogue, what kind of fluid are we talking about? "Water" means the flow of that positive polarized energy which we call holiness, an energy that is very much like the energy of the Voice, an energy that polarizes the things it saturates in the direction of that Voice. Truly, in this sense, one can say that blessing is the substance of the power that makes for salvation.

What moves a human father to bestow his blessing? He has *Nachat*. *Nachat* refers to an exhalation. a sigh, a centering down and skin-tingling energizing of fingertips, a transfer of that which is in the father's hands onto the child's head, a transfer of power, that makes for a certain committed deliberateness as a young *Panim* faces an experienced-furrowed *Panim*. The blessing saturates its recipient, a few of the many lines of the bestower transfer themselves to the recipient—at least this is what a child confronts in facing his father's voice. As he humbles himself he receives the inflow of blessing.

If the positive flow of energy is a blessing, then a negative flow of energy would seem to be a curse, but it isn't.

Good and Evil—Ham and Eggs

Matter is recalcitrant. It does not conform easily to the polarization of the good. Matter is far more at ease when it can avoid polarization, when it can remain "-*and*-evil." In the world's prize boner, Adam and Eve, we, are turned into hopeless suckers. The hawker's promise then was that we (like God) would be knowers of good and evil. At least, this is what we thought. We would know good clearly and absolutely, and we would know evil clearly and absolutely, and we would be able to embrace the good and avoid the evil.

We, however, want to experience life. So we continue to think that the wider our exposure to loyalties of all sorts, the more God-like our knowledge will be. But exposure tends to contaminate us with polarizations of attachments to things which we face and to energies which possess them. As a result, we do not know good and evil, but, in all things, only *good-and-evil*. We are affected and infected and cannot escape innocently from any exposure to good-and-evil. Whereas, before our exposure, before the primal sin we, mankind, Adam and Eve, needed no *persona*, no mask to hide behind, we now feel naked without one. Having exposed ourselves to so many things makes us anxious about our exposure. The very fact that we have to assume roles vis-à-vis given immediacies (or else shrink into bottomless anxiety unmasked), means that we are now incapable of immediate relationship. Our mask interferes with our immediacies, so that it is almost impossible to relate spontaneously in an unqualified manner.

Even in this sense, the manner in which we must turn our skin into "leather garments," has our sin become the dividing wall between us and the other. We cannot face God as we are. We can only face Him in one of His roles into which we construe Him, and in one of our roles into which we construe ourselves vis-à-vis Him. In this good-and-evil fiasco, not only have we become contaminated but so has every bit of the matter which surrounds us and it, too, faces us not as it is in itself but as a "something." This "something" we define in terms of usefulness, pleasure, or libido-object. Even the world plays the roles assigned to it by our conceptualization as if it were an end in itself. Would that Berkeley were right! How easy it would be then to live and to choose!

The Eminence of Gray

We seldom face either of the two ends of the continuum of good and evil; most of our choice challenges fall somewhere in between. Pure blacks and whites would have made choice a mere automatic act. However, the many shades of gray place us in an insoluble predicament. In the gray we discern a little bit of white, and our pity for the little bit of white causes us to accept much of the black in the good-and-evil mixture. Our predicament stems from the fact that we are not too sure whether it is the white in the gray that attracts us or whether we are genuinely attracted by the black in the gray and are offering the white as a mere rationalization for choosing the gray.

No, that is not quite true: our attraction for the little bit of white is not merely a rationalization. We do not have any real inclination to choose the black; the white really gives the black its only appeal for us.

However, we ourselves are not objective, for we discern with eyes that are also gray and with a mind which interprets what our eyes discern, a mind which does not escape its own lack of polarity. Thus, we have no criteria which can come to our aid; we cannot quite gauge the scales of gray by matching them to an inner hierarchy. Due to the grayness of our own mind, to the good-and-evil restlessness of black and white in our own being, the standard for a hierarchy is constantly shifting. Hence good and evil are patterns which we cannot assess even momentarily. Good and evil are shifting shadows generated by a high-lighting equipment over which we have no control and whose location we do not know.

The Jeopardy of Caprice

Order is holiness and purpose. Order is plan and system. Order stands for harmony. Disorder is impurity and discord. Even a totally evil tyranny is an order and partakes of some of the virtue of order. However, it is not a total order, for it is not harmonious with all that is. Its good is not coherent, for it does not allow every other good to stand next to it. Yet tyranny, a man-made evil system, is at least an attempt at ordering chaos. A carcinoma, very much like tyranny and fanaticism, is the result of miniature order-making. Despite the evil of tyranny, the stark evil which appears in dictator-ship is nearer to the good than existent blind, orderless caprice, which is a curse. Tyranny and dictatorship are evil because they are a mockery of freedom, and the dictator is a mockery of God. Orderless caprice, the curse, is anti-God. Orderless caprice—*tohu*—is a world which has turned into a ghost town its master has forsaken, abandoning it to chance.

He who approaches evil deliberately deserves the directed curse of *'Arur*. In this sense, the participle of the past, *'Arur* denotes not retaliation by God but the inevitable result of man's deliberate choice to derive his energies from chaos. In this sense must Deut. 27: 15-26 be understood.

The worst punishment that the author of Leviticus could conjure up was not *'Arur* but "If you will go with me *Keri* I will go with you in the anger of *Keri*." Hasidic masters interpret this to mean a *mikreh*, an accident, chance, mere probability. Hence, they read it: "If you are related to me in a capricious, accidental, and haphazard manner, so will I in turn relate to you." *Keri* is thus the disease of the grays, the evil which disguises mere means as divine ends. *Keri* is the taking lightly of life which leaves every *datum* to a *fatum*.

Pain is not a curse as long as it is inflicted by a rod held in a father's hand. Thus, "Thy *rod* as well as thy staff—they comfort me."

Pain is often purposive and good; it is the warning signal system of an organism. One cannot equate pain with evil unless one has yielded to catch-as-catch-can sensate hedonism. No *Hasid* ought to say, "It is bad—*'shlekht.'*" Instead the Baal Shem Tov said he ought to say, "*Ez iz bitter.*" For the good Father never gives evil but often must administer a bitter medicine.

The Pact Against the Covenant

Random energies attaching themselves to such as attract them by using them are evil. At first, these energies come as diverting guests and playmates. They stay on, however, as tyrannical obsessions. Folklore always saw demons in this manner. At first they are useful and worthy of exploitation, like a fire in a stove, but as soon as fire changes from a way of cooking or warming to an all-consuming end, it acts out of a *hubris* of Promethean self-expansion and it becomes a *Molokh*.

Almost always, the price for excesses and the exploitation of random energies is the loss of soul. He who turns to these random energies, even if he arranges with himself the possibility of repentance after exploiting them, will find that he can no longer turn away. To allow himself to be fooled by the promise that the eternally Feminine would ultimately redeem Faust, is the price that Goethe paid to Mephistopheles for having helped him to write the play. Both Faust and Job (as popularly understood) are fictions which tranquilize the average reader to identify with the hero out of a self-deceiving consolation that "Peace will be mine, for in the dominion of my heart I will proceed" (Deut. 29:18).

Does the King Send His Son to War Without Arms?

Assessing our predicament: the fact that we must choose; that even God Himself is a dimension of our predicament; that we have so many choices before and in us; that we must choose today; that blessing is difficult to find uncontaminated; that means at first exploited turn into idolatrous ends; we are ready to yield to despair. All our experience has taught us that it is impossible to do anything about our predicament. We cannot trust any person's best intentions, nor can we trust our own. We do not think anyone capable of really choosing.

However, on the level where we hear the challenge, we are also given an assurance that not only must we choose, ought we choose, but we can choose and make the choice stick. The challenge is harmonious with the statement of our sages, "God does not tyrannically abuse men." Our very predicament carries within itself enough life-space to make choice possible and worthwhile. The Voice trusts us more than we trust ourselves. Perhaps we are not able to find an answer to the question: *Why does it trust us?* or *How can it trust us?* Nevertheless, the nature of the challenge and of our predicament make it very clear that it *does* trust us, with an intense loyalty which amazes us and embarrasses us and obligates us as a result of its costliness. We would be encouraged by the Voice if some of the co-ordinates of our predicament: God, the hierarchy of our values, our role constructs, the flickering highlights would hold still long enough. But if they held still, they would all be static and arrested and this would mean our death. To be alive one must live in the shifting highlights and trust the cosmos for its trust in man. As long as one is alive one can make a fresh start, paradoxically learning from experience that one must forget all that has happened before, because this time it can really work. (See Milton Steinberg's "Our Persistent Failures" in *A Believing Jew.*)

A Program for Heavenly Days upon Earth

Like *Panim*, the word *Hayim*, life, does not occur in the singular. We do not live one homogeneous life. Our life is a number of flowing streams, some which are above the ground and others underground. Often those above the ground submerge and those below emerge, as in *emergencies*. Life is keying up and tuning down. Life for us is made up of "sitting in thy house, going on the way, rising up and lying down." In all of these we are bidden to make sure "that these words which I command thee today be upon thy heart; and thou shalt teach them diligently to thy children." While there is a promise attached to the challenge that we may some day live "heavenly days upon earth," there is no way in which we can make life stand still long enough for us to shape it to that heavenly form.

The Jewish tradition into which we were catapulted by the fact of our birth as Jews offers us a vital and viable way of living, polarizing energies positively rather than offering us an atavistic glorification of a salvation achieved only in death.

Death solves many logical problems. To write one's philosophy is to write one's last will and testament. The static conclusiveness of thought partakes of the anatomy of a corpse. Whatever lives organically must face dangerous complexities. We cannot help choosing life.

So we do not wish to commit ourselves to a static philosophy. We wish to be able to live and grow, we wish to be able to reply to the challenge as living beings, but we must turn our face in one direction, and we must be able to understand the direction in which we are turning. We cannot dismiss philosophy altogether; neither can we make our philosophy static.

Home Is Where the Deep Will Resides

Minds have a primary set. It is the set of a deep decision.
The set of the mind is occasioned by the deep-seated will. In
no way can the surface will to descend to that level, nor can
a surface assertion or affirmation change the set of one's
mind. This primary set stems out of a primary decision. It is
an *'Eruv*, an anchoring to one's deepest personal domicile.
One establishes one's domicile *Halakically* for the Sabbath by
an *'Eruv*. Once one has by an *'Eruv* anchored his domicile to
a particular locale, his permissible Sabbath orbit is established.
An *'Eruv* is a guarantee that the person who established it is
to be found around there at least on the Sabbath.

Thus a Hasidic interpretation of Ps. 119:122 reads as follows: "Anchor Thy servant in goodness, then wickedness will
not abuse me."

The problem is how one moves oneself from one anchoring
place to another, a process often called conversion which
has preoccupied many mystical and ethical writers. The inner
psychology of the spiritual life is built around this principle.
For what one needs in order to effect conversion is no less
difficult to achieve than fixing Archimedes' world-wrenching
lever.

The Baal T'shuvah—An Outsider

There is a set of the esoteric mind which is opposed to the
exoteric mind. The person with an exoteric mind does not
see himself in need of an overwhelming and general desire for
T'shuvah. He may recognize that there are many times in
which *T'shuvah* is required of him, but generally he is at
home with God. We may classify such a person as having
the *Hakham* type of mind (very much like the "wise son"
of the Passover "four questions"). His rightness is measured
in terms of Torah behavior and the mutual approval of the

pious. The *Hakham* approach in Jewish theological problems is detached, as if merely re-examining already concluded philosophical business. He advocates the study of Maimonides' *Guide to the Perplexed*, if at all, in terms of studying the answers before the questions—and then only in order to know how to answer the heretic. The *Hakham* tends to be quantitative, form-following, seeking the obvious. He is content to function with a dormant motivation which derives from a past decision. It is not that he is unconcerned about God, but that he is too busy doing God's will. The *Hakham* is basically democratic. According to the Torah dictum he seeks the majority opinion. He defines his thought in terms of quality and essence. The *Hakham* looks to the past for justification. He is more a student than a disciple. He wishes to walk through the world with a cool head rather than with a heart afire. He is content to align his conceptual thought with a great authority, and leave it at that.

The other type of mind is not "at home," is uncomfortable. If his is not yet the heart afire, it aspires to become fervent. It is more concerned to increase its present holdings than to maintain them. The *Baal T'shuvah* is intoxicated with his yearning and feels depressed unless he can maintain his intoxication. To live in the stress of the *Baal T'shuvah*'s psychology is emotionally expensive. Not many souls can bear this expense, and sooner or later they align themselves with one or another form of being, having arrested the process of becoming. From that moment on they are not in a *Baal T'shuvah* relationship to Judaism; they have become *Hakhamim*. The *Baal T'shuvah* must tap very deep resources in his own soul in order to be able to maintain himself in this emotionally expensive atmosphere. He truly is a heart afire in a thornbush that is never consumed.

The *Baal T'shuvah* lives in an atmosphere of crisis. He sees the world as in balance, and by his act of Torah observance, he wants to weigh the scales of the world on the merit side. His own sin is not just deviation from Torah-true behavior; it is a cosmic cataclysm. Merely to square himself with *halakic* criteria is not enough for the *Baal T'shuvah*. He is not satisfied with mere *halakic* justification. Like the Seer of Lublin he asks himself: Will God take delight in my action? He places himself before the visage of God. This does not mean that the *Baal T'shuvah* has reached such high levels of contemplative vision that he is sure of God's qualities or attributes. He is sure only of his yearning for them. He has no criteria other than "not yet, not yet." The *Baal T'shuvah* is not concerned with any rational proof of God's existence. God exists for him in his dissatisfaction with his present, somewhere at the end of his strivings. He seeks not so much to know God as to find Him, and he finds Him in seeking. It is often difficult to communicate with the *Baal T'shuvah*. He is impenetrably esoteric, highly symbolic. The *Hakham* often accuses him of doubletalk. But the repentant communicates his concern and his striving.

The *Baal T'shuvah* is not satisfied with dormant motivation. He strives always to bring it to full awareness. He lives in a state of tension. The consent of the majority is far less significant to him than the discipleship he seeks in one who has already trodden his path. He is concerned not so much with the *what* of Judaism as in the *how* of becoming a good Jew. No goal in the present can satisfy the *Baal T'shuvah;* he always looks toward the future. He speaks from want of reconciliation, always considering himself in debt. He makes demands upon himself and upon others which seem unreasonable.

These two types of mind stand opposed in this primary set. The esoteric mind wishes to anchor the deep will only in God. The exoteric mind tends to deny the deep will and concerns itself only with the surface ought.

My Son, the Catalyzing Fossil

If we permit ourselves another dichotomy, the poles of the continuum named after two abnormal psychological types, we could speak of the *paranoid* set versus the *schizoid*. We do not intend to say that either of these attitudes is abnormal. In fact these two attitudes make up the normal state of thinking of our time. We will use them only for the insight they give to us in the primary set which we are discussing.

The schizoid personality finds it difficult to see relationship and purpose, design and the origin of design in a number of data. The schizoid mind does not get excited; it shrugs its shoulder and prefers to live in an atmosphere of Apollonian detachment and grandeur. It insists that real history does not exist. It is always unsure of its parentage and origin. It permits polytheistic appeasement. It capitulates before stress, and so it is totally un-Jewish. Toynbee sees in this mind the acme of the higher religions. Obviously Hinduism and Buddhism, seeing in *samsara* an endless cycle of Karmic changes, can find only one way out, and that is to seek *Samadhi* or *Nirvana*. The Japanese variant does not so readily capitulate before stress. It seeks to increase this stress and to reorganize its primary set as a result of the prolongation of the stress. One of the translations for Zen is *distraction*, for it drives itself to distraction until it can become converted in a moment of *satori*. In the Zen *Koan*, the moment of stress is prolonged until the mind bursts into *satori*, enlightenment, that makes peace with *suchness* as it is and allows one to move with creative caprice in the midst of chaos.

Not so the Jewish mind. It is "paranoid" in that it goes to great lengths to seek to see design and purpose. It claims a father and its own sonship to him, though it also is terrified by the father's hiding. This is why even the "rod" is a real comfort, for it points to the father. One of its higher hopes is, "Only goodness and mercy shall *pursue* me all the days of my life." Rain, flood, and drought are not results of atmospheric conditions, but of being judged in the eyes of God. "If you walk in my statutes . . . I will give you rain in due season."

How a yellowed leaf on a tree is to be plucked from its branch and wafted by the wind, and where it is to be set down, is part of divine design. The half-life of a decaying electron is determined by Him in the same manner as "He causes their hosts to go out in their number calling each one by name." Conditions, therefore, cannot be changed by manipulation of symptoms alone. One has to "rise to the source and root of the decrees in order to sweeten them."

A child sits in the rear seat of a car, looks out at the moon, and shouts to his father who is driving, "Dad, the man in the moon is following us." This is the phenomenal reality of the child's experience. Analytical thought would divest phenomena of personal meaning.

The tone of almost all the books of the Bible, of almost all the statements of the sages, of almost all the moral lessons of the pulpit, has been "paranoid."

This does not mean value judgment but rather a functional assessment of a psychological set. Freud has already shown us that on the deepest levels of our being we share much with the insane. We may legitimately if analogically speak of the "paranoid" versus the "schizoid" set.

The secular mind, that of the modern pagan, is "schizoid." In order to maintain a semblance of sanity it must be pragmatically oriented. It sees life as a game, a sport, and its innermost criterion is pleasure. The Hindu, too, sees life and history as the sporting of God. The price for not being a "fossil" is to become a toy, a marionette for the cynical amusement of the capricious "fates."

The Bankruptcy of "Ethics"

The only way one can exist in such a universe is to operate
in terms of enlightened self-interest! If, from time to time, the
secular mind experiences anxiety, it drowns terror in sen-
suousness. How else can it help to conquer anxiety if from
infancy it has learned to still it by "hitting the bottle"? How
can it do otherwise, if it was not reared by a father who is
a repository of values, a father who becomes introjected into
the child as the holder of values systematically demanding
and exacting discipline by reward and punishment? The secular mind suckles at a breast that is too sweet or too sour
because mother never acts but just *re*acts to the environment
in disoriented caprice, the stony breast of an unresponsive
mother or the impersonal consolation of a rubber nipple.
Without the father, the child must learn to deal with mother's
caprice on the basis of momentary and hazardous ingratiation.

The hedonistic mind then is embraced by a process of
education that is empirically pragmatic and analytic, that
never learns to think integrally or to refer to values. As a
result it fails to develop any deep emotional responses. It is
never "sent"; it is "cool" and schizophrenically detached; or,
and this is perhaps worse, it develops deep emotional responses
which remain capricious, chaotic, and manic-depressive. Either
the anxiety of the existential questions is repressed, or it is
drowned in self-pitying sensuous consolations. The secular
mind cannot relate to the word "holy." This word is not
found in the dictionary of the pleasure-driven. In living with
society on the basis of enlightened self-interest, the only coherent construct the secular mind can find is an "ethic."

This mind is far too pragmatic to be able to create. It
may claim to create, but this is merely a rationalization, an
a posteriori adoption of an action that was in fact motivated
by enlightened self-interest. It is not concerned with letting
others live except as part of the formula of "live and let live,"

with an emphasis that loads the word "live" with more energy than the words "let live." The "let live" is merely a necessary compromise. A working hypothesis of "I will scratch your back today so that you may scratch mine tomorrow" does not deserve the word "ethic." Neither does *égotisme à deux* deserve the dignity of the word "love"—nor does the occasional placation of a tribal totem deserve the dignity of the word "religion." If the secular mind preens itself on a philosophy, its life is not bound to its philosophy.

I Plight My Troth to Thee in Righteousness and Justice

The religious mind is a bound mind (*religare*—to bind). It is bound to a co-ordinate and from this binding up, from its anchoring, it derives principles. It cannot "travel now and pay later." It is not free, because it is maintained in covenantal relationship. The religious mind realizes that the archetypal relationship of the soul with God was misplaced when it was projected on a father of flesh and blood; when an all-too-human father cannot quite manage to personify the values he demands, the religious mind displaces this projection and manages to focus it on Him, the Father who first fashioned the need for this projection.

The religious mind has opted for seeing all anxiety as the "echo that daily radiates from Mount Horeb calling 'Return, ye wayward children.'" It is impossible to still this anxiety, which is the carrier wave of His Voice, with sensuous consolation. The religious mind is not responsible to a pleasure principle. It is responsible to God. Thus it must seek its solution within the matrix of Torah. Often the religious mind is misunderstood by the secular. The secular mind cannot see in the word *Torah*—direction—a prime co-ordinate for shaping the chaos, but only a legislation which compounds man's chaos by piling a huge amount of new debris in his path.

The Torah Is Not a Tranquilizer

"Straight are the ways of the Lord." *Yesharim*, the religiously minded, walk on it. *Posh'im*, the secular-minded Promethean rebels, stumble on it. The religiously minded see in a step the possibility of going higher. The secular see in a step nothing but an obstacle.

To one who is not involved in Torah, it is impossible to expound by the mere use of the printed word the process of studying it. He who has not recited a blessing which involves the Giver of the Torah in the teaching process sees only a legislation like all other legislations, which represents the social compromise, "as long as one does not get caught . . ."

As a social compromise the Torah is a failure. The Torah is not designed to ease the pursuit of pleasure and to make this pursuit more effective in terms of sensuous consolations. It does not intend to adjust man to the lowest possible tension among his various drives, in the face of other men seeking to fulfil the same aim. It is not concerned with "living and letting live" but with being holy, for "holy am I the Lord your God." The word "holy" is to the religious person the branch that connects the fruit to the tree, the fetus to the womb, the soul to God. And that is all the steadiness that the religious mind seeks, for it relies on the teleology inherent in the life that streams into his being, and the religious man allows it to form him into a shape that he by his own outer will cannot achieve.

Thus the religious mind, after announcing that "The world is a spinning die and everything turns and changes; man is turned to an angel and an angel to man; the head to the foot and the foot to the head. Thus all things turn and spin and change, this into that and that into this, the topmost to the undermost, and the undermost to the topmost," can also say that "at the root all is one and salvation inheres in the change and return of things." Thus, where the schizoid mind cannot discern a pattern, the paranoid mind manages to see a pattern, a *Gestalt*, in the most chaotic mess. For the religious mind even the good is not absolute in itself. Surely "good" is not a euphemism for the pleasurable or for that which produces a game of life, but rather is that which is good-in-the-eyes-of-God.

Evil Is a Husky Husk

And evil is that which the religious mind as it faces God must learn to disown. All good is related to the process of thou-ing—facing God without a mask as a Thou. The Non-Thou, the absence of personal relationship, is for the religious mind the source of all evil. Evil then is found where, instead of a person, one is a mere shell, a mask, a *K'lippah*. And so too does evil get its energy from a non-personal, non-thou, assignment, which is also nothing but a shell, of the energy that comes from God.

It may seem that good and evil are not ontological realities but verbal polarities of direction. One could say that good is what *goods*, and evil is what *evils*. But this is not quite so. The religious mind sees in these words "good" and "evil" a problem. It is "paranoid" and it sees in everything the image of God. Being at home with the statement "Know you therefore today and set it to your heart that the Lord is God *and there is nothing else*," it is at once obliged to blame Him for evil. The religious mind goes so far as to say, "Former of life, Creator of darkness, Maker of peace and *Creator* of *evil*." He is All, and evil is part of the All, therefore that part of the All which is evil is also He. This relentless logic is a problem that only the most bound mind can face without breaking the bond and receding into the schizoid set.

The religious mind does not move from its premises. It remains anchored to its set, and shouts "In spite of it all and in the very face of it," and proceeds to ask God in prayer,

"What is it you would have me do? What is it that you would
have me not do?" The religious mind has experienced discovery by a Voice that speaks, saying, "Thy intentions are
desirable but thine acts are not." The religious mind therefore
does not want to decree its own acts.

If Y're So Committed, How Come Y'aint God?

The problem of good intention which, in spite of itself,
brings evil results preoccupies the ethical thinker but not the
religious mind. The religious person "daily at all times and
at each hour" commits himself to the covenant and its principles. The problem of the religious person is the problem
of the act. He is only too painfully aware of the results of
his acts and thoughts. He knows that despite the best intentions he is not God but a finite person and that many good
actions bring results that are not good. The intentions of a
given act may be pure and good; the results as they show up
in interaction with the social world are not always good; and,
since the religious person cannot continue to exist in a world
where any act, even with the best intention, is bound to have
evil repercussions, he must consolidate his responsibility and
be answerable only to One and not to many. William James
calls this attitude the attitude of one who takes a "moral
holiday." Stefan Zweig in his masterpiece, *The Eyes of the
Undying Brother*, explores an ethic which seeks unfailingly
good results. Like the hero of his story, any such person
could not help but, in frustration, renounce the world and
become a keeper of dogs. If one does not wish to take the
moral holiday, what is the alternative? He must be God and
take all responsibility to himself. Jean-Paul Sartre, who cannot
take a moral holiday because his God is dead—and he wishes
it were not so—must take all responsibility himself and do so
in the face of the utter fear of non-being.

The religious mind does not stand beneath the sword of
Damocles but beneath a poised Mount Sinai which threatens

to crush him unless he accepts the Torah. The Torah-bound religious mind cuts the Gordian knot of good result–ethics. It gathers all a person's investments (cathexes) and bets them on Pascal's wager. It trusts the "straight laws" that issue from God, but prayerfully, begging God for help.

To Pray Is to Be Destitute

Our society does not tolerate beggars. How paradoxical is its moral tone! While Protestant, and thus centered not in the deserving of grace gained by good works but in the free grace of God, it abhors the flesh-and-blood beggar. The *Shnorrer* becomes an institutional fund-raiser. He never knocks on our door hoping to satisfy his hunger. He feeds on our own hunger for belongingnesss.

We may spend a great deal of our budget on "entertaining friends," but we do not invite the hungry for a meal. The real beggar is not fed but referred to a social agency.

At a time when we turn from the poor, it is terribly difficult for us to pray.

How often rabbis in pulpits insist that the Jewish meaning of prayer derives from self-judgment—*Hitpalel*—and not from the Latin *precare*, precarious, beggar-like existence. Nevertheless the praying person, while making any request to God, begs. Even if he builds God a magnificent temple it does not entitle him to negotiate a "deal," for "from Thine hand have we given to Thee." It does not matter whether he begs for material or spiritual benefits. In praying for either he says, "The needs of Thy people are all so many and their minds are all too small."

In the realm of the holy, the dichotomy between matter as evil and spirit as good does not exist. From a Jewish point of view it takes very little audacity to insist that matter is more holy than spirit. Physical *"Mitzvah"* substances (leather *T'fillin*, woolen *Tzitzith*), when utilized by a commanded person in the covenant relationship, are almost more holy than the spiritual substance of angels. And it does not matter whether one fulfils the duties of the body or the duties of the heart.

We cannot glibly divide matter and spirit, nor can we glibly insist that in prayer we judge ourselves but do not beg.

At this moment both writer and reader are utterly frustrated by the merely descriptive material available on prayer. The Voice bursts out with threatening impatience, demanding that talk *about* prayer be stopped and that prayer begin. One is frustrated by hearing what the message of the prayer ought to be without being initiated into the process of speaking it. We cannot hesitate and defend ourselves against this urgency by ordering and polishing the verbal niceties of our intended prayers and thus escape from uttering them.

At moments when we face God, words fail us. The body does not know which attitude to take. A Jew casts a sidelong glance at an imagined Catholic kneeling before a crucifix and wishes that he, too, could kneel. At the same time, he knows that it would be all wrong and that kneeling would amount to anatomical apostasy. But then to sit in one's chair and to imagine that one is in the synagogue or to settle for formalized responsive reading is equally unsatisfactory.

Somewhere in the back of our mind we remember an ancestor wrapped in a *Tallith*, his eyes closed, his body swaying, his hands raised in a heaven-storming gesture. But we are blocked in our self-consciousness and are ashamed before our own *persona* since we who see God outside of ourselves think Him to be so far away. One does have to descend into that desolation in which the modern Jew, who completely lacks a repertoire of prayer, finds his soul. Reading further will not help him. Meditation, at this point, is also an escape. Writer and reader have to become beggars and stop before God.

You God have . . .

I need . . .

Give . . . !

From the Sanctuary to the Study Hall

If writer and reader have prayed, they have come away with the conviction that "the righteous will live by his faith" or "He had told you, O man, what is good and what does the Lord require of you but to do justice, to like loving action and to walk hidden with your God."

Receding more from the prayer experience, the generalization gives way to particulars. Because one acts for Him, by Him, and with His help, one does not construct general principles but executes particular *Mitzvot*.

The responsibility ends as far as we are concerned when we complete the commanded act. Only those who are demonically beset by scruples will not be able to relent and relax. Only wise and loving souls can exorcise the demons of scrupulosity in themselves and in others. Part of the comfort is contained in that man who knows that it is not only he who bears the yoke of the commandment, but that the Divine Commander also bears the yoke of the command and, especially, the responsibility for the results. Thus the *Mitzvah* is not a means to an extrinsic end but the fulfilment of His will, and it is from the fabric of *Mitzvot* that the pattern of good is woven.

The Reward of a Mitzvah Is Man's Gift to God

Here is another logical paradox which nevertheless is a functional reality; on the one hand, God does not become real for any man except in the modification of that man's behavior and in the culmination of that behavior in *Mitzvot*. On the other hand, man cannot begin to do a *Mitzvah* in effectuality unless God is real to him; that is to say, unless he relates to God as a Thou facing him in a relationship which we call "holy." Then God is commanding at the moment of the act and observing the fulfilment of the commandment in the moment of the act and rewarding with his relationship the person fulfilling the act. To the secular mind objectively essaying the situation this is a hopeless chicken-and-egg cycle.

To the religious mind which makes that leap of action which is also a leap of faith, which is also an entering into the covenant, which is also a receiving of the law, which is also becoming disciple to a Teacher, an apprentice to a Master, the contradiction yields to committed beginning. For inasmuch as man is absolved of the responsibility for his *Mitzvah* acts he is not promised the result of his acts, nor is he given the fruits of his action. In fulfilling a *Mitzvah*, the fruit of that *Mitzvah*, the reward as it were, is presented to God as a votive offering. Every once in a while a religious person must defy the temptation to look back for results, a temptation to slide back into the pragmatic trap of demanding a messianic consolation.

One can respond only by fulfilling the command, and this one can only do deliberately. Being commanded, one can now live because being commanded is altogether different from being coerced. In the divine motivation for the creation of man there is no coercing. God does not wish to *live* man but to live *with* him. Such a relationship is possible only in reciprocal deliberateness. Why this should prove to be so delightful to God we may never know. What we may be given to know is that it is delightful to man.

To Do a Mitzvah Is to Admit God into One's Life

The Kotzker once embarrassed his Hasidim by posing the question, "Where is God?" and to a shrug on the part of his Hasidim and to their reply, "Where is He not?" he replied, "God is wherever He is let in."

Values reside in man only inasmuch as he has given life space within himself to significant persons to whom such values are important. To be holy means that one has given the power of attorney to God over one's entire life space.

Our sages call the life space that each person occupies "the four ells." Furthermore, the sages say, since the temple was destroyed, the Holy One, Blessed be He, has no more space in this world than the four ells of *Halakah*. These are the four ells which God and man occupy when man lives under the compunction of divine commandments. In occupying man's life space, God is not a nasty boarder. He not only pays "rent," He becomes a member of the family, indeed the *paterfamilias*. The rent which God, as it were, pays to the householder is the consolidation of all his values and holdings, the cessation of tensions and strife, for it is He Who has now assumed the burden of the responsibility for the ultimate rightness of our acts. No more need we please either our environment or the society we live in, for even these relationships are part of His command. Whatever "sunning" or "mooning" is to be done, is done as a result of His commandment, for it is He Who rules each day.

A Wise Son Says What?

Part of being in the disciple-apprentice position is to ask *questions*. The raising of objections is inappropriate to disciple-apprentice relationships. The question seeks to elicit information in order to complete the conceptual system, but an objection seeks to destroy the very skeleton on which the information is hung. He who seeks information has emptied himself of his own opinions, he is aware of their inadequacy, and he thus becomes a receptacle capable of containing the information; whereas the objector is full of his own opinions which are to him the only criteria of acceptance and rejection of information. The newly committed disciple-apprentice is a catechumen and the answers to his questions may be called catechism. A catechism is the kind of teaching that is given by "those who know" to those who have to be initiated. It is not that the catechumen must receive information. If it were merely this, we could use modern educational methods which would begin with the motivation inherent in the pupil. But because the motivation of the pupil is bipolar and his cognitive apparatus is bipolar, he must be taught in an organic way. The catechumen literally has to swallow what he is fed by his master and teacher.

To the opinionated objector, the catechetic way of teaching is wholly unacceptable, no matter what one's religious situation is. Prometheus never asks how man is to merit fire, he never begs and prays for it; he begins with his objection to a situation in which man does not have fire. Prometheus cannot be a catechumen.

Tell Him Even About the Laws of the Aphikomen

Every new item of information into which the Jewish catechumen is initiated makes terrible demands on him in terms of behavior change. The Jewish seeker is therefore less free to be convinced by the truth of a dectrine because, convinced, he becomes convicted of actual misdemeanors. The objections that a Jew is bound to raise to his instructor are therefore more often of a pragmatic nature than of an intrinsically aesthetic or logical one. No wonder, then, that the truths which are most readily confirmed by one's inner criteria are those that vote in favor of "the fatherhood of God and the brotherhood of Man" and "democracy." It is very easy nowadays for Jews to become convinced of neo-orthodox liberal Protestant Christianity, whose value structure he has imbibed with his ABC's. He can even become "committed" to it, for it will not demand a radical change in his style of life. But what if the disciple-apprentice is exposed to Jewish indoctrination? It is not logic that will object but the introjected image of parents, spouse, and children, business associates, and others. Introjected as they are, they own a considerable emotive investment. Therefore these introjected factors are far more difficult to deal with than are logical objections.

The reality of the introjected significant persons is more profound than the reality of the values of neo-orthodox liberal Protestant Christianity, because they are not merely conceptual and because they are in powerful control of one's *persona*. But the apprentice-disciple must be capable of jettisoning past roles if he is to be instructed further. For most people this is too harsh a demand, unless they receive not the catechetical instruction of tradition and its accumulated know-how, but a sugar-coated reasonable Judaism. Alas, there simply is no way of acquiring the information that those who have transformed their own lives from the dualistic to the monistic position can share with us, except by changing one's behavior. Otherwise, even to acquire information from *Zaddikim* who have realized God in their life here is an impossible task. One cannot listen to them long enough without losing patience, not because of what they say, but because of what they do *not* say, because of what their information demands in terms of behavioral change. Thus we are prone to raise objections before we have fully given *Zaddikim* a hearing. And yet what they say bears the authentic seal of that Voice which challenged us in the first place.

Concepts Are Thought Handles

Neat theories are based on neat conceptual systems. There is one neat theory that holds that evil is an illusion. All is good because God is good. Man in his error invents evil. This theory begs the question how it came about that man fell into this error, because the creation of the very possibility of man falling into such error is evil.

Another theory holds that evil is as much a reality as is good. A good god opposes an evil god, and man is a poor creature caught in between a dual reality. But how could the good god be God if there is room for an evil one to oppose him?

In between these two theories there are a number of

others. Some of them are closer to the first, such as theories that hold that yesterday's good is today's evil in the upward rising movement of man. In this gnostic view, the closer one is to earthy things the more embedded in evil one is. But somewhere, way on top, there is no evil at all.

Who made the "below"? Not a good God of course, but an evil demiurge who wishes to play god and who has trapped us on a Ferris wheel in which evil keeps forever bobbing up and down and from which we must escape to the good God. Such a view exonerates God. It removes Him from the ken of man and turns His world into a hell. The world and the things in it are vile beyond the possibility of becoming sanctified.

Another view divides evil into two categories. One is natural evil, such as the kind of cataclysm that insurance companies blame God for. But there is also another kind of evil that is incurred by man as a form of punishment for his transgressions of immutable cosmic laws, be they natural or moral. Natural evil is justified as a bitter pill, a temptation, an opportunity for heroic generosity and sainthood. The other evil, which comes as a punishment, is the response to man, like a ricochet bullet which is deflected by the target and hits the man who pulled the trigger. Natural evil then comes as a *grace*. Moral evil has the rigor of *justice*.

Evil as K'lippah

There is much to be said for these views, but there is no way in which the truth of any of these propositions can effectively be demonstrated. Yet in a pragmatic way one could perhaps show that there is some "cash value" in the Hasidic system which combines some of these, adds depth and relationship to them, and comes out with a system which is not as simple as any of the other views and still bears in itself the seeds of deliberate action which help man to "turn from evil and to do good." This is the doctrine of the sparks—

Nitzotzoth—and of the two energy systems, the system of
K'dushah—holiness—and the energy system of *K'lippah*—
shell—husks—or *Tum'ah*—the defilement.

The world can in this system be the place where God is
truly present, so that "in their oppression is He also oppressed." A person can, by taking a physical object, fulfil
a commandment and do God's will. In this system man is
also able to do *T'shuvah*, turning, and through an act of
T'shuvah man can convert past evil into meritorious good.

We are aware that the presentation of the Hasidic system
may raise many more questions than it answers immediately.
Moreover, few if any of the subtle points could be made
without the use of concepts, each of which needs prerequisite
concepts. So we cannot really promise to give a complete
account of the Hasidic view. At best we can tease the appetite
of those who may be called to delve deeper into these teachings with the help of a Hasidic guide.

God, IT Exists; So What?

We seat ourselves at the feet of the sainted masters of
Hasidism and the Kabbalah. They invite us to start with the
promise of an Infinite God in an infinite number of co-ordinate dimensions. Three of these infinite dimensions are: the
dimension of IT, the dimension of the HE, and the dimension
of the THOU. By calling them "co-ordinate dimensions" we
indicate that we are dealing with conceptual tools, whose
descriptive utility helps us to systematize our thinking.

We define the IT dimension of God as the concept of the
Supreme Being, the philosopher's God, all powerful and all
fulfilled. This God of consummate Equilibrium, not needing,
not seeking nor wanting anything, is traditionally called
Eyn Sof (the Endless) in the Kabbalah. In the *Eyn Sof*
there is no distinction between Creator and creature, since
in IT neither of these terms applies. There is no differentiation between "space" and "time," since the Infinite fills and

is all. The *Eyn Sof* existed before the "Prime Mover" moved anything, for in movement time began and space was "made"; the endless remains the very same *Eyn Sof*.

The simplicity of the One rules supreme; He is the God Who was and Who will be, without change and without peer. This is the God of the mystic and the atheist. While the atheist insists that the God in Whom he does not believe could only be an IT, the mystic is intoxicated with an Absolute which the IT concept of God implies.

HE Creates the Best of All Natural Worlds

The HE of God stands for the Creator of Nature and the universe, the Prime Mover, the Planner and Originator of space and time. To the HE of God we can give a name, the Biblical name *Elohim*. *Elohim i*s a plural form and provides room for the plurality of existence and for a God Who emanates creation and Who is Omnipotent. We refer to Him as a divine object, as a Someone Who is not turned to us but Who is busy creating constantly. So preoccupied He seems, and so turned away from us, that He is not to be influenced by any one of His creatures and therefore He cannot be reached by any of our prayers. There is no way of making Him change the laws of His creation. As a result, He is "blamed" for permitting suffering.

But HE is the God Who causes evolution and being, without Himself becoming involved. HE *exists* without *being* and relating. HE is a permissive God Who cannot be said to care. Moral and ethical criteria do not apply to Him. HE creates man only to forsake him, as it were. HE is the scientists' God. HE is the expert Designer Whose mind is discernible in His works. But in our human predicaments, we have no concern for the purposes of His plans. HE overwhelms us as HE squelched Job. We stand in awe before His unbendingness, and cannot do anything but submit to Him. We conclude that HE has some purpose, but this purpose cannot be discerned by us. And, just as we cannot reach Him, we cannot elicit a response from Him. Consequently, other than realizing His plan and design, an intellectual need (or luxury?), we as human beings have no need of Him.

The God Who can help and Who relates to us, cannot be found in the HE dimension. We must look for Him on a different level, the level of THOU. Consider the apparent contradiction between chapters 1 and 2 of Genesis. First we hear that in the beginning *Elohim*, or HE, created the heavens and the earth. Later we find *HVYH-Elohim* made earth and heaven. Rashi informs us of the opinion of our earlier sages that "In the beginning HE wished to create the world with His attribute of law. When HE saw that the world could not exist in this manner HE wedded the attribute of mercy to it."

God, THOU Enterest into Thy World to Be with Us

God as THOU is Father and Helper. HE needs us as much as we need Him. HE is the moral God Who cares enough to reveal Himself and to relate to man. HE wedded mercy to justice as part of His original creative plan. Once man exists, God it not only an IT and a HE; HE has become a THOU.

THOU is the One Who even redeems.

THOU is the One Who redeems, for THOU is also called into exile. THOU redeems man and man redeems THOU. Relating to us as THOU may seem to lessen the majesty of His omnipotence, but HE restricts His power because HE as THOU so loves us that HE joins us in our limitations. Jewish tradition identified the THOU with the *Sh'khinnah*, the Divine Presence which we are capable of encountering. THOU is the God Whom our grandmothers addressed as *"Gottenyu,"* of Whom the Bible says that "In all their oppression was HE oppressed" (Isa. 63:9). All our striving, our life and our love, relates us to THOU. Whenever we cry out "God" and wish to reach Him, we seek Him as THOU, as One facing us and hearing us. Whenever the answer comes forth from the depth within us, it is the THOU who answers "that Thou harkenest to the prayer of any mouth"; "before we call Thou answerest us." Without us as persons who face Him as Thou, He could never be a Thou. To angels He is always a third-person entity. Only as THOU can He enter relationship.

Since THOU relates to us, THOU demands a THOU-like life, and sets conditions for His dwelling with us. THOU is the loving Father Who hears the prayers of His children and helps them. THOU is the Benign King Who directs the lives of His subjects. THOU is the Teacher. THOU is He Who remains forever our Father. And THOU is person, if by person we mean will, drive, intelligence, feeling, joy, and empathy.

The Lord Our God Is One

A prayerful approach now yields the attitude in which it is possible to think of IT, HE, and THOU as One.

The motive of the personal THOU and the infinite potential of the transcendental IT explain why HE creates the actual universe. In the HE-created universe, the IT cannot be met save as THOU. The THOU and the HE derive their Divine transcendental value from their identity with the Divine IT.

The existence of evil in the universe filled by God is a philosophic scandal, but we can now begin to see that the scandal was of our own making. Because we flattened (at least) three dimensions into a one-dimensional line, we created "scandalous" contradictions. Perpendicular concepts relate in a "plastic" manner. Their angular coherence constitutes no inner contradiction. Besides resolving the "scandal," this approach helps us in other ways also. An absolutist's concept of God leaves little room for man to act. His questions are often answered, "My thoughts are not your thoughts" (Isa. 55:8). A purely immanentist relativism leaves us without the "Highest." For the traditional THOU, one claims on the one hand utter transcendence—"I, *Adonai*, have not changed" (Mal. 3:6)—while at the very same time, His transcendence *is addressed to man.*

Infinite Minus One

THOU is the Infinite-minus-one, never quite finite. THOU makes room for man in the cosmic scheme of things. THOU challenges man to add his own *one* to the Infinite-minus-one. THOU is the self-limitation of the IT-HE, in Whom we see ourselves as true partners sharing with God the anticipation of a blessed state of things; His efforts to bring about this state; and His care for the conversion of evil. But in giving room to man, THOU has, by allowing non-THOU, given up His omnipotence. Man suffers as THOU suffers also, and THOU suffers because of His foregoing the IT imperturbability. Only when man makes the great unification—by sanctifying every life aspect—by filling all his life space with only THOU, not leaving any life space at all to non-THOU, then, at least for him, THOU has all the HE energies, from which union all "miraculous signs" come. Thus, the *Zaddik* decrees and God fulfils. Man has so joined with the divine IT, that in the unification he becomes oblivious of the non-THOU and suffers the "pangs of love." Such a man has merged with the "being of the King" so that the THOU-HE-IT are again unified.

For the whole world this unification comes only with Messiah. Then the "whole world will be filled by the glory of God as the waters cover the sea." It is only when one realizes the identity of the waters and sea (trees: woods) that one is rid of non-THOU and there is no longer IT-THOU-HE but "on that day *Adonai* will be One and His name [all outer conceptions] One." But as long as non-THOU exists for man or mankind, evil is starkly real. The root of real evil (not merely the evil which results from an absence of good) inheres in His self-limitation to become a THOU. IT is not opposed by *non*-IT; HE is not opposed by a *non*-HE; IT and HE are Infinite. But THOU is THOU only when faced by the "I" (of man). When man does not face THOU, he faces "non-THOU," another side of reality, the *Sittra Ahra*.

One Man's Meat May Be Another Man's K'lippah

There are two kinds of *K'lippah*, absolute and relative evil. Acts forbidden by the Torah bring about complete enslavement to *K'lippah* that yields only to the most drastic measures of *T'shuvah*, turning. Relative *K'lippah* energizes all "permitted" acts. It depends on intention, which can turn the permitted into good or into temporary evil. By Thou-ing, man can eat and sleep, enjoy physical pleasures, and complete the circuit, for the immanent and the transcendent release sparks from bondage and brings about God's *Nachat*. By not Thouing, he temporarily enslaves these energies which can be freed only in the next *Mitzvah* or *T'shuvah*. Dialogue is not limited to speech but functions in dialogic *Mitzvah*-action (contrary to Buber?) in which the whole man speaks through actions.

The energy systems of non-Thou hold us in defilement. On the one hand, holiness may be commonplace, for the most commonplace act can be sanctified and serve to close the circuit between the Infinite-minus-one and the One. Thus it is in the commonplaces of life that God can be freed, rather than in an ecstatic flight to a transcendental realm where God needs no freeing. On the other hand, evil is as much at home in the commonplace as in the ecstatic.

However, on the ontological level, non-Thou is a vast energy system in its own right. While boldly real (on the Thou continuum), it has no transcendental reality of its own. Its main function is to energize the man who chooses not to face the Thou. It is dynamic, because when enough men yield to its charms (and these are great because they allow man to live in self-centered conceit not answerable to a Thou) it grows to catastrophic proportions. Man is the cosmic valve which can divert He-energies to the "other side." Or, if man chooses to yield his will to the Thou, the slow redemptive process of *T'shuvah* begins. Not only is man redeemed in "turning" to face the Thou but God is also extricated from the energy system of non-Thou.

All this has social consequences. We are not in isolation when we work with other "ones" of the Infinite-minus-one equation. "Love thy neighbor"—who "like Thyself" is capable of redeeming ME; "I am *Adonai*" Who stands in need of being redeemed by man. The Torah is not only not Man's theology, but it is the guide to God's anthropology. It shows how man, facing a chunk of reality, can call the Thou into the four ells of *Halakah*, which our sages termed God's sanctuary in an upset world. In the face of such Divine need, Israel has no choice but to say "We shall do and obey" (Exod. 19:8). Were it not for the messianic hope that "On that day He shall be One and His Name One" (Zech. 14:9), one would despair. The hope that the non-Thou will ultimately be annihilated, the growing joy which little victories gain by *Mitzvot* against the non-Thou afford, are, to one sensitive to the Thou's plight, reward enough.

Job and Eichmann

If God exists, and if He is what a God is supposed to be, how could He permit Hitler, Eichmann, and the death camps?

Hitler and Eichmann represent an accumulator for the discharge of non-Thou energies which potentially suffuse our corner of the universe. A saturation point was reached. Jews, the most vulnerable people in this universe, were an opposite pole, attracting discharge like a lightning rod. The highest positive potential was in Russian and Polish Jewry, because they were suffused more than anyone else in *K'dushah*, holy energies. It is not for us to estimate the amount of spark liberation that took place as a result of Jewish Thou-ing in death. Only Hiroshima and Nagasaki remained as the pinpoints of discharge of non-Thou energies on the side of the Allies. With eastern European Jewry no longer a lightning rod, with non-Thou energies daily mounting in furor, what awaits the world now is far worse than the Second World War, unless we can manage by a mass *T'shuvah* to neutralize non-Thou energies, to free them, and to convert them into Thou energies.

This may represent the metaphysical fact, but is psychologically inadequate. The holocaust could also be explained as a premessianic necessity. But to the individual in *Todesangst* such views will be inadequate. Rabbis have often pointed to the book of Job as an explanation. Job may not explain very much, but it offers an example of yea-saying in the face of a terrible God Whose ultimate purpose is not conceived but believed. "Even though He slay me, still do I trust in Him." A well-fed Rabbi to a well-fed and well-cushioned congregation may "holler like hell because the argument is weak," and achieve a momentary nod of agreement which says nothing more than "Here is an explanation so that we don't have to be uncomfortable."

I, the Man, Saw Pain at the Rod of His Anger

But Job is no answer because, unlike us, he had no guilt whatsoever. Both the prologue of the book and the development of the theme past the comfort, point to this. But *we* do have guilt. There is much in the "empty" consolation of the comforters which applies not to Job but to us. We have presumed, we have sinned, and we do not deserve to fall under the category, "Hast Thou considered my servant Job for there is none like him in the world"! There are many sinners like us who require comfort.

Jeremiah did not console by preaching the Job ethic. He introduced us to a sentiment of the deepest religious significance, the sentiment of lamentation. We do not have much lamentation today. We do not sit on the floor, shoes removed, ashes on the head, admitting our shame and guilt, exclaiming "How hath this faithful city become like a harlot?" Sackcloth and ashes are outer manifestations of the sentiment of lamentation. But lamentation cannot be assumed; it must be experienced in terms of real grief and pain, accompanied with cathartic weeping, with pain, "abreacting" sinful pleasure in mournful distress.

Cry for Your Teeth

To lament is not merely to cry over one's own woe. The sainted Rizhiner once asked a person who wept bitterly after reading the Book of Lamentations on the Ninth Av of his motive for crying. The man replied, "Why should I not cry if the Temple was destroyed?"

Said the Rizhiner to him, "What does that really mean to you?"

Embarrassed, he answered, "I am a *Cohen*—a priest."

Said the Rizhiner, "Is it merely a question of meat, that you now have less to eat? Stop crying and I will buy you ten pounds a week."

Further embarrassed, the man replied, "But, Rabbi, is it not written that since the Temple was destroyed all the taste that was in the meat is now in the bones?"

"So I will buy you a whole heap of bones. Stop crying!"

Even more embarrassed the man replied, "But my teeth are gone."

Said the Rizhiner, "Then stop weeping for the sanctuary, weep for your teeth!"

All lamenting must be personal, must be sincere and self-referred. But even that is not enough.

In the lament one must be able to sympathize with the *Sh'khinnah*, for she too suffers and her suffering is not finite. Hers is not limited to only one body, one place, or one time. Her pain is in everyone who suffers, for "in all their oppressions was He oppressed." Those who shake an accusing fist toward heaven and cite the six million arrogate to themselves a position where they claim that only they suffer, forgetting that all the agonies were felt by God. Unless

Sh'khinnah is redeemed by us and by Him, and the redemption redeems not only the future but also the past in one retroactive jubilee, God's spirit is in agony.

Perhaps we have managed to understand evil somewhat; understand, that is, but not condone it. For no matter what paradoxes inhere in the ambivalences of choice, we must confront evil and contest it. Moreover, we must lament evil and join it in its own lament. For, as the midrash perceives it, the "lower waters" constantly raise their lament to God saying, "We who could have been before the King have been set below the firmament."

If we are to confront and contest evil, there are two kinds of evil which we must clearly separate. While one type demands that we contest it and redeem it through our involvement with it, there is another kind that becomes more and more tenacious and substantive the more we become involved in it. The second kind must be unmasked, confronted, and abandoned. Hasidism calls the first process *Birrur*, clarification, and the second *Nissayon*, temptation.

Israel—the Wrestler

Birrur means clarification and separation, analysis. It describes the manner in which we are to deal with a nature not yet committed to evil in its essence. To reject the world because it faces us unsorted would mean the cowardice of escape. Usually the *Yetzer ha-ra* seeks to prevent us from grappling with it and tells us to be humble; not to attempt a job that is greater than our capacity; to leave well enough alone; to seek tasks which, though not ours, are easier to bear. It is precisely in the uncommitted social sphere that evil which challenges us to *Birrur* resides. To be responsive to the outcry of the oppressed, to seek equity for them as well as for us, to work at one's profession or trade in a manner befitting one who has become a THOU-ing partner with the Infinite, to live with others and their weaknesses, to try to help them transcend themselves without being censorious, in other words to be active in a sphere where one can reply to one's own question, "Is this my real place and task?" with a "Yes" that nevertheless is uncomfortable and would much rather be "No": all this is *Birrur*. *Birrur* is the way in which the vanquished faces the victor and the way in which the victim faces the oppressor, too.

The death camp inmate had a responsibility toward his executioners. Seldom did he discharge it. He escaped into terror rather than facing the oppressor and saying to him, "What you are doing is wrong. I submit not to you and will not be coerced by you. My responsibility is to God and I am responsible not only for myself but also for your spark." He would have been put to death just the same or, what is worse, been made to suffer for speaking in this way. Passive non-resistance is escape and not *Birrur*. Violent resistance seldom is good *Birrur*. Non-violent resistance which speaks with compassion for the oppressor's spark, with concern for that one's soul: this is *Birrur*. *Birrur* would have said to the oppressor, "I cannot co-operate with you; neither can I resist you, for I have not the means of resisting you; nor do I consider it my task to resist you with violence. *Birrur* is not only my task but also yours." We have no way of estimating the spiritual salvage that could have been accomplished through such words.

Birrur is a *freedom ride*, for it represents a sorting, an imposing of pattern on the crazy quilt of prejudice. *Birrur* is a *peace corps* for there, too, it sets the pattern of good on a haphazard crazy quilt of raw need.

Birrur is eating the permitted in a sacrificial manner. It is begetting children and making love in honor of *Shabbat*, it is plucking what is good, delightful, and useful and offering it to God. But *Birrur* is never the responsibility of man to the matter which he must separate and sort, not even to the spark hidden in that matter, but always only to God.

The neutral is no longer neutral after *Birrur;* it is now

good. *Birrur* does not handle opaque evil in which God is negated and blocked. Opaque evil is essentially evil *K'lippah*. Neutral, translucent evil yields to *Birrur*—and when transformed into good it becomes transparent, not merely translucent, to God's radiance and light.

Nissayon

One way of translating this word is to call it temptation. Another way would be to call it an upraising, an ascent, "for the Lord your God tests you, raises you up." The evil one faces in *Nissayon* is absolute. It is reinforced by an absolute arrogance that claims: "Even this can be redeemed and you are the man to do it."

The *Baal Shem Tov* said once, "*Shabbetai Zvi* had a great soul: I once tried to redeem him but his pride was so great that he wanted to swamp me with it too." *Nissayon* arrogance would say, "Everyone could not possibly redeem evil such as this. It would be very dangerous for others but not for *you*. Not only are you an exception, but it has been waiting for you all these years."

The truth is that absolute evil which disguises itself in a tempting form *cannot* be redeemed by man. Its residual reality is anchored to the pole opposite holiness. It must always be there to leave choice open. It is there also for those who have transcended themselves and entered into the universe of the One. For as Reb Nachman tells us, "Even a *Zaddik* has a *Yetzer Hara*, but his is a holy angel." It is basically fantasy and not reality which one faces in *Nissayon*. It is a fantasy rich and seductive for the person tempted. It is also a fantasy in that it claims that it would yield up its sparks if treated in the same manner as *Birrur*. Such evil is real enough if man rejects it as "fantasy," for it is then that he is capable of redeeming the lofty sparks inherent in it.

The arrogant would-be redeemer of total evil suffers from a Messiah complex. He thinks that he can grapple with it and redeem it by his own promethean powers. Poor Rabbi Joseph de la Reina who chained a phantasm and lost his mind!

The true *Zaddik* is not a heroic redeemer; he is content to serve God. Whatever is not part of his service he is content to leave for God. But a manic-depressive Saul, whose head is higher than that of everyone else among the people, knows—so he thinks—better than a Samuel who says that God seeks humble *Birrur*, obedience, not unbidden sacrifices. In a *Birrur* or a *Mitzvah* God inheres as Helper as well an immanent Animator. The promethean hero tries to do it all alone. Man can redeem the *Sh'kinnah* only with God's blessed help.

Fantasy becomes as real as man allows it to be. Once it has energized man, it cannot be shaken; like pitch, it sticks and defiles. The promethean hero is chained to his fantasy and cannot be freed. He will be damned before he calls on God to help him, and so he remains damned.

But T'shuvah and T'fillah and Tzedakah Remove the Evil Decree

He who, out of his fear and anxiety, returns to God, can turn the evil willed into a forgivable unintentional act. Out of anxiety for a sin one comes to realize that one lives a driven, non-deliberate, unconscious life. This realization thus has the power to transvaluate the past; but not completely. One is transported to a less incriminating category before God, but the past is not yet altogether redeemed. The palliative was not a cure.

But if one faces God in His utter preciousness, if one does not care so much for one's own safety but rather is utterly contrite at having offended Him, and if one anchors himself and his deep will in a passionate reparative love relationship, then the very passion of sin is transmuted into the present passion to be at one with Him. The passionate sin of the past becomes present merit.

This doctrine is less antinomian than it seems. If one is passionately lost in God, one cannot deliberately expose oneself to sin and hope to do *T'shuvah* afterwards. He who sins deliberately finds the passionate return not at hand. The cool sinner may become nothing more than a tepid penitent.

But the man of passion is redeemed by his passion when his object is God. And with his love he can turn back time, turn sin into merit. To this love even the fantastic evil yields. The *Baal T'shuvah* has as his wedding gift all the gems of the sparks in his soul which now knows that the IT, the HE, the THOU, and he himself, with God as his own Self and Center, are One.

For the passionate *Baal T'shuvah*, the Messiah has come—alas, only for himself alone! For he is lonely, the *Baal T'shuvah;* the righteous do not stand with him; they are scandalized by his "merits." The *Zaddik* still lives in a dualistic world. He too loves God, but in a premessianic, historic, exiled way. The *Baal T'shuvah* has transcended history, joined IT and THOU to HE, abolished polarities. Like the *Sh'kinnah* on Sabbath eve, he is the one facing the One.

But there is more than this. Opaqueness is not altogether bad. Metal allows no light to pass, but if burnished and polished it not merely reflects a few rays but mirrors the whole sun. *The passionate Baal T'shuvah mirrors the whole God*, while some *Zaddikim* are at best transparent only to a transcendent IT, a harsh impersonal HE, or a less-than-infinite THOU. The light that is mirrored back to God by the penitent who holds the polished and burnished opaque mirror toward heaven brings Him to resplendent joy.

But Until You Get to the Inn You Still Need a Little Bit of Gin

What the *Baal T'shuvah* feels is a private experience. Matter is still recalcitrant, and mirrors sometimes rust. Evil is still very much with us, both as *Birrur* and as *Nissayon*. The work of *Birrur* is difficult, and the withstanding of *Nissayon* takes every bit of our sanity. Death is close, and loneliness is the price of becoming a *Baal T'shuvah*. Probability seems more real than conviction. What are we to do until the Messiah comes, when even the inanimate world will awaken into organic oneness?

Let this be our consolation: We are able to do *Mitzvoth* and may leave cosmic politics to God. We are able to fight evil in *Birrur* and free many a holy spark. We are able to play our part in the game of *Nissayon* hide-and-seek. We are able to beg God humbly for everything we need. Even if He wanted to forsake us, He could not; for as long as we are, He makes us be and inheres in us. We can love Him not only as He can be loved in this world, or in the next, but as He will be loved in the time of the Messiah.

If the way to the inn is obscure, and we do not know how much further we must go, there is always a bit of gin available on the way. There is a *Shabbat* every week, when we princes can choose life, be armed for the next week, and dwell in Him Whom we love in His domain of the One. For on *Shabbat* the tensions cease, the wicked are released from Hell, and the Voice teaches Torah distinctly and clearly. On *Shabbat* there is enough hallowing—*kiddush*—to allow us, even after the "separation," to enter the world of *Birrur* and *Nissayon*, to forage through patterns of good and evil seeking gems for the crown of our Beloved.

Christianity and
the Contemporary Jew

A NUMBER OF YEARS AGO, one of my oldest friends, now a minister, told me of his hope of establishing a community church which would attract many of the Jews in New York City who no longer have any religious commitment. "Will you have a cross at the altar?" I asked.

"Of course," he replied. "It is a universal religious symbol."

"That is where you are wrong," I said. "Even to the non-religious Jew the cross is a symbol of the anti-Semitism from which the Jew has had to suffer."

Martin Buber tells that when he first went to school in the Austro-Hungarian Empire, all his teachers wanted to be tolerant of the small group of Jewish students and no attempt at conversion was ever made. Yet the recital of the trinitarian formula, during which the Jewish students stood looking at the ground, morning after morning for eight long years, stamped itself upon his soul more seriously than any intolerance could have done. "To have to participate as a thing in a sacral rite in which no dram of my being could take part," he said, resulted in a lifelong antipathy to all missionary effort among people with religious roots of their own.

What was so difficult for Buber in this situation? It was not that his religious position as a Jew was attacked but that it was ignored. This "unanimity" of the majority which overlooks the presence of another vital attitude remains a central problem for all Jews trying to come to terms with Christianity. One result has been an unconscious disparagement of Judaism which is so much a part of our culture that the average secular Jew shares it—a tendency to look on "the religion of the Old Testament" as a lower, inferior religion with its jealous, wrathful God in opposition to the New Testament's religion of love. Another is that even liberal Jews are often quite unable to have an honest dialogue with Jesus, Paul, and the New Testament.

Yet if Judaism is to come of age intellectually in our day, it must be able to enter into this dialogue without fear of losing itself. This fear leads many Jews, including rabbis, to suppose that Martin Buber's deep influence on contemporary Christian thought must somehow mean that he is not really Jewish. But real dialogue, as Buber himself teaches, means both going out to meet the other and holding your ground while you meet him. Speaking of Hasidism Buber writes:

> It has often been suggested to me that I should liberate this teaching from its "confessional limitations," as people like to put it, and proclaim it as an unfettered teaching of mankind. Taking such a "universal" path would have been for me pure arbitrariness. In order to speak to the world what I have heard, I am not bound to step into the street. I may remain standing in the door of my ancestral house: here too the word that is uttered does not go astray.[1]

The Sermon on the Mount

My first significant encounter with Jesus was through my Christian pacifist friends; my second through Christian mysticism; my third through the study of the comparative records of the synoptic gospels (Matthew, Mark, and Luke) in discussion groups run by the Sharman method.[2] Finally, I returned to encounter Jesus again from the standpoint of biblical, normative and Hasidic Judaism as I had come to under-

stand them. In all of these encounters the Sermon on the
Mount (Matthew, Chapters 5-7) has had an important place.
This is not because I imagine that Jesus gave this sermon as
such. The evidence, on the contrary, is that it is made up of
many fragments, and I am inclined to credit the Sharman
view that Luke's "Blessed are ye poor" is more probably
Jesus' form of address to the simple fisher folk in Galilee
than is Matthew's "Blessed are the poor in spirit." For all
this, I have come back to the Sermon on the Mount again
and again because it forms a whole, because it is central to
so much of Christianity, and because it raises basic problems.

One of the most clearly basic is the use of the phrase "the
kingdom of heaven." This is often taken by Christians, as
a matter of course, to refer to heaven in the Christian sense.
I am more inclined to believe, from both the usage of the
day and the context in which it is used, that it refers to
Malchut Shamayim, God's kingship. Certainly the emphasis
in later Christianity upon this world's being a forecourt for
the sake of gaining admission to heaven is hardly borne out
by Jesus' emphasis upon the present. "Take no thought for
the morrow, for the morrow shall take thought for itself . . .
Sufficient unto the day is the evil thereof." To be sure, this
passage is prefaced by a contrast with laying up treasure on
earth where thieves break in and rust destroys, but the meaning of this passage is made unmistakable when Jesus adds,
immediately afterward, "No man can serve God and mam-
mon. If the eye be single, the whole body is full of light."
Jesus' emphasis is clearly upon loving God with all one's
heart, soul, mind, and might, and such love means an unconditional trust which does not suffer the present moment to
be used as a mere means to a future end. Jesus does not
disparage the need for food, clothing, and shelter. Rather he
says, "Your heavenly Father knows you need these things,"
and adds, "Seek ye first the Kingdom of God and all these
things shall be added unto you." The Kingdom of God, or
the Kingdom of Heaven, is not thought of here as an afterlife

but as finding authentic existence in the present through
bringing one's life into dialogue with God. "Ye are the salt
of the earth," says Jesus. "If the salt hath lost its savor, wherewith shall it be salted?" Man is the being who gives special
meaning to the earth, yet if he has lost that authentic humanity which makes him man, nothing else—not prosperity nor
power nor prestige—can make up for this lack. For Jesus the
Kingdom of Heaven is in us, and it is also among us.

Jesus begins the Sermon on the Mount with a series of
paradoxes, on the basis of which some have assumed a dualism
between the material and the spiritual. But little or nothing
in all of the synoptic gospels confirms this interpretation.
Rather, as Jesus says, "Narrow is the way, and strait is the
gate": the road to authentic existence is a difficult one—and
yet so easy since it means trust which leaves to God the
"morrow" as do the lilies of the field. This trust is a continuation of the biblical *emunah*, that unconditional trust in the
relationship with God that characterizes Psalm 23 ("Though
I walk through the valley of the shadow of death, I shall fear
no evil") and Psalm 91 ("He shall not suffer thy foot to
stumble"). It is this latter verse that Satan quotes to Jesus
as the second of the temptations in the wilderness. He takes
him to the top of the Temple and invites him to throw himself down, as proof that it is he of whom this was said.
Jesus' reply, "Thou shalt not tempt God," is not only a
quote from Deuteronomy, referring to the people's tempting
Moses to strike the rock with his staff and produce water;
it is also thoroughly Biblical in spirit. *Emunah* is not a magic
security, a guarantee that *God* will have to protect his favored
one. It is a trust that remains constant even when we walk,
as we must, through the valley of the shadow of death.

What are we to make of the series of contrasts in the
Sermon on the Mount? "Ye have heard it said . . . But I say
unto you." Most of them are from the direction of outer
action to inner intention, but one of them at least (that
concerning divorce) is in the opposite direction. The empha-

sis on *kavanah,* or inner intention, was nothing new in Judaism; it appears not only in the Pentateuch but in the Prophets and in the Pharisees. What appears new is the valuing of purity of intention above purity of action. "Who shall stand on God's holy hill?" asks Psalm 24. "He who has clean hands and a pure heart"—not one or the other but both. Does Jesus in fact mean what Paul later taught—a dualism between the outer action "that killeth" and the inner spirit "that quickeneth"? "Ye have heard it said that ye shall not commit adultery," says Jesus. "But I say unto you that he who looks at a woman to lust after her has already committed adultery with her in his heart." What are we to make of this statement? If it be taken as the realism that "as a man thinketh, so he is," we can only call it a fair extension of what the commandment already implies. If we take it as a call to kill all lust within the soul, it becomes a counsel of perfection appropriate to the Christian saint but not to the Jewish image of man forever tempted anew by the "evil urge" whose passion he must direct into the service of God. If we take it to mean that adultery is all right just so long as it is not committed with an impure heart, we fall into an antinomian gnosticism that is clearly far from Jesus' intention. If we take it to apply to the Christian image of man in general, we run head on against a dominant strain in Christianity which sees man as given over to "original sin," associated by both Paul and Augustine with lust. So far from hoping for perfection for all men, Paul urges the average man to compromise, since "it is better to marry than to burn."

How in the midst of all this are we to get back to what Jesus himself meant? I do not know. But it has always seemed to me that Jesus never spoke against sex or marriage as such, as Paul did, but rather asked his disciples for total allegiance in response to the unusual demands of the hour. This is that "ethic of perfection" to which Albert Schweitzer points as associated with the expectation of a speedy coming of the kingdom. Nor can I see Jesus' statement so much opposing as supplementing the commandment he cites. If it is taken in the traditional sense of striving for purity of heart (which to a medieval Christian would mean spiritual‾perfection and to a modern Freudian, sublimation), and if Paul's statement on marriage is taken as the real opposite of the belief in perfectability implicit in this striving, then the Jewish position occupies a middle point—one in which purity of heart can never be attained entirely, since temptation and the "evil urge" remain real, yet one in which the "evil urge" never becomes "original sin" that necessitates man's sinfulness unless redeemed by unmerited grace. This middle position, familiar in all the lineaments of Judaism, is beautifully illustrated by a Hasidic tale, "The Limits of Advice." The disciples of the Baal Shem Tov, the founder of Hasidism, asked his permission to visit a man in the neighborhood who had a reputation for sanctity and scholarship. On receiving permission, they asked the Baal Shem, "How can we know if he is what he is said to be?" The latter replied:

> Ask him to advise you what to do to keep unholy thoughts from disturbing you in your prayers and studies. If he gives you advice, then you will know that he belongs to those who are of no account. For this is the service of men in the world to the very hour of their death; to struggle time after time with the extraneous, and time after time to uplift and fit it into the nature of the Divine Name.[3]

Emunah versus Pistis

Whatever the difference between the everyday ethic of the Pharisee and Jesus' ethic of perfection, and whatever his notions about his own messiahship, Jesus did not call on his disciples to have faith in him but in God. Paul, in contrast, begins with *pistis*, faith in a proposition, faith with intellectual content. Paul also knew *emunah*—the first Epistle to the Corinthians is a great statement of it—but it is a trust that is always "through Jesus Christ our Lord." Due to his

profound experience of inner division and a still more profound conversion experience that delivered him from it, it is
through Jesus only that Paul knew the love of God, and it
is only thus that he sees others as knowing it. Immediacy is
now broken by original sin, and it may only be restored
by faith in Christ. "Wherefore, as by one man sin entered
into the world, and death by sin; and so death passed upon
all men, for that all have sinned." The "law" is no longer
the Torah which guides man in his dialogue with God, but
a part of a fearful dialectic in which man's consciousness of
the law makes him "exceedingly sinful" so that only unmerited
grace, not in response to man's action but in place of it, can
redeem him. This means the abolition of the immediacy between God and man which had been the essence of the
Covenant and the kingship of God. " 'I am the door' it now
runs (John 10:9); it avails nothing, as Jesus thought it would,
to knock where one stands [before the 'narrow door']; it
avails nothing, as the Pharisees thought, to step into the open
door; entrance is only for those who believe in the 'door.' " [4]

Both types of faith are present in both religions, but
emunah is the starting-point of Judaism, *pistis* that of orthodox
Christianity. Yet Christianity begins with Jesus. Does this
not mean that *emunah* is also the starting-point for Christianity? I think it does, unless we are to make an unbridgeable
dichotomy between the Jesus who lived and died a Jew and
the Christ of Christian theology. Putting it another way, if
Buber's contrast between Jesus and Paul is a valid one—and
I think it is, though most Christian theologians do not—then
both *emunah* and *pistis* must be fully present in Christianity.
Consider the use of miracles in the New Testament. We are
told that when Jesus was crucified and gave up the ghost, the
veil of the Temple was rent and many other wonders
happened "in order that ye might believe." Jesus, however,
speaks differently of miracles. He tells the woman who touches
his robe and is healed of an issue of blood that it is her faith
that has made her whole, and he tells his disciples that if they

have but as much faith as a grain of mustard seed, they can move mountains. In other words, for Jesus miracles are not the cause of faith but at most the product of faith.

Much in Judaism has had the character of *pistis*. Revelation and law may originate in the dialogue with God, but they have again and again become possessions and dogmas. The danger of any religion of revelation, Buber remarks, is the tendency to turn the *being* of religion into the *having*. This is a danger built into any tradition. The dialectic of continuity and change means a holding on to the forms that have been, to some extent, and the renewal of those forms in the fire of the new moment and the new situation. "To be a spiritual heir one must be a pioneer," Abraham Heschel has written, but he also urges one to hold on to the inherited forms until one can fill them with *kavanah*. Every form of tradition is a Thou which will become an It, but which can again become a Thou. Similarly, every image of God may point the way to the imageless God until it swells itself up and blocks the road by claiming itself to be the divine reality. It would, therefore, be utterly inaccurate to think of Judaism as a religion of pure trust which does not cling to tradition, or to speak of Judaism as a religion in which God is imageless as opposed to Christianity in which God is imaged.

The problem is subtler. It is whether Christianity prevents God from hiding himself, as Buber suggests, by *fixing* him in the image of Christ. Idolatry does not arise through images of God but through any one image being taken to be God. "They take the finger pointing at the moon for the moon itself," says a Zen Buddhist text. Certainly the imagelessness of God has been a central emphasis in Judaism, yet there has been no lack in Judaism of talmudists, philosophers, and *Halakists* who have wanted to fix God in one image or another. "The Torah warns us," said Menahem Mendel of Kotzk, "not to make a graven image of anything the Lord our God has bidden us." The problem, once again, is not whether the imageless God reveals himself, as he must if there is to be a relationship to him, but whether these revelations are taken as universal, objective attributes of God or as God's relationship to man in concrete situations, capable of being transformed and renewed in still other concrete situations. Abraham Heschel's category of the "divine pathos" in his book *The Prophets* is constructed on precisely this contrast. God does not reveal *himself*, Heschel tells us. Rather he reveals his concern for man. He speaks into human situations and the prophet is one who responds.

Judaism has no fixed midpoint of revelation, Buber tells us, whereas Christianity does. But is the uniqueness of the revelation of God to the people at Sinai any different from the uniqueness of the revelation in Christ? Again Buber would say yes, since to him the moment of revelation is not Sinai (or the burning bush) but our present perceiving of Sinai or the burning bush. Is this not true for Christianity, too? If the Passover Haggadah has the good son tell "what the Lord did for *me* when he brought *me* out of Egypt," St. Patrick's hymn extols the presence of Christ in the believer: "Christ within me, Christ before me. . . . Christ to comfort and restore me. Christ beneath me, Christ above me, Christ in quiet, Christ in danger, Christ in hearts of them that love me, Christ in mouth of friend and stranger." The Friends carry this knowledge of Christ's presence so far that they need neither ritual, nor symbol, nor preacher to persevere in the immediacy of Christ's ministry.

A few years ago I took part in a remarkable dialogue with an English Quaker, who is perhaps the leading theologian in the Society of Friends today. The dialogue was before an audience, but the audience was not invited to take part, in order that the spirit of the dialogue might not be injured. So far from seeing Christ as an article of faith that one must hold to (*pistis*), this theologian fully subscribed to Buber's I-Thou relationship as the only means of relating to God or Christ. What is more, in contrast to both the universalists and the fundamentalists among the Friends, he and I saw

eye to eye on the meaning of the Bible as a history of unique
moments of revelation, as demand and response in concrete
historical situations. He did not deny the revelation of God
at other times and situations than that of Christ nor could I
remain indifferent to his witness to Christ: it was a deeply
moving statement from a truly religious man that I could not
fail to honor. In short, his point of view was much closer
to mine than to that of many Quakers, and my point of view
was much closer to his than to that of many Jews.

Where then was the difference between us? At one point
only, a point which perhaps illuminates the subtle difference
between image and imagelessness of God in Judaism and
Christianity. If he had only wished to witness that for him
the fullest, most complete, and most perfect revelation of God
was in Christ, I should not have been troubled by this witness, even if I could not share it. But when he objectified his
witness into the theological statement that Christ *is* the fullest
conceivable revelation of God, he had in that moment gone
over from *emunah* to *pistis*. "Ye are my witnesses, saith the
Lord," we read in Isaiah, but the Hasidim add, "If ye are not
my witnesses, then I am not the Lord." What is this but a
reiteration of the covenantal relationship in which we witness for God through bringing every aspect of our lives into
dialogue with him? The Jehovah's Witnesses have objectified
this "witness" into something that can be handed out in
pamphlets, in memorized speeches, in phonograph records.
Just such objectification takes place if one claims that the
Jews *are* the "chosen people" in abstraction from the Covenant—that dynamic relationship and falling-away-from-rela-
tionship which can lead Hosea to name his son *Lo-Ami*, "Not
My People," when Israel has turned away from God.

Prophetic versus Apocalyptic

Another category of Buber's thought that has entered into my own thinking about Judaism and Christianity, although he has not applied it thus, is the contrast between the prophet, who *speaks* to the people in the historical situation and calls for a decision that may affect the character of the next hour, and the apocalyptic *writer*, who sees the future as already fixed and is only concerned with foreseeing it. Actually Ezekiel, Daniel, the apocryphal texts, and many elements in the *Kabbalah* are clearly apocalyptic, while Christianity has a great deal of the prophetic in it. We come back, necessarily, to the contrast between Jesus and Paul—a contrast which is blunted, to be sure, by the fact that Jesus undoubtedly did expect the speedy coming of the Kingdom. Jesus nonetheless stands in the tradition of the prophets who called on the people to turn back (*t'shuvah*) and thought they had the power to do so. Paul, on the other hand, despairs of himself and of other men and sees the initiative as necessarily coming from God, not just in the address to man but even in the grace which enables one to respond to it. The contemporary Pauline theologian, Emil Brunner, sees man as sundered from God by his original sin and turns Buber's I-Thou into a Thou-I relationship, in which God bridges the gap with his grace while man receives but cannot initiate. Certainly Paul's cosmic view of all men becoming sinful through the giving of the law at Sinai and of being redeemed from sin only at Golgotha removes the possibility of turning back to God and receiving forgiveness, which was always open to man in the Hebrew Bible. Some strains of Christianity have emphasized the apocalyptic more, some less. But insofar as Pauline Christianity has held man unable to do any good thing of himself and has seen him as entirely dependent upon the grace that comes through belief in Christ, the apocalyptic lineaments of the despair of man in history

and the "Good News" coming from the supernatural breaking into history are there.

Very often, of course, as in the thought of Reinhold Niebuhr, both elements are subtly mixed. Niebuhr strongly
objects to what he regards as Paul Tillich's equation of the
creation with the fall. Creation is good, says Niebuhr, and
the fall comes not through man's existence as flesh but through
his will, which tries to absolutize what is in fact only relative.
Niebuhr rejects "original sin" as any sort of biological inheritance, à la Augustine, but he affirms it as our social inheritance
and as the sinful overstepping of creaturely limitations that
man not necessarily but most probably will fall into again
and again.

That the prophetic and the apocalyptic strains are also
mixed in Judaism, and even in Hasidism, Buber makes clear
in his Hasidic chronicle-novel *For the Sake of Heaven*. In
this chronicle the Seer of Lublin and many other saintly
men join in theurgic magic to strengthen the cause of
Napoleon, whom they identify as Gog of the Land of
Magog who will force God to send down the Messiah. In
opposition to them the Yehudi, the Seer's disciple, says that
the coming of the Messiah depends not upon our magical
prayers but upon our *t'shuvah*, our turning with our whole
heart to God. When Buber was five a man told him the Messiah was a beggar waiting at the gates of Rome. "What is
he waiting for?" the young boy asked. "For you!" was the
man's reply. Insofar as modern Judaism has turned from
the literal belief in the coming of the Messiah at a specific
time, it has turned from the apocalyptic. Insofar, however,
as it has turned to a "messianism" which is equivalent to automatic progress toward universal ideals, it has *not* turned
toward the prophetic. It is a lamentable fact that a great
deal of modern Jewish thinking is far less concerned with
the prophetic reality of historical demand and decision than
a great deal of modern Christian thought.

What has been said here about *emunah* and *pistis* and

about the prophetic and the apocalyptic can be brought together through a legend of the Baal Shem, called "The Tree of Knowledge":

> They say that once, when all souls were gathered in Adam's soul, at the hour he stood beside the Tree of Knowledge, the soul of the Baal Shem Tov went away, and did not eat of the fruit of this tree.[5]

If this legend is taken to mean that the Baal Shem's followers saw him as perfect in a way that other, fallen men are not, then we have here *pistis*, or faith in a proposition, and an apocalyptic view of what is foredestined that are little different from the orthodox Christian faith in Christ. This interpretation would be entirely incompatible, however, with that other story of the Baal Shem that we have cited. What the legend expresses, rather, is the wonder that simple people felt before a man who was tempted like them but who did not regularly fall into sin as they did, because he had succeeded in serving God with the "evil urge." In this latter sense, the story is still compatible with *emunah* and the prophetic. As long as the *zaddik* remained the man who brought his followers into greater immediacy with God, he remained true to these two attitudes. But when he became the mediator who lived in showy splendor, performing splendid miracles, then *pistis* and the apocalyptic had their hour.

The Old Covenant and the New

Israel, to the Hebrew Bible, means the actual people Israel who became a people through the Sinai Covenant and who remain one insofar as they are faithful to this covenant. This covenant, in the words of Exodus, is to become "a kingdom of priests and a holy people." A holy people does not mean a collection of well-meaning individuals but a true community; imitating God's justice, righteousness, and holiness in the life between man and man *and* in the social, political, economic, and international life of the people. There is no distinction here between the religious and the social, since the religious for biblical man is not a separate dimension transcending history but the demand that the Transcendent places on man in history. The unity of these two spheres, which have come apart in modern life and thought, is clearly grasped by Jesus when he gives as the first commandment, "Thou shalt love the Lord thy God with all thy heart, soul, mind, and might," and as the second, "which is like unto the first," "Thou shalt love thy neighbor as thyself." Many uninformed Christians do not realize that these two commandments were quoted by Jesus from Deuteronomy and Leviticus. It was with amazement, however, that I heard so eminent a Christian thinker as Pastor Martin Niemoeller say that what was unique to Jesus' teaching was putting the two commandments together. From the Lord's reply to Cain, "Thy brother's blood cries out to me from the ground," to "Thou shalt love thy neighbor as thyself. I am the Lord" these two dimensions have always been joined in the Hebrew bible, as in Judaism in general.

If we recognize this, we still have the question of how the old and new covenants differ, since Jesus himself stood so clearly in the tradition of the Hebrew biblical covenant when he cited these two commandments together. In terms of Jesus himself, it must be said that he addressed men as individuals rather than as the people Israel, largely, no doubt, because he lived after the historical age of the Hebrew prophets. So far as orthodox Christianity's understanding of the covenant and Israel, however, the difference is a more radical one. For Christianity there is a new Israel, the Corpus Christi, or invisible Church that unites all who have been reborn in Christ. This new Israel differs from the old in that it is not an actual community able to respond to a demand placed upon it as a people, but a spiritual bond of widely separated individuals whose communal and social lives are lived in practical distinction from their membership in the invisible Church. The one covenant is associated with a task—the realization of the kingship of God through which Israel may serve as the beginning of the kingdom of God. The other is associated with a fulfilled reality—the partaking in the redemption through Christ which is already there for all who share in this communion. In the face of these differences, it is incomprehensible to me how Will Herberg, a Jewish theologian with a profound understanding of Christianity, can maintain that the doctrines of the people Israel and Israel as the organically united Body of Christ are concepts of the same nature.

The understanding of the Messiah is a corollary to the understanding of Israel and the covenant. For Judaism, the Messiah is not a divine figure who can bring redemption in himself but a man who can lead the people or a remnant of the people in turning back to God, fulfilling the covenant, and making real the Kingship of God. This is evident from the passages on Immanuel in Isaiah in which Immanuel is associated with the tasks of justice and righteousness to which the prophets had continually called the kings. It is also clear in Deutero-Isaiah where the suffering servant takes over this task of leading the remnant in the renewal of the covenant. The suffering of the servant may best be understood, in my opinion, not as vicarious suffering for others but as the terrible suffering which the hidden servant takes on himself by turning back to God while remaining a member of a faithless community.

The Christian conception of the Messiah is very different. The root of the word in "the anointed" no longer signifies a tie to the task of realizing the kingship of God. Instead Christ is the divine figure, the Son of God, who in His oneness with God steps on the other side of the divine-human dialogue and effects a redemption which takes the place of, rather than fulfils, the task of becoming "a holy people." This is not the Messiah who leads men to the redemptive turning, but the

Messiah who has already redeemed them through his crucifixion and resurrection, if they are ready to accept this grace
through their faith in Him. One of the saddest aspects of
the Jewish-Christian dialogue is the failure of even such
eminent Christian thinkers as Jacques Maritain to recognize
the essential difference between these two concepts of the
Messiah. As a result, they regularly attribute the Jewish refusal
of Christ to a desire for a materialistic Messiah who will
lead them to military victory. This dualism between the
spiritual and the material is so strongly ingrained in some
strains of Christianity that it is difficult for many Christians
to understand the Jewish concept of the Messiah, to which
such a dualism is entirely foreign.

But how about Jesus himself? Did he think of himself as
the Messiah in the Jewish sense or the Christian sense? The
texts are far from univocal, but it is as unthinkable to me
that Jesus thought of himself as the Messiah in the Christian
sense as that he said, "Take up your cross and follow me,"
with foreknowledge of the central significance of the cross
after his own crucifixion, or that he said to Peter, "On this
rock I have founded my church," and meant by it the Roman
Catholic Church, a type of religious structure then entirely
unknown in the world.

Did Jesus rather think of himself as the Messiah in the
Jewish sense? Here too the texts are not clear. Buber thinks
that Jesus' "Thou sayest it" in reply to Pontius Pilate suggests
that he saw himself, in the pattern of the apocryphal texts, as
the suffering servant who has had a pre-existence in heaven.
To me the most intriguing interchange is the one in which
he asks his disciples who people say he is and then asks them
who they think he is. "Christ, the Son of the Living God,"
says Peter, and "Jesus charged them that they tell no man
of it." Seen in retrospect, the question is what category Jesus
fits into. Seen from within as a present event it cannot be
that, for the category does not exist. What do the forty
days' wrestling with Satan in the wilderness mean but the

temptations of a man who knows himself called and yet must discover again, in each new situation, just what it means that he is called? For T. S. Eliot's Thomas à Becket, the category of the martyr, the objective and selfless instrument of God, is there readymade for him to fill. Jesus, on the contrary, had to go through the terrible tension of a unique call which he could not know objectively but only as he responded with his whole being to the unheard-of demand of the new moment. When he prays in the garden of Gethsemane, "Father, if it be thy will may this cup be taken from me" he is not, like Eliot's martyr, a man who has lost his own will in the will of God. Rather he is a man in anguish who wills to live, if it be God's will, but who is ready to accept God's will if it is not. And when he prays on the cross, *"Eli, Eli lama sabachthani!,"* he is not merely reciting a psalm, as those Christians who wish to see him as very God but not as very man suppose; he is experiencing again the terrible anguish of the unique vocation in which he has answered the call but in this moment experiences no confirming answer himself. Once I remarked to a Catholic student that the life of Jesus was tragic in the sense that he was not opposed to marriage and ordinary family life but had to forgo them because of the demand of the hour. "Jesus' crucifixion was not tragic," she replied. "If it had not been for it, we could not have had holy communion." I was struck by the reversal which made the timeless ritual drama the essential matter and the unique historical phenomenon that it celebrates the mere occasion, of no intrinsic meaning in itself!

It has been customary for many liberal Jews who wish to show their broadmindedness toward Jesus to enrol him in the ranks of "the prophets" or "teachers" of Israel. In a broad sense of the term, we can share their feeling. But he was no prophet in the exact meaning of the term, and though he was certainly a teacher, he played a unique role in his life that bursts the bounds of any such category. A Jewish protest against Jesus often is that he spoke in his own name—"But

I say unto you"—and not in the name of God, as did the prophets. At the end of the Sermon on the Mount, we read that the people were astonished, "for he taught them as one who had authority, and not as their scribes." But the prophets also taught with authority and not as the scribes. "I am no prophet and no son of a prophet," says Amos, "but when the lion roars who can but tremble, and when the Lord God speaks who can but prophesy?" Jeremiah never tires of belaboring the false prophets while being able to evince no authority of his own other than, "Of a truth the Lord hath sent me." Still, prophets do speak in the name of God, and even Moses, who is pictured as closer to God than any other man, spoke to the people only in the name of God and not in his own name.

But does Jesus speak in his own name as if he were God? The texts do not bear this out. "Not every one who says to me, 'Lord, Lord,' shall enter the kingdom of heaven, but he who does the will of my Father who is in heaven,'" says Jesus in the Sermon on the Mount. And even John, the most theological of the Gospels, says, "Why callest thou me good? Only God is good," and "If I bear witness to myself and not to him who sent me, I witness false." When Jesus cites the two great commandments, he speaks of loving God rather than of loving or believing in himself. Jesus' awareness of a unique calling undoubtedly contributed to the ring of authority in his voice. But equally important, surely, is the reaction against the scribes, who carry on tradition without *kavanah* or inner intention, and the fact that, as George Foote Moore has pointed out, this was the age of an individual piety to our Father in Heaven—a piety which Jesus exemplified in a uniquely intense way. Jesus spoke "I" in such a way that God was simply Father and he was simply son, says Buber in *I and Thou*.

It is still not easy for a contemporary Jew to have the sort of dialogue with Jesus that Buber speaks of when he confesses, "From my youth onwards I have found in Jesus my great brother. . . . My own fraternally open relationship to him has grown ever stronger and clearer." [6] It is not because Jesus is a person so difficult for a Jew to understand. Even if we do not claim to understand him from within, in his Jewish being, as Buber does, we can see parallels enough in messianic leaders such as Sabbatai Zvi in the Hasidic *rebbe* who told his sons to pray for their enemies as the greatest of all service to God, in the figure of the Yehudi who stands in the center of *For the Sake of Heaven*. Buber defends himself against the charge of having christianized the Yehudi on the grounds that the resemblances between him and Jesus come from the fact that both stand in the shadow of Deutero-Isaiah's suffering servant, whom Buber interprets as neither Israel nor the Nazarene but one of a series of "servants" from Abraham down.

The fact that Buber has had to defend himself against the charge of christianizing from the side of Jewish scholars, while Christian scholars have taken exception to the supposed familiarity of his calling Jesus his "great brother," shows how difficult it is to relate to Jesus apart from the categories of Judaism *versus* Christianity, Judaism *or* Christianity. Even Buber is obviously trying to rescue Jesus for Judaism. "I firmly believe," he writes, "that the Jewish community, in the course of its renaissance, will recognize Jesus; and not merely as a great figure in its religious history, but also in the organic context of a Messianic development extending over millennia, whose final goal is the Redemption of Israel and of the world." [7] I believe this too, but the task seems to me difficult and the result necessarily ambiguous. We shall not extract Jesus from Christianity by recapturing him as a Jew, and though he made no conscious break with Judaism (as the Buddha did with Hinduism) we cannot ignore the fact that it was through him that the crack opened up through which the great break came. We are, therefore, compelled to add what Buber himself adds to the two statements just quoted: As to the recognition of Jesus' place in Israel's Messianic development: "I believe equally firmly that we will never recognize Jesus as the Messiah Come . . . In our view, redemption occurs forever, and none has yet occurred . . . For us there is no cause of Jesus; only the cause of God exists for us." As to the acknowledgment of Jesus his great brother: "That Christianity has regarded and does regard him as God and Savior has always appeared to me a fact of the highest importance which, for his sake and my own, I must endeavor to understand."

The God of Wrath and the God of Love

One of the most important stumbling blocks in the relation of the contemporary Jew to Christianity is the widespread tendency to regard "an eye for an eye and a tooth for a tooth" as the description of a vengeful God rather than as elementary social justice, and the tendency to contrast this passage with "Love thy neighbor as thyself," as if the latter did not also come from Leviticus but originated in the New Testament. Christianity has rejected the Marcionite gnosticism that wished to cut off the Old Testament as the product of an evil Creator God, but there has lingered in Christianity just enough of the Gnostic apologetic to stamp indelibly in the popular mind the notion that the God of the Old Testament is a God of wrath as opposed to the Christian God of love. The texts, of course, do not bear this out. There is no end of "gnashing of teeth and wailing in the outer darkness" in the New Testament, whereas in the Old there is no suggestion of a hell where the wicked are punished. The loving kindness, mercy, and compassion of God are emphasized in countless passages throughout the Hebrew Bible, and God's wrath is but minor in comparison: "For a little while I hid my face in wrath but with long suffering compassion I have loved thee," says Deutero- or Trito-Isaiah. And there are a thousand sayings of the Fathers and of the Hasidim that one might adduce in addition.

No amount of citing texts is going to remove this mind-set, however. It can only be removed, if at all, by a new way of thinking. One fruitful way of thinking is given us by Heschel in his concept of the "divine pathos":

> To the prophets, the attributes of God were drives, chal-lenges, commandments, rather than timeless notions detached from IIis Being. They did not offer an exposition of the nature of God, but rather an exposition of God's insight into man and His concern for man. They disclosed attitudes *of* God rather than *about* God.[8]

Heschel makes a trenchant application of the divine pathos to the meaning and mystery of God's wrath. God's anger and his mercy are not opposites but correlatives, he points out. God's anger is *suspended love*, mercy withheld or con-cealed for the sake of love itself, in order that compassion may resume. In contradistinction to the Christian theologian Rudolph Otto, who sees God's love as "nothing but quenched wrath" and who sees wrath itself as arbitrary and irrational, Heschel insists that normal and original pathos is love or mercy and that God's anger is a moral judgment preceded and followed by compassion.

> The anger of God must not be treated in isolation, but as an aspect of the divine pathos, as one of the modes of God's responsiveness to man. It is . . . conditioned by God's will; it is aroused by man's sins. It is an instrument rather than a force, transitive rather than spontaneous. It is a secondary emotion, never the ruling passion, disclosing only a part of God's way with man.[9]

"I the Lord make peace and create evil," says Deutero-Isaiah, probably in conscious opposition to whatever Zoro-astrian dualism had filtered into the culture. To affirm God's oneness is to affirm that there is no realm or power separate from God, that there is no "devil" in the Christian sense, that Satan is no one other than God himself tempting man, and tempting him not to damnation but in order that he may realize hitherto unfulfilled possibilities of dialogue. It is this basic existential trust that underlies the *emunah* which says, "I shall fear no evil for thou art with me." Job, to be sure, was tempted in such a way that he saw God as mocking the calamity of the guiltless, but he never "appealed from God to God," as the Christian scholar Robert Pfeiffer assumed in his interpretation of "I know that my redeemer liveth." Even in the tension between his trust in God and his insistence on justice, Job never ceases to affirm that dialogue with God into which *all* the evil that he experiences must be brought.

When it is no longer possible for man to hold this tension, then Job's question does lead to the Gnostic dualism in which creation and the God of creation are seen as evil, and redemption is redemption *from* the evil of creation and not *of* it. This is the dualism which is embodied in Dostoevsky's "Grand Inquisitor" passage in *The Brothers Karamazov*, in which the merciless justice of Ivan's Inquisitor is complemented by the completely unconditional forgiveness of his Christ, who places no demand of wholeness or authentic existence on the Inquisitor, but leaves him sundered into a being whose actions betray Christ while Christ's kiss "glows in his heart." "My God is a nicer God than Amos'," said a freshman student in one of my classes. "Why is your God nicer than Amos'?" I asked. "Because he forgives *everything*," she replied. I thought about this for a moment and then asked her, "If he forgives everything, then what is there to forgive?" The answer was obvious—it was the guilt she had accumulated in that other, everyday sphere of life ruled over by parents and teachers, which was utterly withdrawn from God's mercy! Even if she had not confessed that she kept her God in the closet when she was a child, it would be evident that we are confronted here with the sort of practical dualism that leads guilt-ridden people like Ivan to imagine (in utmost contrast to Jesus himself) a Christ who

CHRISTIANITY AND THE CONTEMPORARY JEW 233

forgives everything and demands nothing. Surely it is such a dualism between God and creation that leads Kierkegaard to his unbiblical "suspension of the ethical" and his equally unbiblical picture of Abraham as the "knight of faith" who renounces and receives back the finite (Isaac) in lonely relation with the transcendent.

The true mercy of God in the Hebrew Bible is that he cares that we become human, that man live a true life, that Israel make real the covenant and the kingship of God by becoming a holy people. It is this caring and concern that lies behind God's anger. It is a demand placed in a situation rather than an attribute of God. The meaning of man's life is found in the dialogue with God; the meaning of Israel's existence as a people is found in the covenant. For God not to ask Israel "Where art thou?" as he asked Adam, would be a "mercy" that was no mercy, for it would abandon us to meaningless and inauthentic existence. God's calling man to account *is* his mercy. It is no cutting off, such as the Gnostic dualists fear. Adam and Eve must leave the Garden of Eden, Cain must become a wanderer on the face of the earth, Jacob must flee from Esau's wrath in the wilderness, Moses must stop short of the Promised Land, the suffering servant must die in disease and ignominy, Israel must be defeated and dispersed, but God is with them all in their exile. To seek a God who is all-merciful in the face of an existence that is anything but, is to settle for a practical dualism in which God must make up for the God-forsaken creation into which we are flung. To accept the real terrors of existence and bring them into the dialogue with God is to understand, as Job did at last, the mercy that is contained even in God's anger. Not to understand conceptually, of course, but in the uniqueness of one's dialogue with God, as Levi Yitzhak of Berditchev understood when he prayed, "O Lord, I do not want to know why I suffer but that I suffer for Thy sake."

The Covenant of Peace

Deutero-Isaiah links the trust in God's long-suffering compassion with the "covenant of peace" that God will not take from man. Considering that Deutero-Isaiah is as central a Christian text as it is a Jewish one, are we justified in seeing this "covenant of peace" as in any way different from Christian love, Christian social action, and Christian pacifism? I think we are! Christian love is *agape,* the divine love or grace that descends to man and makes it possible for him to love his fellowman. Love in Judaism is rather the imitation of God's *hesed,* or faithful loving kindness, man's response to God, whom he loves with his whole heart, and to his fellowman who is created in God's image. It is not a divine love that passes *through* man to other men, but a human love that passes *between* man and man. It is a concrete and realistic love, as in the story of the Hasidic rabbi who learned to love from two drunken peasants. One of them repeatedly asked the other, "Do you love me?" and when the other as often assured him that he did, he sullenly replied, "How can you say you love me when you do not know what I lack?"

Love in Judaism (and in Hasidism) must be distinguished from Christian love, even that so impressively present among the Quakers, by the fact that it is not spiritualized love but a love of the whole person. By the same token, it is not a purely forgiving love but one that places a real demand upon the other—the demand of the relationship itself. The "hallowing of the everyday" means making the concrete relations of one's life essential, and real relationship includes both mutuality and passion. Mutuality means that love does not simply flow forth from the loving man to others; rather it moves back and forth within the dialogue between them, and is the fullest expression of that dialogue. Passion means that one does not suppress one's humanity before bringing oneself into relation with the other, but, on the contrary, directs one's "evil urge" into that relationship in such a way that, without losing its force, it ceases to be evil. It is the sanctification of the profane in which every natural urge is hallowed.

If one defines Jewish messianism in terms of becoming a holy people in real community, one must say that an impressive number of small Christian brotherhood groups—such as the Friends, the Brethren, and the Mennonites—come much nearer to this goal than the modern Jewish community center, which often has all of real living together except actual community, on the one hand, and the central Covenant, on the other. Nonetheless, we cannot regard the Christian brotherhood group as the true inheritor of the biblical covenant, for it stands on the ground not of an uncompleted task but of an already accomplished redemption in which it is the presence of the resurrected Christ which unites and transforms. Similarly, the Christian peace movement, impressive as it is, cannot be identified with the "covenant of peace." The former is based either on Jesus' teaching of non-resistance to evil, on Gandhi's teaching of non-violent resistance, or on universal ideals of peace and brotherhood. Isaiah's vision of peace, in contrast, grows out of the real multiplicity of nations and is inseparable from the covenant. It is only when all nations come to Zion to learn the law, i.e., to take part in the covenant, that men shall beat their swords into plowshares and their spears into pruning hooks, that "Nation shall not lift up swords against nation, neither shall they learn war any more" (Is. 2: 2-4). Isaiah's "universalism" is not an alternative to the task of the people but a continuation and fulfilment of it. His vision of peace is an integral part of the historical covenant between God and Israel, an integral address from God to the people in a new historical situation. The God who speaks is not a God who guarantees a universal moral order but the God of the Ten Commandments whose "Thou Shalt" is apprehended by the individual person and

by the group only in the unique and concrete situation, the
ever renewed present.

Out of the biblical covenant grows the covenant of peace.
The covenant of peace is not only Isaiah's vision of peace
"at the end of days." It is the comfort that God gives man
now, "the very present help in time of trouble." It is *emunah*,
unconditional trust, that enables the man of the Bible to
enter into the new historical situation without guarantees or
security and yet know that there too he will meet his "cruel
and kind Lord." "The mind stayed on Thee, Thou keepest in
perfect peace," says Isaiah. This is "a peace that passeth
understanding," but it is not a peace beyond history and
daily life. The biblical covenant of peace is not a consolation
at the end of history or an eternity above it: it is an integral
part of history, of the tension between present and future,
a dialectic between comfort and demand.

The covenant of peace cannot mean an "absolute" pacifism,
accordingly, for in history there is no room for absolutes.
"You believe in faith and love," one kindly Friend remarked
to me. "Are not these absolutes?" "No," I responded. "These
are relations to the Absolute. The only Absolute is God."
Any pretense to rest one's life on "absolute" ideals is a denial
both of one's situation as a creature in history and of the
word of God that may come to one in that situation. Even
the Ten Commandments are not universal norms, but, as
their language clearly attests, a dialogue between the "I"
of God and the "Thou" of man in which man learns in
each situation anew what is asked of him. They do not say
"*One* must not kill," but "*Thou* shalt not kill." They do not
impose this command on man as an abstract universal pre-
scription to be applied to particular situations but speak it
into the concrete situation of each man in such a way that
both the word of command and the response of the person
commanded are really new and unique.

The covenant of peace is not the Grand Inquisitor's morality of compulsory order and compulsory good, but neither is

it the morality of the Christ in that tale—the morality of a freely given love which does not ask that man bring his inner feeling and his outer social behavior into one unity. It is not the morality of absolute pacifism and liberal perfectionism. It is not the morality of any "ism" at all, but of the concrete historical situation. Yet neither is it the morality of those like Reinhold Niebuhr who make the moral demand relevant to "immoral society" only as a judgment but not as a call, in Buber's words, to "drive the plowshare of the normative into the hard soil of political fact." It is not the morality of easy choice but of tragic contradiction and of the reconciliation which grows only out of the soil of that contradiction. It is not a sentimental good will toward men that overlooks the real difference between them but a recognition of conflicting claims—a confirmation at once of togetherness *and* of otherness, and the acceptance of the fact that one cannot rise above that situation. It is the living embodiment of biblical creation, in which man is really free yet remains bound in relation with God. "In a genuine dialogue," writes Buber, "each of the partners, even when he stands in opposition to the other, heeds, affirms, and confirms his opponent as an existing other. Only so can conflict certainly not be eliminated from the world, but be humanly arbitrated and led towards its overcoming." [10]

The Biblical and the Greek: Emunah versus Gnosis

When the contemporary Jew looks at modern Christianity, he is bewildered by its variety and seeks in vain to find a key that unites it in all its differences. This same variety extends to contemporary Christian thought, but here at least one key comes to the service of the contemporary Jew: the understanding of Christianity as a mixture of the biblical and the Greek, in which the proportions and method of the mixture determine some of the most outstanding differences. When he then looks at the spectrum of modern Judaism, he finds almost as great a range if not so much variety, and when he looks at contemporary Jewish thought, he finds some of the very issues in the mixture of the biblical and the Greek that he has found in contemporary Christian thought.

A helpful typology for approaching this mixture of the biblical and the Greek is the contrast between two types of knowing: *emunah* and *gnosis*, the direct knowing of trust and the contemplative, comprehensive, or indirect knowing of philosophical and theosophical faith. We shall certainly not be able to apply this typology as a simple key to the differences between Judaism and Christianity, since much of Christianity has been characterized by the simple knowing of a trust relationship, whereas *gnosis* has again and again entered into Judaism, from Philo's platonizing allegory of the Bible through the *Merkabah* mystics to the medieval Jewish philosophers and the *Kabbalah*.

For the Judaism of the Hebrew Bible, of Hasidism, and of such contemporary philosophers of Judaism as Martin Buber, Franz Rosenzweig, and Abraham Heschel, knowing is, to begin with, a reciprocal contact, as when "Adam knew Eve" or God knew the prophet Hosea. This knowing takes place within the relationship of trust, the biblical *emunah*. Faith and knowing are not opposites or separate spheres for these types of Judaism, therefore, as they so often are in Christianity. Biblical man does not find his *Torah*, or guidance, in the order of the cosmos—the Greek *moira*—but in the unmediated dialogue with God Who alone causes the sun to rise up and seals the stars. "He goeth by me and I perceive him not." Therefore, the beginning of wisdom for biblical man is not *gnosis*—whether that means theology, cosmology, ontology, or even Plato's noetic vision of the Good—but "fear of the Lord," awe before the Reality that we can meet but cannot comprehend. This awe is not primitive superstition, as the Russian Orthodox philosopher Nicolas Berdyaev thinks, but the givenness of existence itself, which leads Heschel to declare that the beginning of religion, knowledge, and art is awareness of the ineffable. "All religious reality," writes Buber, "begins with the 'fear of God,'" but this is not a dwelling, as Christian theologians from Kierkegaard to the neo-orthodox have thought, but a dark gate through which the man of *emunah* "steps forth directed and assigned to the concrete, contextual situations of his existence." [11]

The fear of the Lord has never led in Judaism, as it has in some types of Christianity, to putting away knowing. It has led, rather, to the Talmudist's recognition that a wisdom which is not grounded in existence will not stand, to the essential Rabbinic belief that all debate which takes place "for the sake of Heaven" endures, even though opposite and mutually incompatible points of view are put forward, to the recognition that the *doing* of the people in the Covenant with God comes before the *hearing*, that hearing what is asked comes out of entering into the dialogue with God. This is a truth which one does not possess but to which one relates. It is not theology, in the traditional sense of the term, for it gives no knowledge of God as He is in Himself—neither proof of His existence nor description of His nature and attributes. Revelation is never something objective that God hands over to men, any more than it is a mere subjective inspiration. It is address and response in which, as Heschel points out, the response is as much a part of the revelation as the address. It is the word of God, but not Karl Barth's Word that comes to man from the distance of the Wholly Other. God and man may be radically separate, but as Franz Rosenzweig has said in criticism of Harnack and Barth, the Word of God and the word of man are the same word. They *must* be the same, for that is the very meaning and existence of the word. The Word does not exist in some hypostatized substantiality, like the *Logos* of Plato, but is a lived reality of the "between." It comes to man not out of the hyperborean blue but in the concrete, contextual situations of history.

The meaning of history, in consequence, is not an objective one that may be seen from above, but that of dialogue. The meaning of history tells me only what history's challenge is to me, what its claim is on me. This is not subjectivity. It is, rather, the refusal to lose sight of the given of our concrete situation—our existence face to face with a reality that comes to meet us and to which we can respond but which we cannot subsume under a single order or the process or chain of cause and effect. To preserve the existential reality of the present means to preserve history as dialogue. "Lord of the world," said the great Hasidic *zaddik* Rabbi Levi Yitzhak of Berditchev, "I do not beg you to reveal to me the secret of your ways—I could not bear it! But show me one thing; show it to me more clearly and more deeply: show me what this which is happening at this very moment, means to me, what it demands of me, what you, Lord of the world, are telling me by way of it." Levi Yitzhak concludes this prayer with the sentence we have already cited: "Ah, it is not why I suffer, that I wish to know, but only whether I suffer for your sake." [12] "Why I suffer" means here *gnosis* —an objective knowledge of the order of things which would enable Levi Yitzhak to place his suffering in relation to some over-all scheme of cause and effect, reward and punishment. "That I suffer for thy sake" is a meaning found in the dialogue itself—a meaning which cannot be divorced from dialogue and objectified, but which is, nonetheless, a real knowing and not just a statement of blind faith. It is *emunah,* and the knowing that arises from this *emunah* is the open, dialogical knowing of the prophet, rather than the closed monological knowing of the apocalyptic writer or the isolated philosopher.

This does not mean that there is no room in the knowing of *emunah* for the word that is objective, abstract, or conceptual. It is a question, rather, of the status of the abstraction. Is the universal the basic reality of which the particular is only the exemplification? Or is the "universal" only a quasi- or secondary reality that grows again and again out of the concrete event and, rightly understood, points back to it? Is ultimate reality found through the comprehension of the universal or through the meeting with the particular? Put in the terms of Buber's "I-Thou" philosophy, it is a question of which is basic: knowing the I-Thou relationship or the "I-It." To understand this question aright we must recognize that words and symbols are both—direct and indirect, immediate and mediate knowledge. The "word" may be identified with subject-object, or I-It, knowledge, while it remains indirect and symbolic, but it is itself the channel and expression of I-Thou knowing when it is taken up into real dialogue.

Tillich and Buber

An excellent illustration of this problem and one which helps our comparison and contrast between Judaism and Christianity is provided by a juxtaposition of the thought about God of two contemporary religious thinkers whose deep affinities underscore the subtle yet important differences between them. To Buber, God is the "Eternal Thou" who cannot become It, "the Being that is directly, most nearly, and lastingly over against us, that may properly only be addressed, not expressed." To Paul Tillich, in contrast, one must go beyond God as Thou to the "Ground of Being," the "God above God." One of the reasons why Tillich sees this as necessary is his opposition to what he himself calls "primitive theism" and his failure to grasp any third alternative like Buber's paradoxical understanding of God as the "Absolute Person" who *is* not a person but who *becomes* one, so to speak, in order to know and be known, to love and be loved by man. More basic still, however, is the fact that the reality of the "between" is never so real to Tillich as it is to Buber, that the biblical word between God and man is ultimately for him a metaphor symbolizing the non-symbolic reality of the Ground of Being in which one participates through knowing oneself as accepted and therefore acceptable. In the end, knowing for Tillich is not biblical but Greek, not *emunah* but *gnosis*. It is not knowing in the relationship of faith, but the knowledge which gives the ground for that relationship. Tillich changes the ontology implicit in biblical faith—that of the dialogue between God and man—to the ontology which he makes explicit in his doctrine of a Ground of Being apprehended through the ontological analysis of the self.

Buber, too, recognizes the importance of ontology, but the ontological, the "really real," to him is the sphere of the *between*, and this sphere is not something that can be detached and objectified but a reality to which one can only point. For Buber, ontology is only meaningful as it leads us to "the life of dialogue," the reality that is open and accessible in "the lived concrete." For Tillich, in contrast, ontology becomes the basis for both ontological analysis, on the one hand, and the I-Thou relationship of faith, on the other, or in his own terms, for both "controlling" and "receiving" knowledge.

The issue between the two men, finally, is one of *dialogue* as opposed to *dialectic*. In dialogue, as Franz Rosenzweig has pointed out, the other person has not only ears but a mouth. He may say something that will surprise you. Dialectic, on the other hand, takes place in the mind of an individual thinker. All dialectic originates in dialogue, just as all knowledge originates in knowing the other, the Unique, the Thou. But when the dialogue is internalized, the reality of the other person, the other consciousness, the other situation is lost and the second voice of the dialectic is neutralized into an idea, a hypothetical "point of view." This means to forget, like Job, the reality of the creation before which one stands. It is the attempt to substitute for biblical *emunah*, which tells one only that one will meet the Thou *as* one meets it, the *gnosis* that offers one comprehensive formulae and analyses. This tendency to substitute dialectic for dialogue is trenchantly described in a criticism of Tillich by one of his closest friends and disciples, the late David Roberts:

I have always been mystified as to how he could be so flexible, concrete, vital, and "close to home" on the one hand, and so schematic, abstract, and remote on the other. . . . The schematic aspect . . . is an asset wherever it is used analytically and organizationally, that is, where it is used to clarify concepts and to show their interrelatedness. But it becomes a liability at the point where existential problems, after being high-lighted, are swallowed into an abyss. Somehow Tillich, like God, manages to engulf distinctions without blurring them. He fully realizes (again, no doubt, like God) that such problems are met, in so far as they ever are, by living rather than by constructing systems. But it is a weird experience, which I have undergone many times, to have problems answered with great sensitivity and patience, by being brought into connection with some relevant segment of the system, only to discover later that I do not happen to be the man who carries this system around in his head.[13]

Judaism is, at the least, a warning against impersonal, abstract spirit in which a man may finally be engulfed.

STEVEN S. SCHWARZSCHILD

A Jewish Perspective
on International Relations

THAT A GOVERNMENT bears responsibility only to itself and its country; that a statesman, in the conduct of foreign affairs, must take into account exclusively—or at least predominantly—the interests of the political unit, usually the nation-state, whose executive agent he is; this proposition is a self-evident premise of almost all contemporary political philosophy. I wish to analyze this proposition in the light of Jewish theology.

We can, perhaps, begin our analysis most beneficially by considering this thesis in the formulation and context of Benedict Spinoza. Here as in many other crucial areas of modern thinking (and by "modern" I mean "pre-post-modern") he is, on the whole for ill, one of its most decisive progenitors and advocates. Spinoza says, "If we consult loyalty and religion [*pietatem et religionem*] we shall see that no one in possession of power ought to abide by his promises to the injury of his dominion; for he cannot keep such promises without breaking the engagement he made with his subjects, by which both he and they are most solemnly bound." [1] Spinoza teaches that the state and the individual may, if they have the power and if they calculate that it is also to their advantage to do so, break any promise or contract they wish. Only so long as a commitment continues to be useful to the one who has entered into it must he adhere to it.[2]

For Spinoza this is a perfectly consistent and logical view to hold; it follows from his fundamental equation *deus sive natura*, which in turn leads to the definition of might as right.[3] Ethics, then, is not prescriptive but descriptive, and the state's right to disregard its given word is not so much a moral possibility as an empirical fact. An individual or a society will naturally fulfil a promise if to do so is likely to bring it benefit or if not doing so is likely to cause it greater harm than would otherwise be the case. Spinoza reasons that if a state kept a promise to another state when to do so would no longer bring it any benefit, it would obviously be depriving its own citizens, to whom it has a primary obligation, of potential benefits, and thus be derelict in its duty.[4] In any case, the morality of promises affects only and at best individuals. States act by *raison d'état*. Individuals, when they entered into social compacts, deprived themselves of the natural rights which they possessed in the state of nature where the *bellum omnia contra omnes* prevailed. Since there are no international societies, either in Spinoza's time or ours, the rules of the natural state still obtain in the relations between states. Whereas, therefore, the consent of two parties is required for international peace to be established, the will of only one party suffices to create a state of war. And, even as individual promises are valid only so long as to keep them is more advantageous than to break them, so also peace treaties between states will remain in force only so long as to adhere to them is more advantageous to the state than to break them.[5] As Walter Eckstein [6] points out, in the system of morality of the state as well as in that of the individual, according to Spinozan egotism, the desire to preserve oneself and to increase one's enjoyment of survival is the source of ethics. His phrase for it is *conatus sese conservandi*.

One of the chief objects of attention in the discussion of international affairs during the recent past has been the limited nuclear test-ban treaty entered into between the main nuclear powers and joined by most other countries in the world. One passage in its text did not receive the publicity or the close scrutiny which it inherently deserves. It is a passage in which it would appear that the Spinozistic doctrine we have just considered is put into full effect. Let me, therefore, quote in full the four brief paragraphs devoted to it in an analytical article in the *New York Times* of July 27, 1963—the only discussion of the subject I have seen (despite the wordy fulminations in the "advise and consent" debate in the U. S. Senate). The paragraphs both state the facts and begin to study them for their meaning:

> Possibly the most important feature of the treaty for international law is its escape clause, allowing any nation to withdraw after three months' notice of "extraordinary events" related to the "subject matter" of the treaty that have jeopardized its "supreme interest."

> This concept, officials here said, comes close to acceptance of the doctrine of *rebus sic stantibus*, Latin for things remaining the same. It is a greatly disputed concept that agreements may be broken if the relevant conditions at the time of agreement should ever change.

> Experts here believe it is the first time the United States has admitted such a clause to a major treaty. More traditional escape clauses call for consultation and negotiation before the parties may renounce their obligations.

> Actually, many Senators welcome the clause as a device for protecting the national interest, but Administration officials wish to study its implications before it becomes widely accepted for future arms control agreements.

In a way this passage in the limited nuclear test-ban treaty only confirms the character of the rest of the treaty, namely that, desirable as it unquestionably is, it has not created a single new fact of international political reality or of law but merely put into words prior existing realities. The treaty in effect says that any nuclear power will be entitled to recommence nuclear testing if another nuclear power breaks its word by engaging in unilateral testing anywhere except underground—and our officials have hastened to add that what is true of testing is *a fortiori* true of belligerent nuclear activity.[7] All of this is a situation that obviously obtained before the treaty was initialed and would have continued to obtain if the treaty had never been brought about. The treaty is merely descriptive of a previously existing state of affairs,[8] and it is for this reason that it requires no provisions for enforcement, for it is self-enforcing. Furthermore, strictly speaking, even the verbalization of this state of affairs is supererogatory, since, under the charter of the United Nations which prohibits aggression and various resolutions of the UN that call upon the nations to desist from further nuclear testing, all the various nuclear contingencies had previously been guarded against. There is then little doubt, as all the signatories of the compact have tried to impress upon their own citizens and on the rest of the world, that the limited nuclear test-ban treaty serves a preponderantly psychological purpose at a recent juncture in the cold war, rather than a political or legal one.

This, then, is also entirely true of the escape clause with which we are concerned. We pointed out that Spinoza's philosophical justification of the right of a sovereign state to break its treaties derives from his identification of right with might, of God with nature, of ethics with power (as Hegel's famous dictum has it, "what is is rational"); ethics in principle is descriptive rather than normative, and whatever a state is capable of doing it not only may ethically do but is even obligated to do. Let us once more quote the very words of Spinoza in which, as a general philosophical principle and not merely as a political doctrine, he lays down this rule:

By the right and ordinance of nature I merely mean those natural laws wherewith we conceive every individual to be conditioned by nature, so as to live and act in a given way. For instance, fishes are naturally conditioned for swimming and the greater for devouring the less; therefore, fish enjoy the water and the greater devour the less by natural right. For it is certain that nature, taken in the abstract, has sovereign right to do anything she can; i.e., her right is co-extensive with her power. The power of nature is the power of God, which has sovereign right over all things; and inasmuch as the power of nature is simply the aggregate of the powers of all her individual components, it follows that every individual has sovereign right to do all that he can; i.e., the rights of an individual extend to the utmost limits of his powers as it has been conditioned. Now it is the sovereign law and right of nature that each individual should endeavor to preserve itself as it is, without regard to anything but itself.[9]

Quite in this sense, the clause in the test-ban treaty merely describes and approves what every nation, including our own and not only the "wicked enemy," has always done and would surely have done without the treaty.[10] To quote the words of a *New York Times* analyst, it is "a device for protecting the national interest," and this national interest is left to the government concerned itself unilaterally to define.[11] It is, of course, highly doubtful that any American practicing politician would be prepared to justify this policy in Spinozistic terms. Spinoza merely says that, metaphysically, might is right—and everything else follows from this (in his *Political Treatise* he prominently quotes Machiavelli). But the moralistic tradition of our country would subject a political spokesman who made a statement like Spinoza's to vociferous sermonic attacks. He would have to appeal to other moral justifications (along the lines, for example, that we believe in religious or idealistic or natural morality; that America is essentially identical with such morality; and that we must,

therefore, assert the priority of America which is the priority
of morality, regardless of other subsidiary or technical considerations). The effect, nonetheless, would be the same. The
question is merely which rationalization is more truthful
and more useful.

One way of approaching this latter problem is to compare
Spinoza's doctrine with Hobbes's. It is an established fact of
the history of political philosophy that Spinoza adopted
Hobbes's basic view almost *in toto*,[12] Hobbes, in turn, having
gone to school to Machiavelli: "The liberty each man has
to use his own power as he will himself for the preservation
of his nature . . . and that of doing anything which in his
own judgment and reason he shall conceive to be the aptest
means thereto." [13] The crucial difference between Hobbes and
Spinoza resides not in the substance of what they have to
say on the identity of right and might but rather in the
moral evaluation of this identification, which they make in
terms of their respective general philosophic framework. The
British empiricist Hobbes looks, as it were, at the realities,
or at what he thinks are the realities, with a somewhat
resigned, skeptical eye; acknowledges them; and exhorts his
fellowmen not to blind themselves to the facts with any
ethical illusions. He neither praises nor laments the realities;
he takes serious cognizance of them. It is otherwise with
Spinoza. He does not have the hardboiled empiricist attitude;
he is essentially a metaphysician. As such he immediately
proceeds to integrate what he believes to be the hard, empirical
realities into his metaphysical system, and in this system what
to Hobbes were merely terrestrial, human actualities for him
become metaphysical, divine, eternal, and *eo ipso* ethical
values. Thus "the war of all against all" is for him not merely
an experience of history and psychology but a law of nature
and, therefore, a law of God. Of course, a law of God is an
ethical law.

There are profound differences in the human and moral
influence of two such divergent interpretations. It is at least

conceivable that a disciple of Hobbes might say to his teacher, "I admit that what you say has been true up to now, but my friends and I want to try to change human nature and the rules of society to the end that it will not always be true in the future." No disciple of Spinoza could be reasonably expected ever to make such a statement, for how could any man propose to rebel against natural, divine, metaphysical, eternal, and fundamentally moral law? In short, a conclusion of a British empiricist is, by definition, subject to the categories of time and the changes which occur within it; the conclusion of Spinoza, if true or if believed to be true, is completely beyond the realm of time and human mastery.

This same difference in attitude toward what are presumed to be identically recognized facts leads to very different evaluations of the phenomenon of revolution. Spinoza opposes all revolution, on the ground that "whatever actually is is rational." [14] The Puritan revolution in the England of his time was to him the terrible bogeyman that the French revolution was to legitimacy in the nineteenth century and the Russian revolution to the bourgeoisie in the twentieth. On the other hand, the Jewish philosopher Hermann Cohen, for instance, following the tradition of his teacher Kant who had welcomed the French revolution in his day, pointed to Spinoza's fright at Cromwell as the ultimate proof of his incomprehension of and hostility to political freedom, social justice, and ethical seriousness,[15] and thus aligned himself with the opposite tradition of Locke and the Declaration of Independence. What Stuart Hampshire says of Hobbes [16] is equally true of Spinoza: he was "a pessimistic philosopher of realistic conservatism, the defender of the established order, whatever it may be, against the restless claims of individual ambition and conscience." Our problem today, on the other hand, as we expect to show in the following, is, in the words of W. A. Williams, to conduct a foreign policy of "an open door to revolution."

What I am suggesting is something that the contemporary

schools of "realism" in political philosophy have been saying;
namely, that the more clearly actual political behavior is
seen to be what it is rather than being transmogrified into
religious, philosophical, or ethical ideologies, i.e., the less
we "crusade" but rather cynically confess our real motiva-
tions, the more do we, in the first place, practice the moral
virtue of honesty and truthfulness and, in the second place,
create at least the theoretical possibility of adopting other
attitudes and policies. We cannot but agree with Spinoza
and Hobbes that the highest good of the state is its self-interest;
but we have seen that Hobbes's realism is more helpful
(because open to modification) than Spinoza's metaphysics,
if any of us should happen to believe that the self-serving
politics that states conduct among one another on this pattern
is highly undesirable both from an ethical and a "pragmatic"
point of view. I would raise the question, above all, whether
even Hobbes (and our contemporary political realists) is
"realistic" enough—and I take special satisfaction in raising
this question because I am an unashamed and self-confessed
pacifist, Jewish traditionalist, and theological messianist, all
the things that are regularly described by our realists as
"utopian" and "sentimentally idealistic."

Hermann Cohen begins his *Ethics of Pure Will* with the
statement: "The subject of ethics is man," [17] and he hastens
to add, "Without the universality of mankind, indeed unless
one begin with the universality of mankind, the concept of
man not only cannot be completed but cannot even be
developed or formed." [18] This is what I call "realism." [19] The
human individual is the only real ethical or political *con-
cretum* that exists, and since this is so with respect to every
single individual it follows that mankind as a whole, consisting
of unnumbered concrete human beings, is also a realistic
object of consideration. The individual and humanity, then,
are the subject of ethics, and (not necessarily because politics
or foreign affairs are identical with ethics but because they
want methodologically to be realistic) man and mankind are

also the subject of politics and foreign affairs. Everything else is really abstraction, including the state, the UN, treaties, political goals and means and programs, and the presumed hardboiled facts to which Hobbes and Spinoza and our statesmen pay so much attention. I suggest, then, that true political realism will always have foremost in mind that it must be concerned with individual human beings and with all individual human beings, not with any arbitrary and abstract ideals or associations of individuals. The basic unit of study and operation of all politics is not the state but the human being.

A couple of trivial incidents in international affairs recently illustrated the truth of this dictum. Recently the Netherlands returned to the sovereignty of the West German Federal Republic a minuscule strip of land, comprising one small village which it had retained at the end of the last war as a sort of collateral on the payment of war damages. Now, both in view of the general principle of the sanctity of national sovereignty and in view of what are widely believed to be the pronounced national feelings of Germans and Dutchmen, especially in relation to one another, one would have expected a scream of horror to arise on both sides of the frontier. If Germany and Holland are truly "motherlands," surely no one participates in or even watches the dismemberment of his mother without firm resistance and deep anguish. However, nothing of the sort happened. Neither the world as a whole nor the two peoples directly concerned paid very much attention to the whole transaction. The bulk of whatever newspaper reports there were on the subject concentrated on the fact that the patriotic Germans in the village rather regretted the fact that they were about to lose some tangible economic advantages and took measures to compensate themselves for this by means somewhat less than ethical, though perhaps legal.

Our own country had exactly the same experience. In the summer of 1964 the federal government ceded to the Republic

of Mexico a small strip of land on the Rio Grande that had
been in dispute ever since the settlement of the Mexican
War—and not even the Daughters of the American Revolution nor the American Legion bothered to protest this ampu-
tation of the smallest toe on the foot of American geography
for the purpose of pleasing a neighbor.

The reason for these two phenomena is, of course, that
Germany and the Netherlands, the United States and Mexico,
are rank abstractions. Abstractions can be manipulated, like
putty, into any shape. These four countries, like all other
countries, are defined by their borders, and these borders are,
obviously, lines drawn in the minds of men, ideological constructs and historical accidents. The realities are not Germany,
Holland, America, and Mexico but Germans, Dutchmen,
Americans, and Mexicans. As a matter of fact, even these are
not genuine *concreta*, because, as we have seen, a number of
men in all four categories changed nationality overnight without suffering changes in their personalities or characters. The
only genuine realities, then, are human beings and their
material as well as spiritual wants and aspirations. "The subject of ethics is man." This is not an idealistic but a realistic
statement.

It is, of course, true that to many men in the areas of the
world with which we are most familiar, the nationality they
hold is very important. This, too, is a reality. It is, furthermore, true that their national, cultural, historical, and economic background has very largely shaped the specificity of
these men—and specificity, or concreteness, is what we are
looking for. On the other hand, it is simply unrealistic to
think that this pattern is either in the nature of human existence or even historically true of all or most men at this
particular time. When I traveled across the deserts of Iran
I often wanted to stop and ask some of the natives and
nomads of the area what they thought of the Shah and his
relationship to CENTO: the answer, I am sure, would have
been that they had never heard of the Shah, and certainly

not of CENTO; they would, however, be very much concerned with food, medicine, education, housing, love, and
similar actualities. It is simply not true that, as Spinoza said
and virtually every political scientist in our time repeats,
the first and last responsibility of the statesman is to his
country. His responsibility is to his fellow citizens.[20] Politicians and philosophers may agree on the validity of *raison
d'état*, but human beings merely want a meaningful life. This,
presumably, is what we mean by the old American slogan
that the state is for the individual, not the individual for the
state; and, in the sense of the Declaration of Independence,
"whenever any form of government becomes destructive of
these ends, it is the right [and duty] of the people to alter or
to abolish it, and to institute new government . . ."

I beg not to be misunderstood. I must reiterate that
what I am looking for is a really "realistic" ethic of foreign
policy, not idealistic anarchism. I am not, of course, advocating the abolition of the nation-state, even if this were feasible.
I am highly and wryly skeptical even of the World Federal-
ists, not only because, for the time being and for a good
while to come, they have no chance of succeeding, but also
because they are naive idealists: they work with the premise
that there is such a thing as man-in-the-abstract, universal,
undifferentiated man, or at least the state-in-the-abstract, and
that, therefore, all men or all states can be subsumed under
one heading. This is not so, of course. There is no "man";
there is only this man, that man, and the other man. By the
same token, every state is different and *sui generis*, from
federal political union without ethnic homogeneity to the
totalitarian class-state, from the people-state to some of the
most recent non-states, etc. Nation-states are obviously here
to stay for a long time.

I am only pointing out two aspects of the matter. The first
is philosophical and ethical, namely, that however firmly
the institution of the nation-state seems to be established
today, there is nothing natural, eternal, or inherently ethical

in it. It is a peculiar product of the modern age which, no doubt, will pass away with its age.[21] My second point is ethical and practical: the only conceivable ethical justification of the state is the welfare of its citizens, not its own (*imperii salus summa lex*), and the welfare of human beings generally. There can be and are objective conflicts of interest between states when these are conceived as ultimate criteria; but the authentic conflicts with whose increasing resolution all politics, foreign as well as domestic, ought to be concerned are the conflicts between human beings, not states. Once this is recognized, we are not rid of all our serious problems, but we may, at least in part, find ourselves confronted by new and different, humanly and ethically genuine ones.[22]

Politicians and theoreticians worry about whether America is secure and stronger than the USSR. They discuss such abstractions as democracy, the dictatorship of the proletariat, guided democracy, socialism and the welfare-state, capitalism, and postures of strength. All of their conclusions are ideologies, and real human beings do not really care about them—unless and to the extent to which these affect their real personal existence. To be sure, there are some human beings who are profoundly concerned with such ideologies, but they are hardly "real human beings"; rather they are ideologues, artificial products of our societies of "bread and circuses." There is, then, absolutely no reason why a statesman should define his sacred task as that of protecting the interests of his own state. *Fiat veritas, pereat realitas!*

I anticipate the objection that what I have been saying is incapable of being transformed into a practical principle of foreign policy and even less into a "realistic" foreign policy. Therefore, I want to use one example, that of the problem of intervention in the internal affairs of a foreign state, to illustrate how the overriding commitment to the welfare of human beings would and should—and sometimes even does—find its practical enactment.

I hope that this will also effectively reply to Ernest

Lefever's taunt that the approach to an ethical foreign policy "which has instructed a great number of religious leaders [and which] has emphasized the ideal goals of international peace, justice, and brotherhood" leads to an insistence "upon an absolute ethic based exclusively upon good-will, noncoercion, cooperation, and education," [23] for I am about to advocate a pretty ruthless policy of interventionism, pacifist that I am. Lefever admits that there are exceptions to his thesis, but he then proceeds to forget about them. Lefever's school of "realism," as derived from the Protestant neo-orthodoxy of Reinhold Niebuhr, makes a number of the most fundamental mistakes. It claims that the "national interest" and a foreign policy committed to it is the starting point of national policy. ("It should be borne in mind, however, that the President of the U. S. is directly responsible only for the security of our nation and for the preservation of the values we, as a people, represent . . ." [24]—and all the soft-spoken qualifications do not alter this definition.) The Christian realists maintain that their controverters do not recognize the inherent sinfulness of man nor the reality of power. We are most sensitively aware of the reality of power, but we want it to be used wisely and for the purposes *we* define, rather than they; we are thoroughly conscious of our sinfulness, but we refuse to accept the premature and dogmatic definition of the limitations which our sinfulness puts on our freedom to act which they stipulate.[25] Indeed, I regard such dogmatic pontification as to where freedom and sin clash as an outstanding illustration of human sinfulness: the ambiguity of "Suez"—now replaced in academic discussions by "the Cuban fiasco"—is due not to the conflict of ethics and power but to the realists' political prejudgment that the military success of Britain, France, and Israel was unquestionably desirable.

In terms of Jewish theology, there is no doubt in my mind that the fundamental error of the self-proclaimed ethico-political "realists" is a direct and almost inevitable consequence of an essential and integral Christian doctrine, a doctrine which, as much as any other, has split Christianity from Judaism. "There is a richer, more authentic and enduring Christian tradition free of all the illusions and confusion of the presently fashionable revivalist trend. From Augustine to Niebuhr, Christian realism at almost every point in time has sought to grapple patiently with the perplexities and limitations of the day." [26]

The doctrine at issue, be it noted, is not the doctrine of sin, original or otherwise. Man's sinfulness is biblical doctrine, Jewish and Christian, and no one should any longer make an invidious and incorrect distinction between Jewish self-righteousness, optimism, and this-worldliness on the one hand and Christian humility, faith, and eschatology on the other. The doctrine at issue is a basic Christian dualism (Hellenistic and gnostic in origin) between body and spirit, this world and the other world, the kingdoms of the former and the latter. This doctrine leads to Paul's condemnation of the flesh and all that goes with it—to the transfer of God's kingdom from this world to the other and into the heart of man—and to "Render unto Caesar what is Caesar's and unto God what is God's." Kenneth Thompson is quite right in speaking of this as normative Christian tradition through the ages. It resulted, as Karl Barth pointed out in his famous letter to the French Huguenots, in Luther's doctrine of the two orders and in the divorce of German Lutherans from all political matters, leaving the road open to the princes' ruthless suppression of the peasants' revolt in Luther's time and to the principled indifference of the German church as a whole to the rise of Hitler. In such a world, separated from God's direct sovereignty, it is, indeed, true that God's law is ultimately inapplicable. To try to apply it is really hubris. "There are grounds for arguing that Christian standards have little if anything to do with the course states can pursue . . . ," Thompson confesses.[27]

Judaism, on the other hand, has never abandoned this world to the devil. This is God's world, created by Him, and

His law is specifically and even exclusively meant for it. When, according to a talmudic statement, the angels wanted to stop God from giving His law to Israel because they feared that it would inevitably be blemished on earth, God had Moses, on his celestial mission, answer by pointing out that all the laws of the Bible were useless to angels and only meaningful under human conditions—until the angels conceded and exclaimed (Ps. 8:1), "Oh, Lord, our God, how glorious is Thy name *in all the earth*." [28] Sin is not a matter of materiality but of errant spirit. And the fact of the matter is, of course, that while Caesar is explicitly removed from the jurisdiction of the Christian faith in the New Testament, the Hebrew Bible and Talmud and all of Jewish canon law are full of the most explicit and detailed legislation concerning king, government, and civil concerns. (It is one of the real ironies of the modern situation that Judaism, which indigenously knows nothing of a separation of "state and church," has had to fight for this principle in the Western world, whereas, at least at the present moment, Christian circles, with whom the principle of separation is native, are fiercely resisting the notion of secularity.) Furthermore, whatever the total conception of the eschatological state may be in Judaism, none can doubt that the messianic kingdom is awaited *on this earth*. And thus it follows that, from the Jewish point of view, such matters as foreign policy must be regarded, like everything else, as directly—not "proximately"—under divine command. Judaism is not only monotheistic but also, in this sense, monistic.

What is a little more difficult for me to understand is why sophisticated Christian theologians cannot see the cogency of this view of the matter in their own Christian lights. If "crisis-theology," "neo-orthodoxy," "the new realism"—or whatever it is to be called—has made one great religious contribution to the present age, it surely is its rupture with the easy and humanistic moralism of nineteenth century Christian liberalism and of much of the "social gospel." It offers a new seriousness about the Bible and "Christocentrism." Are the neo-realists then not sometimes taken aback when their dualistic dichotomy between God's kingdom and this world leads them to Christian political positions which sound like quotations from Elbert Hubbard, precisely because they reserve their serious Christian faith for other matters? Listen to George Kennan's conclusion, for example: "A government can pursue its purposes in a patient and conciliatory and understanding way, respecting the interests of others and infusing its behavior with a high standard of decency and honesty and humility . . . sheer good manners will bring some measure of redemption to even the most ill-conceived and disastrous of undertakings. . . ." [29] Just note this catalogue of a boy scout's virtues: patience, conciliation, understanding, respect for others, high standards of decency, honesty, humanity, sheer good manners! And this, at least in the real human social situation, is the upshot of theologically rigorous thinking! I hold that, if the incarnation is to mean anything to the Christian, and creation to the Jew, "Christ" (or Creation) must mean a little more on this earth than such vague moralisms which Greek and barbarian and Confucian gentlemen had proclaimed much earlier and altogether independently.

From this point of view, the gap between a Niebuhr and a Barth is also very instructive. Unlike Niebuhr, Barth forswears the entire apparatus of modern, Hellenistic culture—political philosophy with all other—and attempts to orient himself in the world by the Word of God alone. His resultant "neo-biblicism" sounds in many ways like fundamentalism. But the interesting political fact is spread on the record that Barth's attitudes to the secular problems of people and nations in the modern world have been pretty nearly unassailable—from his opposition to the Kaiser's German imperialism, through his commitment to some kind of religious socialism, his courageous and militant fight against Nazism, to his current advocacy of religious understanding of and spiritual help to the antireligious societies of communism. And in all these positions and the actions he has taken he has always tried to follow immediate biblical command. He has not placed a wall of philosophy, theology, political science, or any other kind of ideological construct between himself and the will of God as he understood it. This has, on the one hand, saved him from the inherent dualism of Hellenistic Christianity, and on the other, bestowed upon him the ability to see all of "the world and the fullness thereof" under the direct sovereignty of God.

Why should not the Niebuhrians also be accessible to this truth which they, after all, proclaimed at the very beginning of their theological revolution? Is it not Niebuhr who has always insisted on the biblical, anti-Hellenistic view that body and soul, matter and spirit, and, therefore, surely also world and God are inextricably intermixed; that this is the meaning of the incarnation; and that, therefore, the Christian must assume responsibility in the world? "Proximate judgments," on the other hand, are, by definition, human acts of prudential wisdom, rather than unqualified commitments to the truth and commands of God. Logically, it is through them that considerations have entered into his and his disciples' decisions and proposals that have removed political matters so far from faith that, as we have seen, the result sounds more like a scout's recital of the bourgeois virtues than the profession of a believer. No wonder, also, that so many of the practicing politicians and theoreticians who follow in his footsteps declare that they accept his analysis of the nature of man and of society but reject the theological foundations or conclusions that are, in Niebuhr's own view, inseparably connected with it. This has often been commented on in a laudatory sense; perhaps, however, it may shed some revealing light on the question of how innately Christian and biblical his world-view really is. Niebuhr and Niebuhrianism have, in effect, become the theological and theoretical wing of the Pentagon; by and large the same things are said in the main building and in this wing, the

difference being that in the wing they are said in the tone
of slightly worried conscience.

Let me now make a political confession: I strongly
opposed our intervention in the domestic affairs of Guatemala, but I was delighted when we kept a warship off the
coast of Trujillo's Dominican Republic. (For me, the difference between the two cases was, of course, that I thoroughly
disliked Trujillo, whereas I had some sympathy with the revolutionary Guatemalan regime.) By the same token, I am convinced that we shall have to restore diplomatic recognition
to Castro Cuba, but—to stay in Latin America—if I could I
certainly would persuade our government to break relations
with Stroessner's Paraguay. (Again, it is clear that I am
biased: I thoroughly hate fascism, whereas I believe that
revolutionary leftism—however malignant and repulsive—is
a perversion of what nonetheless remains a moral search:
communism is a "Christian heresy," something scarcely conceivable with respect to Nazism.) Examples of this kind of
inconsistency could easily be multiplied. It is obvious that
I can be told: either you believe that all *de facto* governments
should be granted diplomatic recognition—and then you cannot distinguish between Castro and Stroessner—or you evaluate governments on the basis of their international morality
and trustworthiness—and then again, though in precisely the
opposite way, you must treat both régimes in the same fashion.
I am, in fact, told that a man either holds to the doctrine of
non-intervention in another country's internal affairs—and
then American meddling is no better in the Dominican
Republic than in Guatemala—or you abandon this policy,
and then you have no leg to stand on when you oppose the
CIA's adventures in Guatemala anymore than you do on the
Caribbean island.

I am a stiff-necked Jew, however. I am aware of my incon-
sistencies and yet stick to them. I must, being a "thinking
man," ask myself: Why? The answer to this question lies, in
part, in my belief that the original sin of mid-twentieth cen-

tury political thinking is the identification of communism with fascism. It goes without saying that I am as aware of their similarities as the next man. I take it that a man need no longer present his anticommunist certification. The fact of the matter is that I believe some of the anticommunism of the American Right to be soft: I would have screamed bloody murder in the mid-thirties when the business community established close commercial relations with the Soviet Union (and it is now again doing so). When America as a whole clasped Russia to its bosom during the Second World War some of us warned that this was merely a tactical alliance, and that the basic conflict between self-righteous totalitarianism and confessedly sinful democracy would re-emerge; I find myself in some surprising agreement with Thomas Molnar that, toward the non-communist world, the basic community of belief and interest of the Soviet Union and Red China will re-assert itself in the long run; I am convinced that the infallible index of communist evil is its cultural policy, that someone ought to publish a book soon in which side-by-side Khrushchev's comments on non-representational painting would be printed General Eisenhower's and the late Representative Francis Walter's criticisms of an American exhibit of contemporary art that was sent abroad on a cultural mission. Despite all this, I maintain that all forms of fascism are a bloody pagan *rejection of the human spirit* and must be dealt with as such, whereas communism, in its rapidly diversifying forms, is a *corruption of the human spirit:* fascism is a demon from another world; communism is a human being gone wrong. It follows that I hold that fascist regimes must be treated differently from communist ones: the former with the final aim in view of totally eliminating them, root and branch; the latter with the aim in view of "socializing" and reforming them.

This, however, is not the sufficient, nor perhaps even the basic, explanation of my inconsistency in judging our behavior toward these two types of national governments. I would here draw a distinction between "formal ethics" and "substantive ethics." Formal ethics is a code of behavior which lays down certain general rules that are then to be applied impartially to all situations within a given category. For example, a formal ethic would declare that intervention in the internal affairs of a foreign government is bad, and a power that commits itself to this ethic thereupon refrains from meddling in other people's affairs, regardless of who the people is or what the affairs are. A substantive ethic, on the other hand, is not primarily concerned with general rules of behavior but rather with certain defined human values, for example, economic advancement or intellectual and cultural freedom. Such an ethic will then say: Wherever the values to which we are committed are enhanced we will offer our support, and where they are harmed we will level whatever opposition we can get away with, regardless of what formal rules of international behavior we violate in the process.[30]

Maurice Samuel, in a book entitled *The Gentleman and the Jew*, drew such a distinction between what may be called the pagan and the biblical man. For Samuel—I think rightly —the ideal of the gentleman is the direct heir of the pagan-Greek hero, the medieval knight, Shakespeare's courtier, the cricketeer on the playing fields of Eton, and the gentleman-boxer of recent times. He has a code, to be sure. The code says that you stick to the rules, to your advantage as well as to your hurt. The knight, for example, would never lance his opponent once the joust was ended, but the specific ethical value of human life meant nothing to him, so that while the joust was going on, for the mere sake of "playing the game," he had no hesitation in killing a man. This is a formal ethic. Biblical man, on the other hand, is committed to the sanctity of human life. The rules of Lord Queensberry mean nothing to him. He will break the splendid ritual of standing at attention before the Queen in order to revive a man who has fallen prostrate because of the heat—and he will slink off the field in disgrace to save his skin rather than be buried with the epitaph that he had been a grand sportsman to the bitter end. This is a substantive ethic.

One could also say that the one is an idealistic ethic, the other a realistic one, for the former is concerned with general rules and the latter with specific situations and values. And, in order to get back to the individual South American cases with which I began (the Guatemalan revolution seen against the dictatorship of Trujillo), it seems to me that the specific ethical value to which the United States ought to be committed—and out of which it should determine its foreign policy—is the value to which its historical heritage, its ideological orientation, and its politico-economic interests predispose it: what W.`A. Williams in the last chapter of his otherwise dubious book, *The Tragedy of American Diplomacy*, calls a "policy of an open door to revolutions." (Justice Douglas has often spoken of this desideratum.) Thus we have arrived at a position exactly opposite to the Spinozistic opposition to all revolution with which we began. This is the biblical morality of "Do not stand by [the shedding] of your neighbor's blood; rebuke your fellow-human [when he sins]" (Lev. 19:16 ff.).[31]

In the attitude to international politics which I have been trying to outline there is another element which I want to try to crystallize phenomenologically. I am convinced that we make decisions and form final judgments in virtually all spheres of life long before we rationalize them. Who can doubt, for example, that the Supreme Court knew, deep in the pit of its collective judicial stomach, that it would rule against segregated schools long before anyone had opened books to check on legal precedents or educational psychology? (To this extent the Southern segregationists who protest against political prejudice are entirely right.) The Court which, at the end of the last century, ruled in exactly the opposite sense had before it, after all, precisely the same Constitution and even the same statutes. The difference between the two courts was the difference of their almost visceral reactions to the reality of segregation. I submit that the same holds true of the determination of foreign policy. We have certain "gut reactions" (which in turn are, of course, caused by all sorts of tangible and intangible influences) to foreign governments, leaders, and their political, economic, and cultural systems. These gut reactions come first, and all pragmatic and theoretical elaborations of policy are usually no more than clever and persuasive rationalizations of them. I have no doubt, for example, that staff members of the State Department, no less than I, have an immediate though perhaps a different reaction to a new administration in West Germany, and everything that follows can be predicted in some detail from their first response. I would again call this a realistic appraisal of what happens in the formulation of foreign policy, as opposed to academic, idealistic verbalizations. I do not deny in the least that I know precious little about either General Stroessner or Mr. Arbenz, but it would take a gigantic amount of evidence to the contrary to convince me that my distinction between a South American *caudillo* and a leftist, intellectual egalitarian is incorrect.

There is only one real question, as far as I can see, and that is how educated a stomach we have. It will be argued, for example, that a foreign policy of the stomach is a terribly dangerous thing, because the stomach only reacts; it neither sees nor thinks. It may, therefore, take a poison and die. As a vegetarian I can confirm that many a nut dish seems to taste like meat, and as a Jew I often shrink from margarine served with meat simply because it looks like the forbidden butter. The political analogue is, for example, that many a man—and especially the mob—immediately places a democratic socialist government in the same class with a Soviet satellite and therefore demands that our government act toward the former as it does toward the latter. I am also exposing myself to the accusation of advocating anti-intellectualism, with all its inherent dangers.

I would suggest that there is a preintellectual and a post-intellectual political and moral stomach. The preintellectual life of the stomach reacts from sheer hunger and brute fear: the other country threatens my resources, security, or power; therefore, I will resist and oppose it with whatever means are at my disposal. Since the time when this was our way of forming national policy, a lot of political, cultural, and intellectual water has flowed down the Mississippi. Political theory and philosophy have filled many libraries, and the political intellectuals have arrived at literally every theoretical position conceivable. The intellect has proved itself to be far from a safe course of political ethics. (One of the traumata in my life was the article *"Nous ne voulons pas mourir pour Dantzig"* published a few days before the outbreak of the Second World War in Europe in *L'Echo de Paris* and signed by Marcel Déat, one of the intellectual leaders of the French socialist movement and later a Nazi collaborator.) Pure men of the spirit have almost invariably been pulled into the maelstrom of political corruption; the intellectuals who fell for the Communist party and justified the Moscow trials; the dedicated products of the American populist tradition whose distrust of Wall Street led them to isolationism and from isolationism to pro-Nazism; the international Socialist movement that broke up in chauvinistic national blocks after Sarajevo, etc., etc.

I want to cite one last and most painful example of this failure of the intellect, Thomas Mann's *Dr. Faustus,* which is really an attempt to analyze the sickness of European society. When I re-read it recently, I remembered that I had somewhere on my shelves a study of this novel by the Marxist critic with the greatest world-wide reputation, Georg Lukacz; I had picked up the book in East Berlin in 1949, long before Lukacz became a short-lived hero of the Hungarian rebellion. On reading it I was shocked in my soul to find that it is—again—essentially a long-winded justification of the Soviet cultural doctrine of "socialist realism" in literature, music, and the arts (the essay is entitled "The Tragedy of Modern Art," and was published in Berlin in 1948). On page 79, written at the height of the Stalinist paranoia, the following paragraph is to be found: "It is a strange coincidence—if it be a coincidence—that the writer of this essay completed the reading of Mann's Faustus novel just at the time that the decision of the Central Committee of the Communist Party of the Soviet Union about modern music was made public. Thomas Mann's novel, with its passages which characterize especially modern music so brilliantly, thus is seen to be spiritual and cultural justification of this decision, which broadly encompasses all of modern art, its problems of expression into their technical details, and its human and social foundations." [32]

The intellect is far from being protection against barbarism. Thus, those who object to my thesis of "visceral politics" leave themselves wide open to the reply: *tu quoque.*

What the nurture of the intellect can, at best, do for us is to educate our stomachs. The starved savage and the refined gourmet have in common that they desire, above all, to satisfy their bellies; but one is satisfied with a piece of raw meat torn from a captive in war and the other demands all the culinary arts of France expended on a sauce. It seems to me that we have come out of the dreadful and cultured era behind us with one lesson: All the political theory and all the knowledgeable sophistication in the world are as nothing compared to the simple and fundamental virtue of compassion —call it pity, love, sympathy, or anything else. I am talking about a visceral hate of brutality and cruelty. I am talking about plain compassion for human beings, a deep disgust at unnecessary suffering, and an infinite yearning for decency and dignity.[33] To this have come all the anguished intellectual debates of the last 200 years. This is where the finespun arguments about historical dialecticism, the dynamics of the capitalist welfare state, social utopianism versus laissez-faire, and all the other ideologies have ended! Compassion alone turns out to be the refutation of anti-Semitism, racial discrimination, and what, in a discussion with John Courtney Murray, I have called "the ghastly vision" of nuclear warfare. I call this true realism because, as distinguished from all the abstractions with which the political scientists of the most hardboiled realistic school occupy their thoughts (states, organizations, treaties, and political platforms), it is above and beyond all concerned with human beings, individual human beings—who are and remain the only *concreta* of society, in our own country and in all the world.[34]

Notes

Lou H. *Silberman:* THE TASK OF JEWISH THEOLOGY

1. An earlier version of this essay appeared in the Central Conference of American Rabbis, *Yearbook,* 1963.
2. G. Scholem, "Mitokh hirhurim al hokhmat Yisrael," *Luah ha-aretz,* 1944/45.

Jakob J. *Petuchowski:* THE DIALECTICS OF REASON AND REVELATION

1. Jastrow, *Dictionary,* p. 104, s.v.; and Michael Guttmann, *Clavis Talmudis* (Breslau, 1930), vol. III, part 2, pp. 9 ff.
2. Genesis Rabbah 26:6.
3. Friedrich Schleiermacher, *On Religion—Speeches to Its Cultured Despisers* (New York, 1958), p. 89.
4. Abraham Geiger, *Judaism and Its History,* translated by Maurice Mayer (New York, 1865), pp. 47–64.
5. Kaufmann Kohler, *Jewish Theology* (New York, 1918), p. 39.
6. Gen. 12:7, and frequently.
7. Gen. 12:1, and frequently.
8. Deut. 4:33 and 5:19.
9. Exod. 4:24.
10. Jer. 7:25.
11. Exod. 20:1 ff.
12. Exod. 3:1 ff.; Ezek. 11:24; and Hos. 12:11, and frequently.
13. Deut. 5:5, and throughout the Bible.
14. Isa. 2:3, and throughout the Bible. See also my *Ever Since Sinai* (New York, 1961), pp. 4–12.
15. K. Kohler, *Jewish Theology,* p. 34.
16. M. Kadushin, *The Rabbinic Mind* (New York, 1952), pp. 57 ff. Kadushin denies that "Revelation," in the sense used by us, is a Rabbinic concept.
17. Lev. 18:5.

271

18. On this whole transformation of "Wisdom," *v.* J. Coert Rylaarsdam, *Revelation in Jewish Wisdom Literature* (Chicago, 1946).

19. B. Shabbath 23a; see my "The Magnification of Chanukah," in *Commentary* (January, 1960), pp. 38–43.

20. Genesis Rabbah 1:1. Leo Baeck, *Aus Drei Jahrtausenden*, 2nd ed. (Tübingen, 1958), pp. 157–75.

21. Harry A. Wolfson, *Philo.*, vol. I (Cambridge, Mass., 1948), p. 141.

22. Tosephta Sanhedrin 7:11, ed. Zuckermandel, p. 427.

23. Baraitha, in Introduction to the *Sifra*.

24. *V.* Saul Lieberman, *Hellenism in Jewish Palestine* (New York, 1950), pp. 47–82; and David Daube, "Rabbinic Methods of Interpretation and Hellenistic Rhetoric," in *Hebrew Union College Annual* (1949), XXII, 239-264.

25. Exod. 6:12; Num. 12:14; Deut. 31:27; and others.

26. *V.* Louis Jacobs, *Studies in Talmudic Logic and Methodology* (London, 1961), pp. 16–37.

27. *Ibid.*, p. 37.

28. *Sifra, Aharé Moth* 13:10, ed. Weiss, p. 86a.

29. B. *Sanhedrin* 56a.

30. Even more striking in its concise form is the old Palestinian version of this benediction:—

Favor us, O our Father, with knowledge from Thee,
and with understanding and discernment out of thy Torah.
Blessed art Thou, O Lord, gracious Giver of knowledge.

Cf. Solomon Schechter, in *Jewish Quarterly Review* (1898), X, 656 ff.

31. B. *Berakhoth* 58a.

32. Erich Fromm, *Psychoanalysis and Religion* (New Haven, Conn., 1950), pp. 45–47.

33. Walter Kaufmann, *Critique of Religion and Philosophy* (New York, 1958), p. 239.

34. *V.* Y. F. Baer, *Israel Among the Nations* (Jerusalem, 1955), pp. 99-117; and Gershom G. Scholem, *Jewish Gnosticism, Merkabah Mysticism, and Talmudic Tradition* (New York, 1960).

35. Cf. the many instances cited in J. Abelson, *The Immanence of God in Rabbinical Literature* (London, 1912).

36. *Sifra Aharé Moth* 13:10, ed. Weiss, p. 86a.

37. Isaak Heinemann, *Ta'amé Hamitzvoth Besifruth Yisrael*, 2nd ed., vol. I (Jerusalem, 1949), pp. 22-35; and Jacob B. Agus, *The Evolution of Jewish Thought* (New York, 1959), pp. 53–61.

38. *Ibid.*, p. 61.

39. See my "The Supposed Dogma of the Mosaic Authorship of the Pentateuch," in *The Hibbert Journal* (1959) LVII, 356-60.

40. B. *Gittin* 60a.

41. *Mishnah Sanhedrin* 10:1.

42. Saadya Gaon, *Sefer Ha-Emunoth veha-De'oth*, Introduction.

43. *Ibid.*

44. *V.* Leo Strauss, *Philosophie und Gesetz* (Berlin, 1935), p. 117.

45. *Kuzari*, I, 25, 87, etc.

46. *Yad, Hilkhoth Yesodé Hatorah*, 8:1.

47. *Introduction to the Commentary on the Pentateuch*, Paragraph III.

48. *Moreh Nebhukhim*, II, 25.

49. *Ibid.*, Introduction.

50. Saadya Gaon, *op. cit.*, Chapter III.

51. *Ibid.*, Introduction.

52. Julius Guttmann, "Vernunftreligion," *Jüdisches Lexikon*, V, 1198.

53. *Kuzari*, I, 67, 89.

54. *Ibid.*, V, 21.

55. *Ibid.*, IV, 13 ff.

56. Julius Guttmann, *Religion and Knowledge* (Hebrew) (Jerusalem, 1955), pp. 66–85. Isaak Heinemann, "Introduction," in his edition of Halevi's *Kuzari: The Book of Proof and Argument* (Oxford, 1947), pp. 9–26.

57. *Moreh Nebhukhim*, II, 33. Malbim, *Commentary on Exodus 20:2*.

58. *Kuzari*, I, 89. *Moreh Nebhukhim*, I, 65.

59. *Moreh Nebhukhim*, I, 66.

60. Emil L. Fackenheim, "Two Types of Reform," in *Central Conference of American Rabbis Yearbook* (1961), LXXI, 209.

61. David Philipson, *The Reform Movement in Judaism* (New York, 1907), p. 491.

62. See the sources quoted in notes 3, 4, and 5.

63. *Sifré, 'Eqebh*, par. 40, ed. Friedmann, p. 79a.

64. Jakob J. Petuchowski, "The Bible of the Synagogue," *Commentary* (Feb., 1959), pp. 142–150.

65. *"A Theologico-Political Treatise,"* Chapter VII in *The Chief Works of Benedict de Spinoza*, edited by R. H. M. Elwes (New York, 1951), I, 98–119.

66. Immanuel Kant, *Religion Within the Limits of Reason Alone* (New York, 1960), p. 102.

67. John Baillie, *The Idea of Revelation in Recent Thought* (New York, 1956), p. 62.

68. See my *Ever Since Sinai* (New York, 1961), pp. 66–83, where this point is developed at greater length.

69. Abraham J. Heschel, *God in Search of Man* (Philadelphia, 1956), p. 260.

70. Franz Rosenzweig, *On Jewish Learning*, edited by N. N. Glatzer (New York, 1955), p. 118.

71. *Ibid.* See also the very important development of the theme of Revelation in Rosenzweig's *Der Stern der Erlösung*, 2nd ed. (Frankfort, 1930), Part II, pp. 88–151. An English digest of Rosenzweig's views on this subject has been prepared by Nahum N. Glatzer and was published in *Judaism* (Spring, 1962), pp. 175-177.

72. Martin Buber, *Eclipse of God* (New York, 1952), pp. 173 f.

73. Fackenheim, *op. cit.*, pp. 219-222.

74. Deut. 29:14.

Emil L. Fackenheim: THE REVEALED MORALITY OF JUDAISM AND MODERN THOUGHT

1. An earlier version of this essay appeared in *Commentary* (December, 1963).

2. Cf., e.g., the famous passage in *Pirke Abot,* I 3.

3. *Bab. Talmud, Yoma,* 67 b.

4. *Fundamental Principles of the Metaphysics of Ethics,* translated by Abbott (London, 1926), pp. 59, 61. I have revised Abbott's translation. When possible, readily available English translations of Kant are quoted; otherwise, the Prussian Academy edition, 23 vols., 1900-56, is the source, and the translation is my own.

5. The "creative morality" interpretation of Kant, given by thinkers from Fichte to Hermann Cohen, has affected quite un-Kantian philosophies, such as those of Nietzsche and Dewey, as well as much popular moral and psychological thinking. Instead of documenting the view that it is not Kantian, which I intend to do elsewhere, I refer only to G. Krueger, *Philosophie und moral in der Kantischen kritik* (Tübingen, 1931).

6. A remarkable nineteenth century Jewish thinker neatly illustrates this dilemma. Samuel Hirsch subscribed to Kantian autonomous morality. Yet he also believed quite literally in revelation. Aware of the possibility of conflict, he sought to resolve it by interpreting revelation (following Lessing) as divine education toward moral autonomy. Hirsch's ingenuity in developing this doctrine does not save it from ultimate failure. Revelation here is a divine guidance the sole purpose of which is to emancipate man from the need for guidance, and hence from revelation itself. Cf. my article "Samuel Hirsch and Hegel" in *Studies in Nineteenth-Century Jewish Intellectual History,* ed. A. Altmann (Cambridge, Mass., 1964), pp. 171-201.

7. Kant returns to this theme on countless occasions. We confine ourselves to quoting one representative passage: "so far as practical reason has the right to guide us, we shall not regard actions as obligatory because they are divine commandments. We shall regard them divine commandments because we are inwardly obligated to them" *Critique of Pure Reason,* b. 847.

8. Prussian Academy edition, VIII, 405.

9. Cf., e.g., Gen. 12:1 ff.; Exod. 3:4 ff., and 19:5 ff.; Isa. 6:1 ff.; Jer. 1:1 ff. When bidden to become a holy nation (Exod. 19:5-6), Israel is, of course, already in possession of *some* commandments in terms of which the content of holiness may be specified. Still, it is of the greatest importance that the bulk of revealed commandments are yet to come.

10. Isa. 6:8; Exod. 24:7. We follow the traditional interpretation of the last passage.

11. Cf., e.g., Isa. 6:4; Jer. 1:6.

12. Whether or not *all* the 613 commandments of traditional Judaism may be regarded as having permanence and intrinsic value is a large question, and one transcending the scope of this essay.

13. Jer., 27.

14. Our brief remarks on this topic (*infra*, section VII) are not, of course, meant to be an adequate treatment of this subject.

15. It is interesting to note that Kant and Kierkegaard use the same Biblical tale—Abraham's sacrifice of Isaac—for opposite purposes: Kant to argue that, since we must judge the claims of supposed divine voices in the light of our moral standards, such voices must be *a priori* either false or superfluous (Prussian Academy edition. VIII, 63 ff.; *Religion within the Limits of Reason Alone*, translated by Greene and Hudson [New York, 1960], p. 175); Kierkegaard to argue that, if revelation is to be a present possibility, there must be, in an extreme situation, the possibility of a teleological suspension of the ethical (*Fear and Trembling* [New York, 1954]). Any Jewish interpreter of the Abraham story will surely be dissatisfied with both the Kantian and the Kierkegaardian accounts. But one must face the fact that if, as Kant argues, a revealed morality is necessarily heteronomous, there is no third possibility.

16. Cf., e.g., *Midrash Tanhuma*, Yitro, and many other passages, in hasidic as well as rabbinic literature.

17. Mic. 6:8. The point made in this section is perfectly expressed in a Midrash in which God is made to say, "Would that they had deserted Me, and kept My Torah; for if they had occupied themselves with the Torah, the leaven which is in it would have brought them back to Me" (*Pesikta Kahana*, XV). Liberal writers are fond of quoting the first half of this Midrash only, thereby perverting a profound statement of the morality of Judaism into a humanistic platitude.

18. *Bab. Talmud, Berakhot* 61b.

19. *Critique of Judgment*, tr. Meredith (Oxford, 1952), p. 110. The translation is mine.

20. According to one Midrash (*Tanhuma, Hukkat*), the righteous do not cease to fear God even though they have received His assurance. According to another (*Sifre Deut.*, Wa'ethanan, No. 32), while everywhere else love drives out fear, this is not true of the love and fear of God.

21. In *Tanhuma, Behukkotai*, God is made to reject the offer of the angels to observe the Torah, on the ground that the Torah is appropriate only for human observance.

22. Cf., e.g., *Bab. Talmud, Berakhot* 31a, *Shabbat* 30b.

23. Isa. 6:6-7; Jer. 1:7-8.

24. As already indicated (*supra*, section IV), for reasons which are beyond the scope of this essay, Kant does not regard the divine will as an *absolute redundancy*. He does, however, regard it as redundant within a purely moral context.

25. Midrash Genesis Rabba, Wayyera LIII 7.

Monford Harris: ISRAEL: THE UNIQUENESS OF JEWISH HISTORY

1. John C. Greene, in *The Death of Adam* (New York, 1959), p. 49, sums up the view of Thomas Burnet (1635?–1715), a prominent churchman, who represented Christian thinking, as follows: "the main events of earth history were the creation, the deluge, and the final conflagration."

2. "Natural" is a doubtful word for a biblical category. "Normal" or "regular" would be better, but these words are so vague that I prefer "natural" despite its non-biblical implications.

3. Jerusalem, 1959, p. 278.

4. There are two Rabbinic traditions about giving the Torah: one to the effect that all nations refused the Torah, and only Israel accepted; the other that God inverted Mount Sinai over them like a vessel and threatened them with extinction unless they accepted the Torah. The first is not, I believe, to point out that Israel was good enough to choose while the nations were not. Its meaning is that it was willingly accepted for if it were *forced* upon Israel then Israel had no choice, consequently, no genuine responsibility. The second tradition indicates that ultimately God made the choice. Both traditions are to be kept together in paradoxical tension. The basic formulation of Israel being chosen is Deut. 7:6-8:

> For thou art a holy people unto the Lord thy God: the Lord thy God hath chosen thee to be His own treasure, out of all peoples that are upon the face of the earth. The Lord did not set His love upon you, nor choose you, because ye were more in number than any people for ye were the fewest of all peoples —but because the Lord loved you and because He would keep the oath which He swore unto your fathers, hath the Lord brought you out with a mighty hand, and .redeemed you out of the house of bondage, from the hand of Pharaoh king of Egypt.

5. Cf. Bertrand Russell, "A Free Man's Worship," in *Mysticism and Logic* (New York, 1929), a rare and perfect statement of modern atheism which shows, unwittingly, the human deflation implied in atheism.

6. Judah Halevi's tempered racism (*Kuzari*, First Mamar, Para. 27) is not to be taken as *the* Jewish view. Isaiah Horovitz (c. 1555–c. 1630) is truer to the tradition, despite his kabbalism. Cf. his brilliant observation and discussion in *Shnei Luhoth Ha'Berith* (Israel, 1959), vol. I, section II, tractate Shavuoth, p. 113.

7. In the Bible, God not only reveals His will to the Hebrew people; He also gives these people insight into themselves. The Bible is not only a revelation of God, but the Jewish people stand revealed there, too.

8. London, 1960. See the chapter, "Political Idealism."

9. *The Jewish Home* (London, 1945), p. 159.

10. My translation is based on the medieval understanding of the text.

11. Cf. J. Rosenthal, "The State of Israel in the Light of Christian Theology" (Hebrew), *Sura* (Jerusalem, 1955–56), II, 106–125.

Arnold Jacob Wolf: PSYCHOANALYSIS AND THE TEMPERAMENTS OF MAN

1. See Ernest Jones, *The Life and Work of Sigmund Freud* (New York, 1953), for the complex and self-sacrificing attitude of Freud toward Jung.

2. *Ibid.*, II, 22.

3. Willy Aron, "Notes on Sigmund Freud's Ancestry and Jewish Contacts," in *Yivo Annual of Jewish Social Science*, vol. XI (1956–57), p. 286, and "Discussion Regarding Sigmund Freud's Ancestry," *ibid.*, vol. XII (1958–59), pp. 297–300.

4. Cf. David Bakan, *Sigmund Freud and the Jewish Mystical Tradition* (Princeton, N.J., 1958).

5. Ernst Simon, "Sigmund Freud, the Jew," in *Year Book of the Leo Baeck Institute* (London, 1957), p. 298.

6. *Ibid.*, p. 292.

7. Hans Meyerhoff, "Nothing New about Freud," *Partisan Review* (1961), XXVIII:5–6, p. 696.

8. Simon, p. 296.

9. Meyerhoff, pp. 701 ff.

10. Simon, p. 293.

11. *Ibid.*, p. 299.

12. Abse and Jessner, "Psychodynamic Aspects of Leadership," *Daedalus* (Fall, 1961), 90:4, p. 693, quotes from Sigmund Freud, "Explanations, Applications and Orientations" in *Introductory Lectures on Psychoanalysis* (London, 1933), lecture 34.

13. Philip Rieff, "The Analytic Attitude," *Encounter* (July, 1962), p. 24. Cf. Rieff's introduction to his edition of Freud's *Therapy and Technique* (New York, 1963).

14. Lionel Trilling, *Freud and the Crisis of Our Culture* (New York, 1955), p. 17.

15. *Life against Death* (Middletown, Conn., 1959).

16. *Ibid.*, p. 9.

17. Sigmund Freud, *New Introductory Lectures on Psycho-Analysis* (New York, 1933), p. 127.

18. *Ibid.*, p. 144.

19. *Ibid.*, p. 142.

20. "Original Sin," in *Handbook of Christian Theology*, ed. Halverson and Cohen (New York, 1958), pp. 349 ff.

21. Brown, p. 14.

22. "Tillich and Freud on Sin," in *Religion in Life* XXVIII (1958-59), p. 223. Quoted in Bernard Martin, *The Existentialist Theology of Paul Tillich* (New York, 1963), p. 139.

23. Niebuhr, p. 350.

24. Alden L. Fisher, "Freud and the Image of Man," *Insight* (Winter, 1963), pp. 13-26.

25. Cf. Will Herberg, "Freud, the Revisionists, and Social Reality," in *Freud and the 20th Century*, ed. Nelson (New York, 1957), pp. 143-63. Herbert Marcuse, *Eros and Civilization* (New York, 1955), pp. 238-74.

26. Harris H. Hirschberg, *"Eighteen Hundred Years Before Freud: A Re-evaluation of the Term Yetzer Ha-Ra,"* Judaism (Spring, 1961), 10, 129-41.

27. Cf. Richard Rubenstein, "Scribes, Pharisees and Hypocrites," *Ibid.*, (Fall, 1963), 12, 456-68; Martin Buber, *Good and Evil* (New York, 1953), p. 97.

28. M. Kasher, *Torah Shelemah*, II (Jerusalem, 5696), pp. 379 ff.

29. Cf. B'reshit Rabbah, 27.4.

30. Vayikra Rabbah, 14.5.

31. Sukkah, 52a, b. Cf. Sh'mot Rabbah, 30.17.

32. B'reshit Rabbah, 22.6.

33. *Ibid.*

34. Solomon Schechter, *Some Aspects of Rabbinic Theology* (New York, 1923), pp. 252 ff. Cf. B'reshit Rabbah, 34.10; Sanhedrin, 91 b.

35. Cf. Shir Hashirim Rabbah, 7.8.

36. Sh'mot Rabbah, 36.3.

37. Schechter, p. 236.

38. Shabbat, 105b.

39. Baba Mezia, 59b.

40. Schechter, p. 264.

41. B'reshit Rabbah, 9.7 Cf. Kohelet Rabbah, 3.3.

42. Yoma, 69b. Cf. Avodah Zarah, 5a.

43. Kohelet Rabbah, 9.8 (Soncino translation).

44. Avot D'Rabbi Natan XVI. Cf. Vayikra Rabbah 34.1; Kohelet Rabbah *ad. loc.*

45. Bamidbar Rabbah, 15.14.

46. Mishnah B'rahot, 9.5.

47. Avodah Zarah, 5a.

48. Schechter, p. 275.

49. Vayikra Rabbah, 24.8; 26.5. Cf. Schechter, p. 292.

50. Bamidbar Rabbah, 10.7. Cf. *ibid.*, 10.10.

51. Sanhedrin, 43 a, b.

52. Kohelet Rabbah, 1.16.

53. Schechter, p. 289.

54. Brown, pp. 78 ff.

55. Vayikra Rabbah, 35.5.

56. Baba Batra, 16a.

57. Sanhedrin, 105a.

58. Sh'mot Rabbah, 41.7. Cf. *ibid.*, 46.4.

59. Cf. Martin Buber, *Between Man and Man* (London, 1947), pp. 196 ff.

60. Sigmund Freud, "Analysis Terminable and Interminable," in *Therapy and Technique*, ed. P. Rieff (New York, 1963), pp. 233-271.

61. See my "Psychoanalysis and Religious Experience," in *The Journal of Religion and Health* (October, 1962), 2, pp. 74-80.

Maurice Friedman: CHRISTIANITY AND THE CONTEMPORARY JEW

1. Martin Buber, *Hasidism and Modern Man*, edited and translated by Maurice Friedman (New York, 1958), p. 42.

2. Cf. Henry Sharman, *The Records of the Life of Jesus* (New York, 1917), and *Jesus as Teacher*, rev. ed. (New York, 1944).

3. Martin Buber, *Tales of the Hasidim: The Early Masters*, translated by Olga Marx (New York, 1961), p. 66.

4. Martin Buber, *Two Types of Faith*, translated by Norman P. Goldhawk (New York, 1961), p. 160.

5. *Tales of the Hasidim: The Early Masters*, p. 35.

6. *Two Types of Faith*, p. 12 b.

7. Address on Leonhard Ragaz, quoted in Ernst Simon, "Martin Buber: His Way between Thought and Deed," *Jewish Frontier* (February, 1948), XV, 26.

8. Abraham J. Heschel, *The Prophets* (Philadelphia, 1962), p. 221.

9. *Ibid.*, p. 283.

10. Martin Buber, *Pointing the Way*, edited and translated by Maurice Friedman (New York, 1963); "Genuine Dialogue and the Possibilities of Peace," p. 238.

11. Martin Buber, *Eclipse of God: Studies in the Relation between Religion and Philosophy* (New York, 1957); "Religion and Philosophy," translated by Maurice Friedman, p. 36.

12. *Tales of the Hasidim: The Early Masters*, pp. 212 ff.

13. David E. Roberts, "Tillich's Doctrine of Man" in *The Theology of Paul Tillich*, edited by Charles W. Kegley and Robert W. Bretall, Vol. I of *The Library of Living Theologians* (New York, 1956), p. 130.

Steven S. Schwarzschild: A JEWISH PERSPECTIVE ON INTERNATIONAL RELATIONS

1. *A Theologico-Philosophical Treatise* in *The Chief Works of Benedict de Spinoza*, edited by R. H. M. Elwes (New York, 1955), p. 208.

2. *Political Treatise*, *ibid.*, pp. 204, 296.

3. *Theologico-Political Treatise*, p. 200; *Political Treatise*, pp. 292, 294.

4. *Ibid.,* p. 310.
5. *Ibid.,* pp. 306 ff.; *Theologico-Political Treatise,* p. 208.
6. "Rousseau and Spinoza," *Journal of the History of Ideas,* V (1944), 285.
7. Actually, the understanding is that, on the strength of the escape clause, either party may use nuclear weapons without waiting for the other to have done so.
8. James Reston, in the *New York Times,* August 21, 1963, put it quite correctly and ironically: "What is at issue is merely that the great men who were not testing above ground have agreed formally not to test above ground, and have done so in a treaty that anybody can renounce if he thinks the other fellow, whom he doesn't trust, is about to test."
9. *Theologico-Political Treatise,* p. 200; *cf.* also *Political Treatise,* pp. 292, 294.
10. That Spinoza is one of the classic fathers of *rebus sic stantibus* has been long recognized: H. Lauterpacht, "Spinoza and International Law," *British Year Book of International Law* (1927), pp. 94–107. The same author also refers to this circumstance in L. Oppenheim, *International Law,* vol. I, ed. 8, edited by H. Lauterpacht (London, 1955), p. 939, note 2; *cf.* the total treatment of the doctrine, *ibid.,* pp. 938–944. The full phrase is *conventio omnis intelligitur rebus sic stantitus.* Lauterpacht's is a very good paper. He makes the penetrating observation that splintered and fragmented Italy in Machiavelli's time was very similar to splintered and fragmented Germany in the nineteenth century, and that this explains why nineteenth century German philosophers and political scientists took so avidly to Spinoza's and Machiavelli's real-political teachings, in the hope thus to be able to bring about the unification of their country as Machiavelli had hoped to do for his (p. 103). In this context he rightly puts Spinoza's influence on Bismarck (as demonstrated in Rosin, "*Bismarck und Spinoza,*" in *Festschrift fuer Otto Gierke* [1911], pp. 383–420). He even comes close to understanding the philosophical identity of Spinoza's doctrine that might is right with Hegel's "what is is rational," and that Hegel's teaching about treaties is therefore identical with Spinoza's (p. 104 ff.). Above all Lauterpacht, the great international lawyer and editor of Oppenheim's standard work in the field, on the basis of his study of Spinoza arrives at conclusions concerning the validity of the *clausula rebus sic stantibus* and on the relationship between a correct understanding of the nature of the state and international peace for which we are also trying to reason here: "To maintain, as does Spinoza, that the contract is valid so long as the will, prompted by the hope of gain, lasts, is to proclaim that the contract is not binding at all. It is a hopeless task to defend such a proposition as the rule of law or equity. . . . In fact, insofar as the application of the *clausula* is dependent upon the discretionary will of one of the parties, its essence is illegality. . . . It has never been recog-

nized as a rule of positive international law, although it may become
so when resorted to by an authoritative judicial tribunal applying
generally recognized principles of law and intent upon giving effect
either to the will of the parties or to higher considerations of common
international good. But this Spinoza did not think" (p. 99). The
article is marred only by the understandable fact that Lauterpacht
is not as good a historian or philosopher as he is an international
lawyer. Thus what to him is a "controverted question, whether
Spinoza was acquainted with the writings of Hugo Grotius," "the
father of international law" and an older contemporary and com-
patriot of his, is answered by the fact that Spinoza had Grotius'
work in his library. (Van Rooyen, Servas, *Inventaire des Livres
Formant la Bibliothèque de B. Spinoza* [The Hague, 1883], pp. 147,
183). Similarly, he does not seem to know that Rousseau was quite
familiar with Spinoza's writings (p. 103, note 2; cf., however, footnote
6), nor that Spinoza's personal morals were far from ideal (p. 106,
note 2; cf., however, footnote 33). More important, because he is
probably not as adept at philosophy as he is at law, he thoroughly
misunderstands the moral preference of Hobbes over Spinoza—as I am
trying to show. He looks at these questions solely from a legal and
political point of view, and therefore does not understand that even
Spinoza's occasional strainings after "optimism" are part and parcel
of the same doctrine *deus sive natura* which makes him a disciple
of Machiavelli and that Hegel's Prussian real-politics follows from the
fundamental nature of his philosophical system (cf. pp. 96 ff.). The
monographic treatment of C. Hill, "The Doctrine of 'Rebus Sic
Stantibus' in International Law," *University of Missouri Studies* (1934),
vol. IX, no. 3, is of interest to us for two reasons. In the first place,
as part of his evaluation of various forms of this highly dubious doctrine, he judges Spinoza's version thus: "Most writers, however,
believe that it is impossible to base the obligatory force of treaties
solely on the interests of the parties because this in fact substitutes
mere utilitarianism for a normative principle and denies the juridical
character of treaties. This definition is of considerable antiquity, although it has never been widely accepted. It can be traced to
Machiavelli and is found at least as one element in the definitions of
Spinoza, Bynkershoek, etc., . . ." (p. 12). In the second place, he
mentions an interesting episode in 1595 when Elizabeth I tried to
invoke our rule with respect to the Netherlands. Grotius and Bynkershoek, both Dutchmen, strongly condemned her for this. Hill quotes
the latter as writing: "The woman made the most absurd answer,
saying, that 'the contracts of princes rested only upon a pledge, and
that they were not binding if they result in detriment to the State, and
other things of the same kind.'" Hill goes on: "He [Bynkershoek]
states that the Netherlands condemned a book in 1669 which maintained
that treaties should be observed only when advantageous" (p. 47, note
5). This sheds some interesting light on an additional reason for the

Netherlands' famous later suppression of *The Theologico-Political Treatise:* Elizabeth of England had almost put one over on them by means of one of Spinoza's doctrines.

11. This is the point at which most international lawyers rebel. Indeed, in the age of the Hague Court and the UN, it might be argued that we have at least the rudiments of an "international society" and that it is high time its agencies were substantively drawn into the processes of international relations.

12. Cf. M. Dessauer, *Spinoza und Hobbes Begruendung ihrer Staats- und Religionstheorien durch ihre philosophische Systeme* (Breslau, 1868); Sigwart, *Vergleichung der Rechts- und Staatstheorien des B. Spinoza und Th. Hobbes,* in Lauterpacht, *op. cit.,* pp. 95 ff.

13. *Leviathan,* II, 1; cf. also XIV.

14. *Political Treatise,* pp. 313, 347, 356; *Theologico-Political Treatise,* pp. 243 ff.

15. "Spinoza ueber Staat und Religion, Judentum und Christentum," *Juedische Schriften* (Berlin, 1924), III: 344, 370 ff.

16. *Spinoza* (Hammondsworth/Middlesex, 1951), p. 182.

17. *Ibid.,* p. 2.

18. *Ibid.,* p. 7.

19. In candor I must admit that Cohen does not draw my conclusion from his own axiom. He distinguishes among "man," "the majority," and "the universality"—the "majority" being the state. This led him, socialist that he was, not only to a theory of the eventual federation of states but even to a raucous support of Germany during the First World War. See my "The Democratic Socialism of H. Cohen," *Hebrew Union College Annual,* XXVII, 429–431.

20. Paul Nitze defines this as the expansion of, e.g., the Secretary of State's duties from those "to the interests of the U.S. as a nation-state" to "those associated with a 'we' group virtually coterminous with mankind as a whole." *The Recovery of Ethics,* Council on Religion and International Affairs (1960), p. 25.

21. "The only state the rabbis were conscious of was the divine state of God." S. Belkin, *In His Image: The Jewish Philosophy of Man as Expressed in Rabbinic Tradition* (London, 1960), p. 120; cf. also pp. 117–119.

22. Cf. Lauterpacht, *op. cit.,* p. 91: "For the relation between political theory and international law is of more pervading character than is commonly assumed. It is the ultimate results of the theory of the state which are resorted to by international lawyers as the foundations of their systems. A political doctrine based on the omnipotence and glorification of the state as an end in itself will naturally result, and has usually resulted, in the negation of the law of nations as a body of rules which, both in its binding force and in its creation, is independent of the will of the state. The present, still rudimentary, stage of international law is not in a small degree due to the prevalence of this type of doctrine. And the time seems as yet far off when the

legal—and, of necessity, also the political and sociological—theory of the state will turn to international law as to the necessary starting point of a truly scientific inquiry."

In a review of Hans Morgenthau's *Politics in the Twentieth Century* (*The Commonweal* [Sept. 20, 1963]) Paul Ramsey admits that Morgenthau, the "old pro" among realists, now acknowledges the true end of the nation-state—although Ramsey tries to salvage some of his vested interests. But the Morgenthau quotations speak for themselves: "The nation-state has outlived its usefulness in the political life of mankind. The state can no longer defend the heartland of the nation, nor effect its policies by ultimate resort to the force in its arsenal. A realistic 'theoretical analysis,' Morgenthau believes, 'can show that the principle of political organization which has dominated the world from the French Revolution of 1789 to this day is no longer valid.' The sovereign nation-state has become obsolete without yet knowing it. This is Morgenthau's 'perfectionism' as a political realist. . . ." Morgenthau uses almost our words: "What has become obsolete is the historically conditioned connection between interest and a passing phenomenon, the nation-state . . ."

23. *Ethics and U.S. Foreign Policy* (New York, 1957), p. 22.

24. *Ibid.*, p. 14.

25. Maurice Friedman, "Martin Buber and the Social Problems of Our Time," *Yivo Annual XII:* " 'I cannot know how much justice is possible in a particular situation,' Buber wrote me in response to a letter from Prof. Niebuhr to me that I sent him, 'until I go on and my head hits the wall and aches. Then I know that no more is possible, but I must go on till my head hits the wall.' The social and political realist, according to Buber, is not the one who knows in advance that nothing or only so much is possible, but the one who knows that history is a mixture of planning and surprise."

26. K. W. Thompson, *Christian Ethics and the Dilemmas of Foreign Policy* (Durham, N.C., 1959), p. 114.

27. *Ibid.*, p. 123.

28. *Talmud, B. Sabbath*, 88.

29. Thompson, *op. cit.*, p. 112.

30. Vice-president Richard Nixon, on the other hand, said on April 29, 1958, "If we openly discriminate between one government and another in Latin America, . . . we would be charged with interfering in the internal affairs of other countries and with trying to impose our system of government on them."

31. I want to make a semantic observation at this point. We speak of "domestic politics" but of "international relations." Have you ever heard someone use the term "international politics" or "foreign politics," or have you ever heard someone use the term "domestic relations" (unless it be with reference to marital problems) or "national polity" with respect to day-by-day political activities (rather than in high-flown and pretty nearly irrelevant *Life* magazine sermons

on American political theology)? The fact is that to the American ear "policy" and "relations" are fine, clean terms, whereas "politics" smacks of municipal graft or, at best, congressional logrolling. By making this terminological distinction we thus raise the discussion of international affairs above the muck of local petty ambitions—a linguistic usage which, in the first place, is obviously unjustified by the harsh facts and which, in the second, represents another case of rank "idealism" by closing its lexicographical eyes to the mud and dirt of ministries of foreign affairs and their call-girls, to military establishments and their venal agents. I therefore prefer to speak of "foreign politics" rather than of "foreign affairs" or "international relations."

32. Cf. George Lichtheim, "George Lukacz—An Intellectual Disaster," *Encounter* (May, 1963).

33. Spinoza's basic premise, on the other hand, permitted him to engage in the private pleasure of watching animals dismember one another. Cf. Freudenthal-Gebhardt, *Spinozas Leben und Lehre* (Heidelberg, 1927), I: 61 ff. Says Hermann Cohen (*Religion der Vernunft* [Berlin, 1929], pp. 162 ff.): his "denigration and rejection of pity" is the inevitable result of Spinoza's doctrine of natural (brute) right.

34. What I have tried to say in this last section is developed with marvelous clarity and technical competence by Manfred Halpern in *The Morality and Politics of Intervention*, Council on Religion and International Affairs (1963). He defines very well the multiple forms of intervention, including non-interventionist intervention which achieves its end by not acting where it could act. (Few historians recognize the consistent policy of economic interventionism that characterizes American history throughout. Cf. W. A. Williams' *The Tragedy of American Diplomacy*. F. Merk's *Manifest Destiny and Mission in American History* is an amusing example of such blindness. His thesis is that not the imperialist doctrine of "manifest destiny" but the moral one of "Mission" motivates American history, and he then proceeds to accumulate evidence which—unwittingly—proves the exact reverse—always assuming that his basic distinction is a meaningful one.) Halpern recognizes the inevitability as well as the desirability of intervention in modern international politics, and he concludes—perhaps in insufficiently clear language—that our commitment to political and economic progress throughout the world has to be the criterion of our positive decisions. He concludes, technician and experienced practical statesman though he is, with precisely my doctrine of the centrality of the individual—which I wish to quote (p. 33): "If we commonly err by confusing God's will with our concrete aims in foreign policy, we usually also err by ignoring the existence of concrete individual human beings in discussing the justice of foreign interventions by the abstract collectivity known as the nation-state. . . . The technicians of power, having shrewdly rejected the illusion that national and individual morality are automatically the same, stop short and do not see that the un-

finished task is to relate national purpose to the kind of international justice that gives security and freedom for justice and love to develop among individuals. Indeed, they tend through the prestigious position of their manipulative power to diminish the citizen's concern with love, 'till he feels embarrassed by the very mention of it in the context of power."

A Note on the Contributors

Lou H. Silberman was born in San Francisco and studied at the University of California, Berkeley, and the Hebrew Union College, Cincinnati, where he was ordained and received a Doctorate of Hebrew Letters. He has written numerous articles on Biblical and Jewish theology, and is at present Hillel Professor of Jewish Literature and Thought and Director of Graduate Studies in the Biblical Field at Vanderbilt University.

Jakob J. Petuchowski was born in Berlin and studied at the University of London and the Hebrew Union College–Jewish Institute of Religion, where he was ordained and awarded a doctorate. He is the author of *Ever Since Sinai* and a frequent contributor to scholarly journals and magazines of opinion. He is at present Professor of Rabbinics at the Hebrew Union College–Jewish Institute of Religion, Cincinnati.

Emil L. Fackenheim was born in Germany and studied at the Berlin Hochschule, where he was ordained, the University of Halle, the University of Aberdeen, and the University of Toronto. He is the author of *Paths to Jewish Belief* and *Metaphysics and History*, as well as numerous articles. He is at present Professor of Philosophy at the University of Toronto.

Monford Harris was born in St. Paul, Minnesota, and studied at the University of Minnesota, the Jewish Theological Seminary of America, where he was ordained, and the College of Jewish Studies, Chicago. He has written for several Jewish publications and is at present chairman of the Department of General Jewish Studies at the College of Jewish Studies.

Eugene B. Borowitz was born in New York and studied at the Ohio State University, the Hebrew Union College, where he was ordained, and Columbia University. He has written numerous articles and is at present Professor of Education at the Hebrew Union College–Jewish

Institute of Religion, New York, and Adjunct Professor of Religion at Temple University.

ARNOLD JACOB WOLF was born in Chicago and studied at the University of Chicago and the Hebrew Union College, Cincinnati. He is the author of *Challenge to Confirmands: An Introduction to Jewish Thinking* and has written for several religious magazines and journals. He is at present Rabbi of Congregation Solel, Highland Park, Illinois.

ZALMAN M. SCHACHTER was born in Poland and studied at Jewish schools in Vienna until the Anschluss in 1938. He pursued his studies in Belgium until 1940, when he was interned in France; he came to the United States in 1941 and was ordained by the Central Yeshivah Tomchei T'mimim Lubavitz in 1947. His articles have appeared in leading Jewish magazines, and he is at present Associate Professor of Jewish Studies at the University of Manitoba.

MAURICE FRIEDMAN was born in Tulsa, Oklahoma, and studied at Harvard University, the Ohio State University, and the University of Chicago. He is the foremost interpreter of the thought of Martin Buber, having translated most of Buber's major works and written *Martin Buber: The Life of Dialogue*. His books on literature and existentialism include *Problematic Rebel* and *The World of Existentialism*. He is at present Professor of Philosophy and Literature at Sarah Lawrence College.

STEVEN S. SCHWARZSCHILD was born in Germany and studied in the United States at the University of Cincinnati and the Hebrew Union College. He is the editor of *Judaism*, the author of a book on Franz Rosenzweig, and a frequent contributor to Jewish publications. He is at present Professor of Jewish Thought at Brown University.